Principia Intellegentia

Principia Intellegentia

The principles governing human and machine intelligence

Roger Kingdon

ALLIED PUBLISHERS PVT. LTD.

New Delhi • Mumbai • Kolkata • Lucknow • Chennai
Nagpur • Bangalore • Hyderabad • Ahmedabad

ALLIED PUBLISHERS PRIVATE LIMITED

Regd. Off. : 15 J.N. Heredia Marg, Ballard Estate, Mumbai–400001, Ph.: 022-22626476
E-mail: mumbai.books@alliedpublishers.com

12 Prem Nagar, Ashok Marg, Opp. Indira Bhawan, Lucknow–226001, Ph.: 0522-2614253
E-mail: appltdlko@sify.com

Prarthna Flats (2nd Floor), Navrangpura, Ahmedabad–380009, Ph.: 079-26465916
E-mail: ahmbd.books@alliedpublishers.com

3-2-844/6 & 7 Kachiguda Station Road, Hyderabad–500027, Ph.: 040-24619079
E-mail: hyd.books@alliedpublishers.com

5th Main Road, Gandhinagar, Bangalore–560009, Ph.: 080-22262081
E-mail: bngl.books@alliedpublishers.com

1/13-14 Asaf Ali Road, New Delhi–110002, Ph.: 011-23239001
E-mail: delhi.books@alliedpublishers.com

17 Chittaranjan Avenue, Kolkata–700072, Ph.: 033-22129618
E-mail: cal.books@alliedpublishers.com

81 Hill Road, Ramnagar, Nagpur–440033, Ph.: 0712-2521122
E-mail: ngp.books@alliedpublishers.com

751 Anna Salai, Chennai–600002, Ph.: 044-28523938
E-mail: chennai.books@alliedpublishers.com

Website: www.alliedpublishers.com

ISBN: 978-81-8424-417-5

Published by Sunil Sachdev and printed by Ravi Sachdev at Allied Publishers Pvt. Ltd. (Printing Division), A-104 Mayapuri Phase II, New Delhi-110064

Preface

Principia Intellegentia makes the case for considering the phenomenon of intelligence in humans to be entirely bound up with their individual ability to learn. It does this by setting out a high-level description of how humans learn, and then showing how this description accounts for many aspects of the human condition. In addition, *Principia Intellegentia* makes the case for applying this same description to the design of learning algorithms for automated computing machines, thereby addressing the greatest intellectual challenge of our age: the quest for artificial intelligence.

This book is a scientific monograph that describes original contributions to a wide variety of fields including neuroscience, psychology, sociology, artificial intelligence, and the philosophy of science. However, it has been written in a style that makes it accessible to the intelligent non-expert, such that it may be classified as 'popular science'. This combination invites comparison with great works of mass appeal such as *The Origin of Species, The Golden Bough and The Structure of Scientific Revolutions.*

The original work described here is the result of extensive research undertaken in my spare time over the last 25 years. Much of this time has been spent in pursuing fundamental questions within the philosophy of science, in an attempt to formulate 'scientific method' as some kind of automatic procedure that could be undertaken by a computer. The discovery of just such a high-level description of learning has allowed the scope of research to be broadened to include the analysis of human learning behaviours. Rapid progress in this latter programme has meant that Principia *Intellegentia* focusses primarily on learning in humans, with machine learning as the secondary theme.

I am a research scientist working for the UK government. Since leaving university in 1987 I have been in continuous full-time employment in a number of government or privatised laboratories, undertaking scientific research in a wide range of applications, the common disciplines being physics, mathematics, engineering and computing. I am the sole author of this book and all of the original research reported in it, none of which has been funded by my employers, past or present. There is no conflict of interest or potential breach of confidence associated with this publication.

Concerning my repeated claim of originality: I have been engaged in scientific research for long enough to know that "there is no new thing under the sun". Accordingly it would not surprise me in the slightest if the publication of this book triggers a number of counter-claims that one or some or all of the insights that I present as original have in fact been extant in the literature for a number of years. It is possible. All I can say is that my search for intellectual precursors has been deep and thorough, and all those that have been uncovered have been duly acknowledged in the text. The rest, I believe, is original.

I am profoundly grateful to my family and friends who have supported and encouraged me during this quarter-century gestation that has been both exhilarating and excruciating in equal measure.

Thank you

Roger Kingdon

London
February 2009

Contents

Prologue

Over the years I have given many different talks on many different subjects to many different audiences. It's something I have to do as part of my day job; it's also something I like to do in pursuing my diverse spare-time interests. When preparing these talks I often try to think about the subject from the point of view of the audience. I ask myself: "If I were in this audience, where would I have come from? What would be my expectations? *What questions would I ask?*" Sometimes I get it right, and on such occasions there quickly develops a lively rapport, giving rise to a veritable buzz of excitement as an infectious spirit of open enquiry takes hold. Usually, however, I get it wrong. My enthusiasm for the subject leads me to neglect the needs of my audience, with dire consequences. I know I've got it wrong when within the first five minutes one of the audience asks:

"What are you telling us?"

or

"How does this fit in?"

or

"How did you get that?"

or

"What's your objective?"

or

"What's your reference?"

or

Words to that effect.

Actually there are only these five questions. The early questioners—a self-selected assortment, often aggressive, irritable or anxious—also fall into five categories:

1. "What are you telling us?" identifies the *Empiricist*, who wants to have a straightforward description of the subject-matter, without interpretation.
2. "How does this fit in?" identifies the *Idealist*, who wants to place the subject-matter within his or her all-encompassing world-view.
3. "How did you get that?" identifies the *Theorist*, who wants to see a detailed derivation of the subject-matter using established methods.

4. "What's your objective?" identifies the *Activist*, who doesn't care what the subject-matter is or where it came from, he or she only cares about whether the subject-matter can be recruited to the mission of achieving certain pre-determined goals.
5. "What's your reference?" identifies the *Conformist*, who wants to place the subject-matter in relation to established works.

I have known them all: the Empiricist, unassuming and innocent in expression, an explorer, keen for new experiences but suspicious of slick packaging; the Idealist, outwardly detached but inwardly neurotic, a mystic, willing to assimilate new information but not willing to contemplate a new perspective; the Theorist, perpetually puzzled, a detective, finding problems in the simplest of propositions; the Activist, impatient or bored, a soldier, only wanting to get on with it; and finally the Conformist, grim and reactionary, a devotee, seeing the world only through the eyes of an adopted authority. Kipling knew them too:

> I keep six honest serving-men:
> (They taught me all I knew)
> Their names are What and Where and When
> And How and Why and Who.[1]

These six servants of knowledge reduce to five when we treat 'Where' and 'When' as inseparable twins, each incomplete and incapacitated without the other, as indeed is recognised in the notion of four-dimensional space-time that was conceived around the same time that Kipling wrote these lines. Thus we have five 'names'—that is, five characteristic phrases—for our five interrogators: "What?" says the Empiricist; "Where and When?" says the Idealist; "How?" says the Theorist; "Why?" says the Activist; and "Who?" says the Conformist.

In order to cater for all styles of enquiry, *Principia Intellegentia* has been written as five distinct books:

1. What?	That which is proposed. For Empiricists.
2. Where and When?	How that which is proposed fits in with its 'frame of reference', that which is currently known or believed to be true. For Idealists.
3. How?	How that which is proposed came to be. For Theorists.
4. Why?	How that which is proposed can be put to use. For Activists.

[1] Rudyard Kipling, *Just So Stories* (1902).

5. Who? How that which is proposed revives the insights of past masters. For Conformists.

If, for example, you consider yourself to be an Activist, and you wish to 'cut to the chase', then you may prefer to start with **4. Why?** But if you feel unable to 'see the wood for the trees' without a 'roadmap', then it is clear that you have Idealist tendencies and you had better begin with **2. Where and When?** And similarly for the other styles of enquiry. Perchance something you read takes your interest, so that you feel emboldened to move beyond the comfort and security of your usual way of interacting with the world, and you take a look at the other books. That's allowed. The books may be read in any order; their sequence has no significance other than it follows that chosen by Kipling, whose reasons were poetic, presumably. Having said that, the books are not entirely independent of one another, and a casual reader not strongly committed to any particular style of enquiry would do well to read the books in the order in which they were written, which just happens to be the sequence **1** to **5**.

My first five minutes are up, and in my imagination certain members of my audience—yes, *you* and *you* and *you* and *you* and *you*—are getting restless. After all, I haven't even told you what *Principia Intellegentia* is about.

Or have I?

1. What?

That which is proposed; IDEAL; IDEAL learning styles; A cautionary tale; Extremism; The five ages of man (and woman); The human condition; The IDEAL model of learning; The Orient and the Occident; Basic data-handling processes; Human learning skills; The quest for artificial intelligence.

That which is proposed

Principia Intellegentia makes the case for considering the phenomenon of *intelligence* in humans to be entirely bound up with their individual ability to *learn*. It does this by setting out a high-level description of how humans learn, and then showing how this description accounts for many aspects of the human condition. In addition, *Principia Intellegentia* makes the case for applying this same description to the design of learning algorithms for automated computing machines, thereby addressing the greatest intellectual challenge of our age: the quest for artificial intelligence.

Definition. The high-level description of how humans learn is called 'IDEAL', an acronym for 'Iterative Dialectic Engine for Automated Learning'[1].

IDEAL

This is IDEAL:

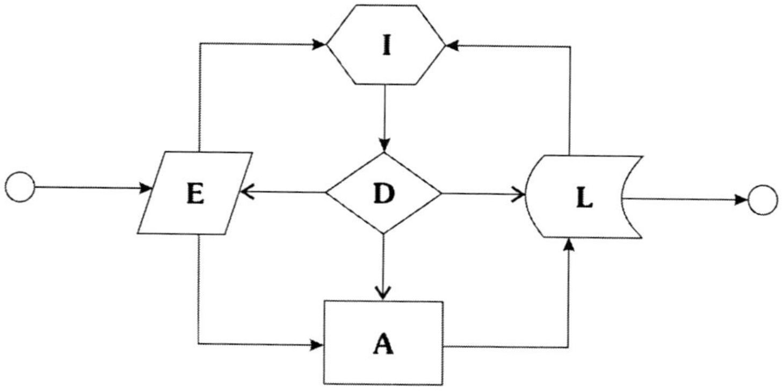

Notation. The acronym 'IDEAL' *also* stands for the five operational components in this diagram:

---

[1] See **2. Where and When?** for a discussion of this nomenclature.

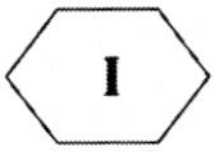

Iteration component.

Decision component.

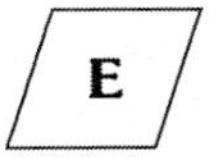

Evidence component.

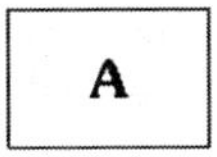

Algorithm component.

Log component.

The functions of IDEAL's components may be inferred from their shapes, following standard flowchart notation[2]:

"PREPARATION. Instruction modification to change program—set a switch, modify an index register, initialize a routine." In this application this symbol is used:

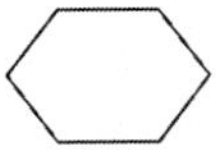

1. To indicate the start of an iteration loop.
2. To define initial parameter values for an iteration.
3. To apply iteration completion conditions.

All these functions involve both **I**teration and data comparison, which are the senses in which this symbol is used in IDEAL.

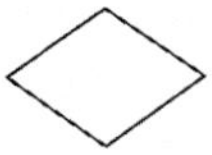

"DECISION. A decision or switching-type operation that determines which of a number of alternative paths followed." In IDEAL this symbol is used to indicate a **D**ecision node that generates a truth-functional statement (True or False) and a consequent control statement, that is, a non-negotiable imperative command such as Go or Stop.

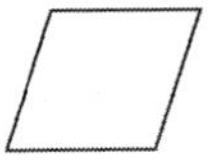

"INPUT/OUTPUT. General i/o function; information available for processing (input), or recording of processed information (output)." In IDEAL this

[2] The *de facto* standard was established *circa* 1970 by the IBM X20-8020 flowcharting template, itself based on a combination of standards in use at that time. The quoted component descriptions are taken from the card envelope in which this plastic template was stored.

function is termed **E**vidence to indicate an input of data from an independent external component.

"PROCESS. Any processing function; defined operation(s) causing change in value, form, or location of information." In IDEAL this symbol is used to indicate the execution of an **A**lgorithm, that is, a sequence of computational operations applied to input data (at the behest of a control statement) and generating results data for storage and further analysis.

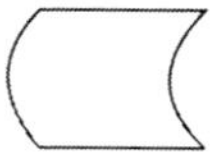

"ONLINE STORAGE. Input/output using any kind of online storage—magnetic tape, drum, disk." In this application this symbol is used to indicate the storage of data. In order to be useful this component must also facilitate the retrieval of stored data, as is possible with a **L**og—a systematic commentary that effectively organises and indexes data—and this is the sense in which this symbol is used in IDEAL.

"CONNECTOR. Exit to, or entry from, another part of chart." In this application this symbol is used to indicate an 'independent external component' that is a source of data for **E** and a repository of data for **L**. Since it is independent, this external component is not included as part of IDEAL's functionality.

The flowline arrows or 'connectors' in the IDEAL diagram show the transfer of two types of information:

Data connector. This connector transfers data in the direction of the arrow. The information thus transferred may be used in a calculation or it may be stored, but it does not constitute a command to any component to commence or cease operating.

Control connector. This connector transfers commands in the direction of the arrow and also admits the transfer of return codes—truth-functional flags indicating the commencement or completion of an operation—in the opposite direction. The command thus transferred will cause the target component to commence or cease a specific operation, but it may not be used in a calculation and it cannot be stored *as a command*. That is, only the codified *description* of the command can be handled as data information.

Whilst the functional components in the IDEAL diagram follow conventional flowchart notation, the definition of two types of connector is unique to IDEAL. Indeed, the related *distinction between data and control* is the key insight that sparked the concept of IDEAL and underpins its derivation[3].

Investigation. To understand how IDEAL works, we look at it from two perspectives:

1. IDEAL has five components, each of which has a specific and distinct function. By analysing each of these components individually, it is possible to build up a picture of their unique contribution to the whole, and to explain what happens when one component is allowed to dominate over the others. This leads to a definition of five *learning styles*, also termed *styles of enquiry*. Using these learning styles it is possible to account for many of the behavioural traits associated with both learning success and learning failure. Indeed, the utility of IDEAL in this application is such that it appears to explain much of what we might call the 'human condition'.
2. IDEAL is drawn as a flowchart diagram that clearly may be used in the design of an operational computer program. By analysing the sequential operation of the connected components, it is possible to define specific *procedures* that may be undertaken using IDEAL. Using these procedures we demonstrate IDEAL's capacity to simulate key human learning skills, thereby making the case that IDEAL may be applied to the design of learning algorithms for automated computing machines.

In the following, IDEAL learning styles and IDEAL procedures are defined, and example applications relating to human and machine intelligence are described.

IDEAL learning styles

Proposition. IDEAL is the mechanism by which humans learn.

Proposition. Different humans use IDEAL in different ways, according to their style of enquiry.

---

[3] See **3. How?** for this derivation.

Proposition. Since IDEAL has five specific and distinct components, it should be possible to define five learning styles based on these components, and use these learning styles to describe and explain human learning behaviour.

Definition. The five IDEAL learning styles are as follows:

1. The *Empiricist*. Empiricists have a preference for using the IDEAL Evidence component.
2. The *Idealist*. Idealists have a preference for using the IDEAL Iteration component.
3. The *Theorist*. Theorists have a preference for using the IDEAL Algorithm component.
4. The *Activist*. Activists have a preference for using the IDEAL Decision component.
5. The *Conformist*. Conformists have a preference for using the IDEAL Log component.

Notation. It is convenient to summarise these and further mappings in tabular form, thus:

IDEAL component		IDEAL learning style
E	Evidence	Empiricist
I	Iteration	Idealist
A	Algorithm	Theorist
D	Decision	Activist
L	Log	Conformist

As stated in the **Prologue**, the above sequence has no significance other than it follows that chosen by Kipling in his poem *I keep six honest serving-men*. For ease of reference this sequence is followed wherever IDEAL learning styles are discussed.

Notation. The names of the learning styles relate to their preferred sources of learning:

1. Empiricists have a preference for learning through *observation*, which is closely related to the data-gathering function of the IDEAL Evidence component.
2. Idealists have a preference for learning through comparing and correlating information within a pre-existing *framework*, which is closely related to the data comparison function of the IDEAL Iteration component.
3. Theorists have a preference for learning through constructing and operating representative *models*, which is closely related to the analytical function of the IDEAL Algorithm component.
4. Activists have a preference for learning through *action and reaction*, which is closely related to the control function of the IDEAL Decision component.
5. Conformists have a preference for learning through *reference* to an established authority, which is closely related to the data storage function of the IDEAL Log component.

IDEAL learning style	Source of learning
Empiricist	Observation
Idealist	Framework
Theorist	Models
Activist	Action and reaction
Conformist	Reference

A cautionary tale

An Empiricist, Idealist, Theorist, Activist and Conformist are lost in the jungle. Eventually, in mid-afternoon, they find a track that they think will lead them back to safety. After following the track for some time through otherwise inpenetrable forest, they come across a small clearing. In the middle of the clearing, directly blocking their path, is an enormous tiger. The tiger is stretched out on his side, his head on the ground. He appears to be asleep.

Empiricist : Oh look, a tiger.
Activist : Theo, where's the gun? Quick!
Theorist : I didn't bring it.
Activist : Why not? It was your job to bring the gun!

Theorist : It needed polishing. Besides, Connie said we wouldn't need it.

Activist : She said what?

Conformist : That's right. In *The Man-Eaters of Noamuk* Barker clearly states...

Activist : Damn Barker! That's a tiger. Do something!

Theorist : Maybe we could poison it?

Activist : *Maybe we could poison it?* Are you crazy!

Theorist : It was just an idea. Do you have a better one?

Activist : Yeah, maybe we could poison you and...

Empiricist : Sorry to interrupt, but I've been watching that tiger, and he's very still.

Idealist : Perhaps he's dead.

Conformist : Unlikely. Barker says...

Activist : Damn Barker! Are you sure, Emma?

Empiricist : Not a whisker. Not even the tip of his tail.

Activist : That's it. He's dead. Come on!

Empiricist : He's a very big *fat* tiger, isn't he?

Idealist : Perhaps he's sleeping off a very big fat lunch.

Conformist : Tigers don't have lunch. Only breakfast. But then they sleep all day.

Idealist : Perhaps he's been dead for days, and he's full of gas.

Activist : How can we tell?

Theorist : Poke him with a sharp stick and see if he goes pop.

Activist : Right, give me that stick...

Idealist : Oi, give it back! That's not a tiger-popper, it's my ley line diviner!

Empiricist : Oh look, the tiger was only sleeping, after all. Run!

Conformist : No need for that. Barker says that tigers never kill more than one person at a time.

Activist : Help!

Empiricist : I must say, he's putting up a jolly good fight.

Theorist : If we skirt round to the left, we can get past while the tiger's busy.

Activist : Help!

Conformist : What about our glorious leader?

Empiricist : He's distracting the tiger so that we can escape. How's that for leadership!

Activist : Help!
Idealist : And what about my diviner?
Theorist : Tell you what: If you leave it, I'll give you the gun when we get back.
Idealist : Does it detect ley lines?
Theorist : I might be able to make the appropriate adjustments.
Activist : Aaa...
Empiricist : He's down. Now's our chance. Come on!
Conformist : I still think we should do something to help him.
Idealist : What would Barker do in this situation?
Conformist : Barker would run.
Idealist : So what should we do?
Conformist : Run!

Moral: *Teamwork.*

Proposition. This cautionary tale illustrates the distinct nature of the five IDEAL learning styles, and begins to show how they relate to one another.

Proposition. Cautionary tales work not because of their setting and plot (which are absurd), but because they focus on characteristic behaviours that we find all too familiar.

Proposition. Through cautionary tales and similar anecdotal 'evidence'—real or imaginary—it is possible to get a more complete picture of the characteristics of the five IDEAL learning styles and how they relate to one another.

Example. By means of an anecdote, the **Prologue** introduced the five different types of question that people ask when they wish to learn about the world or (more likely) impose a familiar mode of discourse:

IDEAL learning style	Question
Empiricist	"What are you telling us?"
Idealist	"How does this fit in?"
Theorist	"How did you get that?"
Activist	"What's your objective?"
Conformist	"What's your reference?"

We thereby recover Kipling's *six honest serving-men*:

IDEAL learning style	Servant
Empiricist	"What?"
Idealist	"Where and When?"
Theorist	"How?"
Activist	"Why?"
Conformist	"Who?"

Example. The above cautionary tale hints at positive and negative characteristics of the five learning styles that may be interpreted as 'virtues' and 'vices' respectively:

1. The Empiricist has an *enquiring* open mind, but also a tendency to *interfere*.
2. The Idealist is *detached* from daily concerns, but can be *passive* in a crisis.
3. The Theorist is *resourceful* in support of others, but often inappropriately *pedantic*.
4. The Activist is a *dynamic* force in society, but often overly *controlling*.
5. The Conformist is *loyal* to a chosen cause, but *reactionary* with respect to alternatives.

IDEAL learning style	Virtue	Vice
Empiricist	Enquiring	Interfering
Idealist	Detached	Passive
Theorist	Resourceful	Pedantic
Activist	Dynamic	Controlling
Conformist	Loyal	Reactionary

Closely related to these virtues and vices are the positive and negative emotional and physical reactions typically displayed by the five learning styles:

IDEAL learning style	Positive emotion	Negative emotion
Empiricist	Attraction	Disgust
Idealist	Joy	Sorrow
Theorist	Inspiration	Fear
Activist	Excitement	Anger
Conformist	Love	Hate

IDEAL learning style	Positive reaction	Negative reaction
Empiricist	Embrace	Flee
Idealist	Proclaim	Lament
Theorist	Create	Fake
Activist	Act	Threaten
Conformist	Serve	Oppose

Proposition. In addition to illustrating the characteristics of the five IDEAL learning styles, the above cautionary tale emphasises the importance of balancing the contributions from each style, both for individuals and for teams.

Proposition. The five IDEAL learning styles may be treated as a 'basis set'. That is, the learning style of any person can be represented by a weighted combination of the five IDEAL learning styles.

Example. Bungalow Bill "went out tiger hunting with his elephant and gun", which makes him an Empiricist/Activist; Eleanor Rigby "picks up the rice in the church where a wedding has been", which makes her a Conformist; and so on:

Friends	Empiricist	Idealist	Theorist	Activist	Conformist
Bungalow Bill	0.3	0.1	0.1	0.4	0.1
Eleanor Rigby	0.1	0.1	0.1	0.1	0.6
Jude	0.2	0.3	0.3	0.1	0.1
Maxwell Edison	0.1	0.1	0.4	0.3	0.1
Michelle	0.1	0.3	0.1	0.1	0.4
Mr. Kite	0.4	0.1	0.1	0.3	0.1
Polythene Pam	0.2	0.1	0.1	0.2	0.4
Rocky Raccoon	0.3	0.2	0.1	0.2	0.2
Sexy Sadie	0.1	0.6	0.1	0.1	0.1

Note that the five weighting factors have been chosen so that they add up to 1 for each person. This 'normalisation' on the basis set is the means by which individuals may be compared with others and with group trends.

Extremism

Whilst it may be supposed that every person has *some* proportion of each learning style, such that no weighting factor is zero, there are instances where a person has become so highly polarised towards a particular learning style that little difference can be seen between that person and the learning style. Such a person is commonly termed an 'extremist'.

Definition. An *extremist* is an extreme exponent of one of the five IDEAL learning styles.

Proposition. This definition of 'extremist' captures *all* aspects of what is considered 'extremist behaviour' or 'extremism'.

Proposition. It is convenient to characterise the five types of extremist in terms of five idealised caricatures or 'archetypes'. Notably, these archetypes are self-appointed to their mission:

IDEAL learning style	Extremist
Empiricist	Explorer
Idealist	Guru
Theorist	Philosopher
Activist	Conqueror
Conformist	Priest(ess)

Investigation. Typically, extremists take pride in their behaviour. Their extreme learning style has netted particular rewards and they see no need to change. Accordingly they ignore advice and warnings to moderate their behaviour and they fail to see the relevance of Kolb's insight that the most effective learning strategy requires a working knowledge of all parts of the learning cycle[4]. Extremists look at the world from a single perspective only, and consequently they do not register any information that would challenge that perspective. Instead, everything they see merely confirms their narrow view, and after a while they cease to learn anything new about the world. Extremism is *stable* in the sense that once a person has adopted an extremist view of the world, he or she ceases to discern any information that might change that view. However, just because extremism is stable, that doesn't mean that it is an acceptable form of behaviour. Learning style extremists are monomaniacs, and monomaniacs are mad, according to Conrad:

> A man haunted by a fixed idea is insane. He is dangerous even if that idea is an idea of justice; for may he not bring the heaven down pitilessly upon a loved head?[5]

---

[4] See David Kolb, *Experiential Learning—Experience as the Source of Learning and Development* (Prentice-Hall 1984), also discussed in **3. How?**

[5] Joseph Conrad, *Nostromo* (1904).

Equally, becoming fixated on *two* of the five learning styles can lead to an identity crisis, which is another form of insanity. The prevalence of this theme in the arts no doubt reflects its resonance to real life[6]. Neither is it any use to simply reject extremism, since an emotional reaction to extremist behaviour can itself be extremist. Thus one often sees people living or working together as 'intimate enemies', each becoming more extreme in reaction to the other[7]. What, then, is the solution?

Definition. The only effective counter to extremism is to engage with all five IDEAL learning styles in a balanced fashion. This effectively defines mature, responsible behaviour in humans.

Maxim. *Omnis extremus, sed non in extremis.*[8]

The five ages of man (and woman)

Extremists start young and never change, but they are partly a product of their environment, and it may be supposed that in a liberal, tolerant and well-knit society extremists are in the minority. The majority of people in such a society would each be able to use a mixture of learning styles, appropriate to the circumstances—*once they have grown to maturity*. This does not necessarily mean that children are extremists, only that they have not yet acquired all the learning styles.

Example. An important determinant of learning in an individual is the adoption of a conceptual framework that sets boundaries within which learning can take place. In the ordinary way of things this conceptual framework is accepted without question by the learning individual. However, there are also times when this 'ordinary' learning is put on hold, so that the conceptual framework itself may be developed[9]. Specifically, the mental development of young children typically occurs within conceptual frameworks that are provided by parents and teachers. These frameworks go largely unchallenged until the teenage years, when they become subject to intense re-evaluation and development, often at

---

[6] See **5. Who?** for several examples of the use of the 'identity crisis' device in literature and the dramatic arts.

[7] Daniel Goleman, *Emotional Intelligence* (Bloomsbury 1995).

[8] "To be every extremist—but none too much."

[9] This is Kuhn's juxtaposition of *normal science* and *scientific revolutions*, applied to individual learning. See Thomas Kuhn, *The Structure of Scientific Revolutions* (second edition, Chicago 1970), also discussed in **2. Where and When?**

the cost of relinquishing mastery in other areas such as physical coordination and effective communication. Finally, a measure of mature adulthood is the extent to which an individual is prepared to develop within a self-selected framework of values, attitudes and practices. From this example it seems that individuals change and develop their learning style as they get older.

Proposition. A description of learning style development may be found embedded within Shakespeare's description of the 'seven ages of man':

All the world's a stage,
And all the men and women merely players:
They have their exits and their entrances;
And one man in his time plays many parts,
His acts being seven ages. At first the infant,
Mewling and puking in the nurse's arms.
And then the whining schoolboy, with his satchel,
And shining morning face, creeping like snail
Unwillingly to school. And then the lover,
Sighing like furnace, with a woful ballad
Made to his mistress' eyebrow. Then a soldier,
Full of strange oaths, and bearded like the pard,
Jealous in honour, sudden and quick in quarrel,
Seeking the bubble reputation
Even in the cannon's mouth. And then the justice,
In fair round belly with good capon lin'd,
With eyes severe, and beard of formal cut,
Full of wise saws and modern instances;
And so he plays his part. The sixth age shifts
Into the lean and slipper'd pantaloon,
With spectacles on nose and pouch on side,
His youthful hose well sav'd a world too wide
For his shrunk shank; and his big manly voice,
Turning again towards childish treble, pipes
And whistles in his sound. Last scene of all,
That ends this strange eventful history,
Is second childishness, and mere oblivion,
Sans teeth, sans eyes, sans taste, sans everything.[10]

---

[10] William Shakespeare, *As You Like It*, II.vii (*circa* 1598).

The last of these ages appears to be the very antithesis of any kind of learning process; and it is significant that Shakespeare calls this age "second childishness", implying that the infant also has no engagement with any *normal* learning process. If we omit these two outliers then we are left with five ages, which would have been a more consistent choice for Shakespeare given that all of his plays are presented not in seven acts but in five, following the custom of the day. These five ages may be mapped to the IDEAL learning styles as follows:

1. The *schoolboy*, "creeping like snail | Unwillingly to school" in Shakespeare's comic inversion, is an Empiricist, wanting to explore the world in his own way.
2. The *lover* is an Idealist, seeing nothing in life save the singular object of his adoration.
3. The *soldier*, "sudden and quick in quarrel" and impatient with intellectual solutions, is clearly an Activist.
4. The *justice*, "Full of wise saws and modern instances", no doubt gleaned from personal experience and from reading many books, is a Conformist.
5. The *pantaloon*, a comic character that has survived into the present day as the wizened and scatterbrained inventor archetype beloved of Hollywood movies, is a Theorist.

Proposition. The reason why Shakespeare's caricatures have survived to this day is that we occasionally recognise their patterns of behaviour in ourselves and our acquaintances. Their comic absurdity has a purpose, in that they show us how *not* to behave. So perhaps it is possible to define another archetype representing the person who throughout his life has avoided the absurdities of each of the ages of man.

Definition. 'IDEAL man' is that person who has lived by the maxim *Omnis extremus, sed non in extremis* through all the ages of man.

Investigation. So much for the ages of man. What about woman? History, and art, has not been kind. Compare William Mulready's depiction of the seven ages of man (1838) with Hans Baldung Grien's view of the seven ages of woman (*circa* 1535, that is, predating *As You Like It*):

Interesting, isn't it, how the simple expedient of representing a woman without her clothes also denudes her of any distinguishing personality or role—other than slave or whore, of course. Lest you think that this cattle-market portrayal of woman's place in society is no longer prevalent, consider the Albert Memorial in London's Kensington Gardens, where Queen Victoria's consort gets to wear fine robes and sit in a chair, but the representative women of Europe, Asia, Africa and the Americas aren't so fortunate. Similarly, statues lined up outside the Musée d'Orsay in Paris depict women of the Orient, Africa, North America, South America and Oceania, all proudly displaying their magnificent breasts. A sixth subject, representing Europe, is more modest in her dress, which speaks volumes about the 19th Century attitude to foreigners. What is disturbing about this frozen beauty contest is not the nudity but the obvious invitation to compare women according to their physical characteristics only. No wonder that a joke currently doing the internet rounds is that the five ages of woman are "Dada, Lager, Aga, Saga and Gaga". Another variant is: (i) To grow up; (ii) To fill out; (iii) To slim down; (iv) To hold it in; (v) To hell with it.

Proposition. The above definition of 'IDEAL man' applies equally to woman.

The human condition

IDEAL has been formulated as a high-level description of how humans learn. As such, it is reasonable to expect that IDEAL accounts for the different sources of learning that people turn to, or the different types of questions that people ask. However, as we have seen, IDEAL also appears to account for aspects of the human condition not usually associated with learning. *Virtues and vices, positive and negative emotional and physical reactions*, *extremism* and *the ages of man* have been cited as examples of human characteristics that can be given a novel, insightful and coherent interpretation using IDEAL learning styles. This impression, of the general applicability of IDEAL to describing and explaining the human condition, is further reinforced by a simple mapping of the five IDEAL components to the five main parts of the human brain[11]:

---

[11] See **3. How?** for a discussion of the mapping between IDEAL and the different parts of the brain.

IDEAL component		Part of brain
E	**E**vidence	Occipital lobe
I	**I**teration	Parietal lobe
A	**A**lgorithm	Temporal lobe
D	**D**ecision	Frontal lobe
L	**L**og	Cerebellum

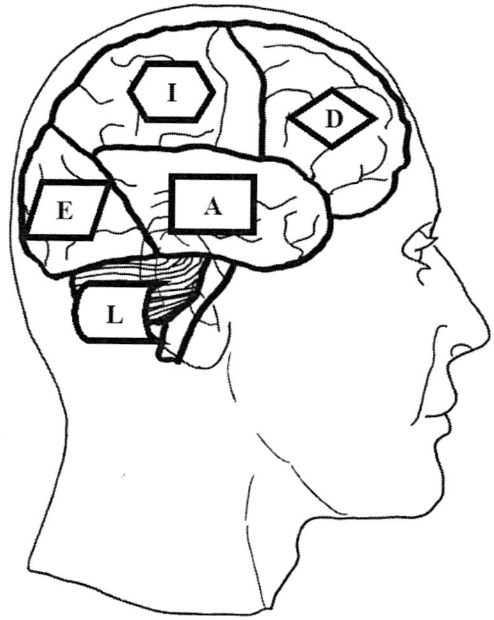

Proposition. The phenomenon of *intelligence* in humans is entirely bound up with their individual ability to *learn*—using IDEAL.

The IDEAL model of learning

The five IDEAL learning styles have been described as a basis set, from which individual styles of enquiry can be constructed, in much the same way as a child can fill a bag of pick'n'mix by selecting from jars containing different sweets. IDEAL is more than a bag of pick'n'mix, though, for unlike sweets the IDEAL components are connected to one another. These connections are specific in nature and they constrain the variety of algorithmic procedures that IDEAL is able to undertake. To understand how IDEAL works as a model of learning, it is necessary to understand the nature of its constraints; and to understand these constraints, we first need to describe more precisely the types of information being passed between the components that make up IDEAL.

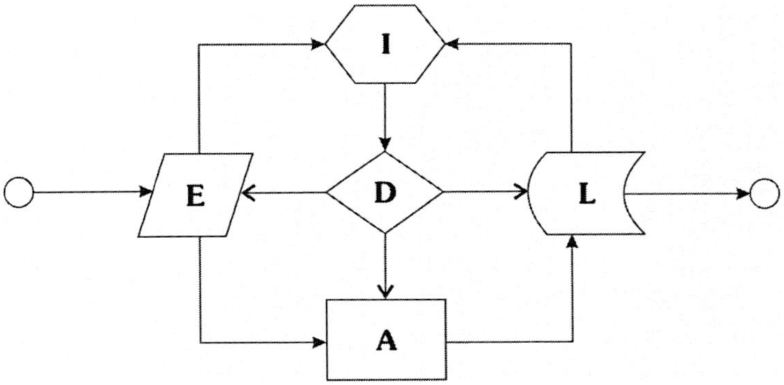

Notation. The letters **I**, **D**, **E**, **A**, **L** and **O** refer to IDEAL's five components and the independent external component:

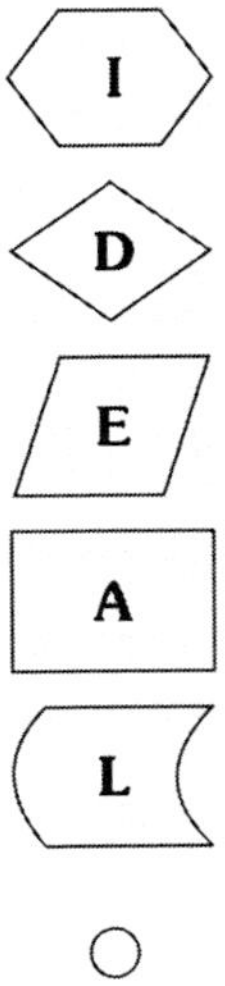

I, Iteration component.

D, Decision component.

E, Evidence component.

A, Algorithm component.

L, Log component.

O, Independent external component.

Definition. An *item of data* or *dataset* is a discrete packet of data transmitted by means of a data connector (solid arrow). A dataset can comprise any of the following:

1. *Input data*, which refers to information received and relayed by **E**. Input data are exogenous, that is, received by **E** from **O**.

2. *Stored data*, which refers to information received and relayed by **L**. Stored data are endogenous, that is, received by **L** from **A**.
3. *Results data*, which refers to information generated by **A**. All results data are sent by **A** to **L**, where they are subsumed as stored data.
4. *Evaluation data*, which refers to information generated by **I**. All evaluation data are sent by **I** to **D**, where they inform **D**'s generation of commands.
5. *Code data*, which refers to codified descriptions of **I**'s data comparison operations, **D**'s command-generating operations (and the commands generated thereby), **E**'s data input operations, **A**'s data analysis operations and **L**'s data logging operations.

Definition. A *command* is a non-negotiable instruction transmitted by means of a control connector (barbed arrow). Commands must be acted upon and thus they cannot be handled in same way as datasets; for example, they cannot be stored *as commands*. However, all human and computer languages codify commands in some manner—symbols, words or gestures, for instance—and this codified description constitutes a dataset that *can* be stored.

Definition. A *return code* is a truth-functional flag indicating the commencement or completion of an operation. It is transmitted by means of a control connector in the opposite direction to the barbed arrow. Return codes can be generated in two ways:

1. Following the commencement or completion of an operation in a component that has received a direct command. For example, if **A** is instructed by **D** to undertake a particular analysis, then **A** sends **D** a return code when this operation has completed.
2. Following the commencement or completion of an operation in a component that has not received a direct command, but which has an inward control connector. For example, if **A** sends results data to **L** for storage, then **L** sends **D** a return code when this operation has completed.

Investigation. It may be observed that each of IDEAL's components has a unique connectivity: **I** has data inputs from **E** and **L** and a data output to **D**; **D** has a data input from **I** and control outputs to **E**, **A** and **L**; and so on. How does this constrain what IDEAL can do? What would we *like* IDEAL to do? If IDEAL is indeed "the high-level description of how humans learn", then it is reasonable to expect that all the information entrusted to IDEAL (*including* code data) can be stored and 'refined' (improved upon) in some manner; and, as part of this, that

IDEAL implements a recognised definition of data storage such as Codd's Laws[12]. To demonstrate this in a transparent manner, we might expect to see all the information stored neatly in one place—that is, in **L**. Can this be done? The answer is *no*. In particular, **D** has no data output, so none of the information 'upstream' of **D** can pass through *as data*. This includes evaluation data from **I**, code data utilised by **I** and **D**, and return codes from **E**, **A** and **L**. In principle it should be possible to address part of this problem by hard-wiring **D** with a general-purpose 'code installer' that instructs **L** to pass appropriate code data to **I** and to **D** itself. However, this 'fix' reduces **I** and **D** to mechanistic automata while expecting **L** to store and refine the code data of **I** and **D** as well as its own, so that **L** becomes a powerful 'brain within a brain'. That is, whilst this solution addresses part of the original requirement of storing all data information in **L**, in the process it creates a new problem that is even less tractable. The obvious conclusion is that IDEAL's design prevents the easy storage of all data information in **L**. Another example of IDEAL's constrained functionality is the unique absence of a control input to **I**, so that **I** is not controlled directly by **D**. However, **I**'s autonomy is tempered by **D**'s monopolistic control over **I**'s output, as part of a system of 'checks and balances' that exists for all of IDEAL's components. The interconnections between IDEAL's components, and the absence of 'Start' and 'Stop' flowchart terminators, ensure that IDEAL's operation is both *iterative* and *self-regulating*, such that internal checks and balances are an inevitable consequence. The reasons for this choice of system are discussed elsewhere[13]; here, we are concerned with the key consequence of this choice, which is that IDEAL is a standalone model of learning. On the basis of the present observations it is possible to formulate the following working definition of this model.

Definition. IDEAL is a *model of learning* that is iterative and self-regulating. Learning takes place through the gradual refinement of all the information handled by IDEAL, including code data (that is, codified descriptions of IDEAL's own operations). In order to do this, the following specific operational rules apply:

1. Once started, IDEAL continues to operate indefinitely, with each component executing its own operations when called upon (by the arrival of data or a command from **D**).
2. The sequence of operations undertaken by IDEAL is determined by IDEAL itself. No component is in overall control, rather control may

---

[12] See **3. How?** for a discussion of Codd's Laws.

[13] See **3. How?** for a discussion of iterative self-regulating systems.

be thought of as a shared asset that passes from component to component, depending on each component's internal operations.

3. Each IDEAL component stores and refines the codified descriptions of its own operations.
4. Evaluation data (from **I**) and return codes (from **E**, **A** and **L**) are either stored by **D** or discarded.
5. All other data are stored in **L**. So that **L** can access input data from **E**, **A** has a 'neutral' algorithm that allows their free passage.
6. Each IDEAL component can access data stored in **L**. In order to do this, **I** has a 'neutral' algorithm that allows the free passage of stored data from **L** to **D**. (A convenient trigger mechanism for this algorithm is the *absence* of matching data from **E** when the stored data arrives at **I** from **L**.) Furthermore, **E** (and therefore **A**) can access **L**'s stored data via **O**.

Investigation. With the benefit of this definition of the IDEAL model of learning it is possible to describe, with some degree of rigour and consistency, the procedures that IDEAL can undertake. We proceed by identifying two core IDEAL procedures and applying them to a range of data-handling tasks, showing that, in principle, IDEAL has the capacity to simulate the key human learning skills of language, physical coordination, awareness, and abstract thought.

The Orient and the Occident

Definition. The two core IDEAL procedures are as follows:

1. The *Orient* procedure, which comprises the upper part of IDEAL.
2. The *Occident* prodedure, which comprises the lower part of IDEAL.

Part of IDEAL	Procedure
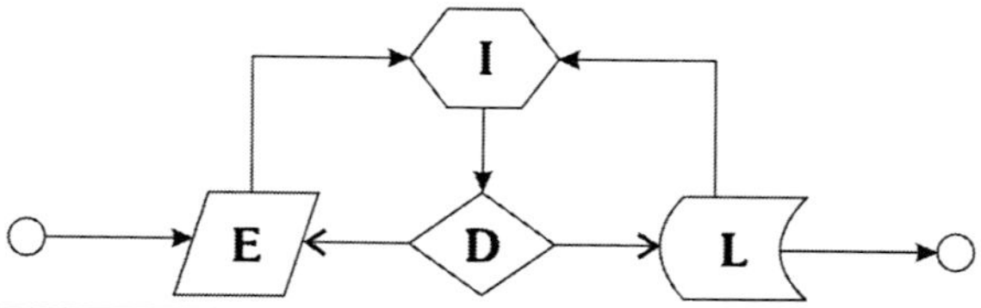	Orient
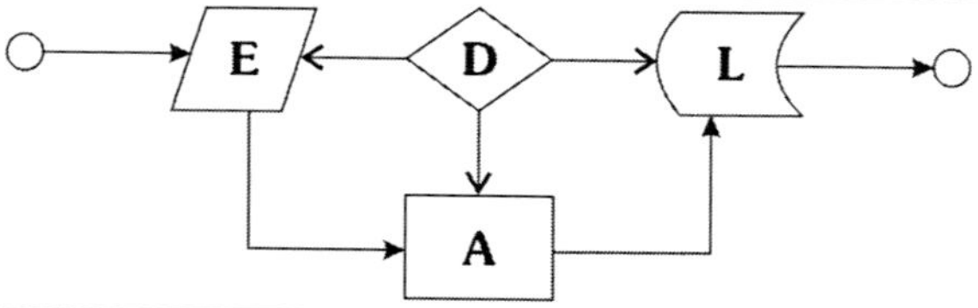	Occident

Notation. The 'Orient' procedure is so-called because it compares or 'orients' one dataset with respect to another. The 'Occident' procedure 'analyses' a dataset by treating it as input to a computational algorithm; it is so-called simply as a whimsical juxtaposition, partially inspired by Kipling:

> OH, East is East, and West is West, and never the twain shall meet,
> Till Earth and Sky stand presently at God's great Judgment Seat;
> But there is neither East nor West, Border, nor Breed, nor Birth,
> When two strong men stand face to face,
> tho' they come from the ends of the earth![14]

'Orient' and 'Occident' is also suggestive of the right and left hemispheres, respectively, with which these procedures have certain functional similarities. However, their greater functional similarity is with the dorsal and ventral visual streams:

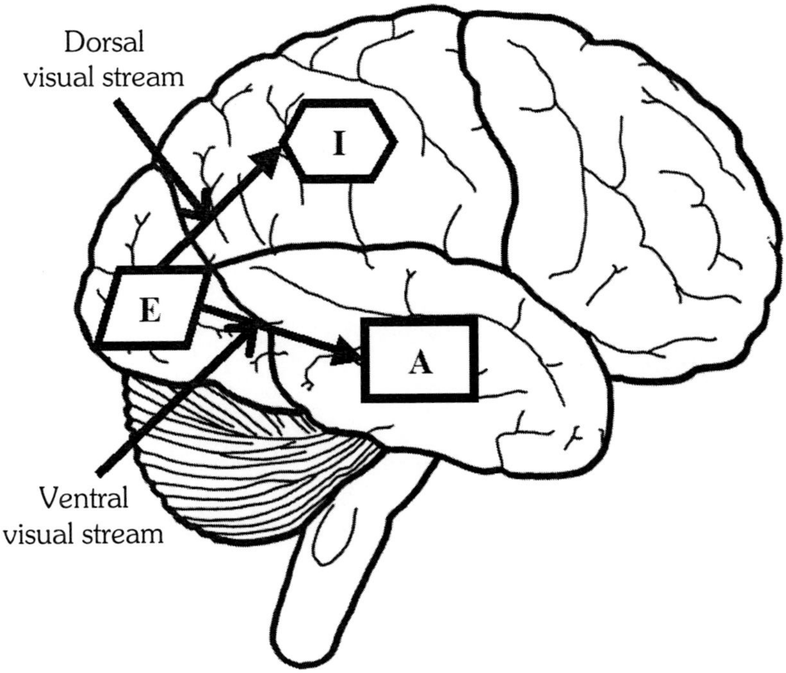

A way of remembering this association is to observe that both the Orient procedure and the dorsal visual stream are uppermost with respect to their counterparts.

[14] Rudyard Kipling, *The Ballad of East and West* (1892).

Definition. The operation of the Orient procedure is as follows:

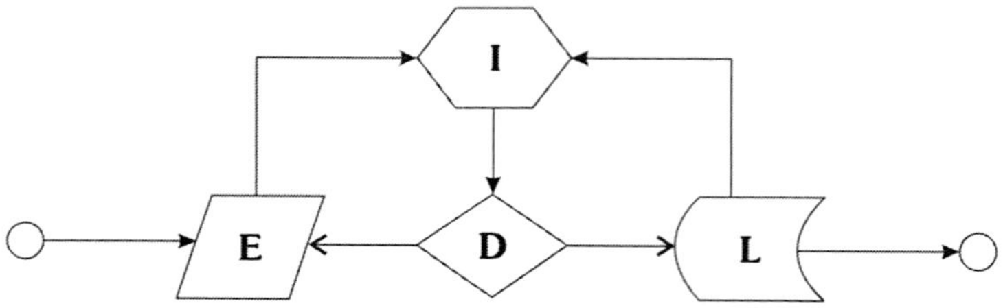

1. **D** initiates the orientation of a dataset by sending paired commands to **E** and **L**. **E** is instructed to input the dataset from **O** and send it to **I**. **L** is instructed to select an appropriate comparison dataset from its archive and send it to **I**.
2. The completion of these operations is alerted to **D** by **E** and **L** by means of return codes.
3. **I** orients the dataset from **E** by comparing it with the dataset from **L**. This comparison might involve anything from a simple calculation (for example, determining the greater of two numbers) to a complex assessment (for example, detecting the similarities between two spatial patterns).
4. **I** sends the results of the orientation to **D**.
5. The completion of the Orient procedure is alerted to **D** by receipt of the results from **I**.

Note that, by convention, this procedure starts and ends with **D**.

Definition. The operation of the Occident procedure is as follows:

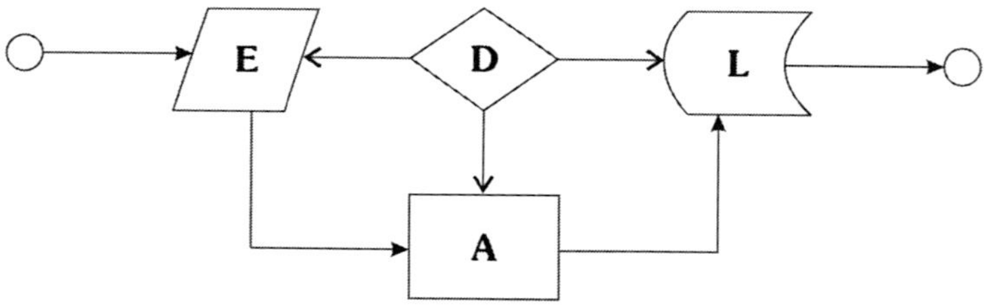

1. **D** initiates the analysis of a dataset by sending paired commands to **E** and **A**. **E** is instructed to input the dataset from **O** and send it to **A**. **A** is instructed to select an appropriate algorithm from its archive for the analysis of the dataset from **E**.
2. The completion of these operations is alerted to **D** by **E** and **A** by means of return codes.
3. **A** analyses the dataset from **E** by treating it as input to the algorithm. This algorithm comprises a sequence of computational operations that might involve anything from a simple calculation (for example,

multiplying two numbers together) to a complex assessment (for example, numerical integration).

4. **A** sends the results of the analysis to **L** for storage.
5. The completion of the Occident procedure is alerted to **D** by **A** and **L** by means of return codes.

Note that, by convention, this procedure starts and ends with **D**.

Proposition. By the nature of their key components, **I** and **A** respectively, the Orient and Occident procedures are fundamentally different. Whereas the Orient procedure is founded in the logic of sets and relations and is mainly concerned with pattern recognition, the Occident procedure is founded in the logic of propositions and arithmetic and is mainly concerned with analytical calculation[15]. In combination, these two procedures are the main prerequisite for the simulation of key human learning skills—as is shown in the following applications.

Basic data-handling processes

Investigation. *Data recognition.* Suppose that IDEAL is exposed to some new information, that is, exogenous data are introduced at **O**. IDEAL's first action would be to attempt to recognise some or all of this new input:

1. Exogenous data introduced at **O** proceed to **E**. The arrival of these data is unsolicited and therefore noteworthy, so this event is alerted to **D** by **E** by means of a return code.
2. **D** can choose to ignore the return code or act upon it. If the latter, then **D** will attempt to recognise the new data by using the Orient procedure to compare them with stored data from **L**.
3. Initially IDEAL knows nothing about the new data, and in order to obtain any positive result **D** must first instruct **L** to retrieve stored data that are broad-spectrum but (to compensate) low-resolution. Positive indications of a match (shown by **I**'s evaluation data) are followed up with further calls to the Orient procedure, on each instance increasing the resolution of the stored data as IDEAL improves the match iteratively. In addition, on each pass **D** can instruct **E** to progressively tune its reception of the input data.

---

[15] *Logic* by Nick Earle (Macmillan 1973) has four chapters: (i) The logic of propositions; (ii) The logic of sets; (iii) The logic of relations; (iv) The logic of arithmetic. The suggestion here is that in practice these systems fall naturally into two groups represented by the Orient and Occident procedures. This is discussed further in **2. Where and When?**

4. When **I**'s evaluation data indicate a good match between input data and stored data (as determined by some threshold value owned by **I** and communicated to **D**), then the input information has been 'recognised' and the procedure ends with **D**.

Investigation. *Data analysis*. Suppose that IDEAL is in possession of recognised data that may be input to a deductive or arithmetical analysis. For example, suppose that the particular instance "Epimenides is a Cretan" has been recognised as a truth-functional proposition that may be input as a premise to a deductive inference. IDEAL may proceed to analyse this information as follows:

1. **D** initiates the Occident procedure by instructing **E** to send the proposition "Epimenides is a Cretan" to **A**, and instructing **A** to use this as input to any appropriate deductive operation.
2. For a typical non-trivial deduction, **A** requires as premises a general principle (GP) of the form "All M are P" and a particular instance (PI) of the form "S is an M", where S is the subject, P is the predicate and M is the medium of the classical categorical syllogism. In this example the PI has been specified as the proposition "Epimenides is a Cretan", but the GP is undefined. Arguably, GPs might be considered to be part of **A**'s 'tools of the trade', with **A** retaining several examples in its own archive; in this case **A** can formulate an appropriate GP by replacing M with "Cretans" and P with some other term from its archive. Otherwise, **A** can call on **L**'s data store by sending the partially-completed proforma GP "All Cretans are P" to **L**, and a "Did not compute" return code to **D**. The arrival of this negative return code from **A** and a "Data received" return code from **L** is an unambiguous combination that may be interpreted by **D** as a request to specify the missing term in the GP. This can be done by **D** instructing **L** to send the GP to **E** (via **O**), then running the Orient procedure (as above) to identify candidate terms for P, then instructing **L** to send those terms to **A** (via **O** and **E**).
3. Suppose that, by the above operation, **A** has been able to specify the GP "All Cretans are liars". **A** then inputs the fully-specified GP and PI as premises to its inference engine:

   All Cretans are liars
   Epimenides is a Cretan

   Epimenides is a liar
4. Finally, **A** passes the premises and the conclusion of this inference to **L** for storage, and the procedure ends with **D**.

Investigation. *Retrieving stored data.* The IDEAL model of learning allows each IDEAL component to access data stored in **L**. For **E** (and therefore **A**) this means retrieving **L**'s stored data via **O**. However, **O** represents an 'independent external component' that is not included as part of IDEAL's functionality. What does this mean in practice, and how does **O** influence the task of retrieving stored data?

One way of understanding **O** is to see it as an 'environment' where **L** may deposit data and **E** may collect data. In this interpretation, **O**'s *effective* capacity is determined by the abilities of **L** and **E** to communicate with it. If **L** has our versatile means of expression (speech, writing and so on) and **E** has our five senses (or equivalent), then from their perspective their common information environment **O** will be indistinguishable from our physical environment. At the other end of the scale, if **L** and **E**'s communication is confined to mutually-comprehensible electronic signals then from their perspective **O** is indistinguishable from a continuous data connector. At one extreme the world; at the other extreme a wire. Somewhere between these extremes is a temporary internal memory space accessible to **L**, **E** and external data feeds (a keyboard and monitor, for example). Thus interpreted as a mediating environment, **O** determines the nature and quality of **E**'s retrieval of **L**'s stored data. How this task is conducted depends on **O**'s 'identity':

1. **O** is equivalent to the physical environment. In this case IDEAL's capacity to retrieve stored data is human-like. This capacity is unlikely to be significantly enhanced by the addition of a temporary internal memory space or a continuous data connector.
2. **O** is equivalent to a temporary internal memory space accessible to **L**, **E** and external data feeds. In this case IDEAL's capacity to retrieve stored data is limited by the characteristics of the internal memory. For example, if **O**'s capacity is similar to a human's short-term memory, then IDEAL is unlikely to be able to compete in data-retrieval terms with a person using her memory *and* the information tools of her physical environment (conversation, books, the internet and so on).
3. **O** is equivalent to a continous data connector. In this case IDEAL's retrieval of stored data is perfect, but both **L** and **E** have lost their mandate to select and translate data. This has its greatest impact on **E**, which no longer has an identifiable role and may be omitted altogether. There are some simple applications where this does not matter—for example, the above analysis of the proposition "Epimenides is a Cretan" would not miss **E**'s contribution—but most applications make repeated use of all IDEAL components, and so the loss of any one of them would be debilitating.

Since IDEAL is a high-level description of how humans learn, only the first of these 'identities' matches IDEAL's requirements. That is, the 'independent external component' **O** is a common information environment indistinguishable from our physical environment. **E** retrieves **L**'s stored data via **O**, hence this description of **O** determines the required features of both **L** and **E**.

Investigation. *Refining stored data.* An important feature of the IDEAL model of learning is that the data stored in **L** must be 'refined' in some manner. In this context, 'refining' is taken to mean the compilation of a log, that is, a systematic commentary that effectively organises and indexes the stored data. The log is not just a cross-referenced list, however. *Effective* organisation involves the prioritisation of data so that anticipated queries may receive a response that is timely, relevant, reliable and self-consistent. Essentially, data prioritisation is a process of demoting or deleting information that is irrelevant to the context, that exists in duplicate, or that can be inferred from a representative set of particular instances. All of these factors are demonstrated in the following example.

Once upon a time there was a wise and well-informed queen called Athene who had a small but determined daughter called Penelope. Each day at breakfast Princess Penelope regaled her mother with tales of the adventures of Percy. Prince Percy was Princess Penelope's imaginary friend who lived far away and had wonderful adventures of conquest and discovery during which he acquired all manner of useful things such as toys and sweets and household implements. One day Princess Penelope described Prince Percy's experiments with his new pet, a puppy called Desmond. Prince Percy was teaching Desmond to run and chase so that when he grew up Desmond could run and chase after escaped convicts. Desmond, it turned out, was a Dobermann. "Oh dear!" thought Queen Athene, but (being wise) she encouraged Princess Penelope to chatter away while she collected her thoughts on how to deal with the question that was sure to follow: "Mum Highness, when are we getting a Dobermann?" As it happened, Queen Athene knew a great deal about dogs, and she knew that a large and vicious Dobermann would not be a suitable pet for the royal household, especially if Princess Penelope were to train it to run and chase after the servants. Queen Athene could think of any number of alternative breeds that would be eminently suitable, but (being wise) she hesitated to appraise her daughter of this information. For she knew that *research* was not Princess Penelope's strongest trait. No: Princess Penelope was much more likely to have fixed her ambitions on a Dobermann because one of her friends owned one. Accordingly, Queen Athene mentally listed pets according to their owners:

Owner	Pet
Archduke Archibald	Alsatian
Baroness Beatrice	Beagle
Countess Constance	Chihuahua
Dowager Delilah	Dobermann
Duchess Deborah	Dobermann
Earl Eustace	Echidna
Farmer Fred	Foxhound

From this list Queen Athene removed pets that weren't dogs, pets owned by commoners, and duplicate occurrences of pets. Then she included information concerning the size and viciousness of each dog:

Owner	Pet	Size	Viciousness
Archduke Archibald	Alsatian	Big	High
Baroness Beatrice	Beagle	Medium	Low
Countess Constance	Chihuahua	Small	High
Dowager Delilah	Dobermann	Big	High

Finally, since it was her daughter's choice, Queen Athene made the Dobermann the representative of all the big and vicious breeds, removing the remainder from her list:

Owner	Pet	Size	Viciousness
Baroness Beatrice	Beagle	Medium	Low
Countess Constance	Chihuahua	Small	High
Dowager Delilah	Dobermann	Big	High

"Penelope, my dear," said Queen Athene, interrupting her daughter in mid-fantasy. "It so happens that your dear friend Baroness Beatrice has invited you to her birthday party this evening. You have my permission to go and enjoy yourself. And keep a beagle eye out for ideas for your surprise gift at next week's Princess Ball." Princess Penelope was perplexed. "I thought Beatrice's birthday was in May?", she wondered. "Yes, that's what she thought too," the Queen replied, "But I know better. Run along now and get ready for the party, and I shall compose a letter of acceptance to Beatrice for her kind invitation."

We note the following:

1. The context of the problem is provided by the anticipated query, "Mum Highness, when are we getting a Dobermann?" This query is a consequence of Queen Athene's foreknowledge of Princess Penelope's personality traits, and it is generated by means of data recognition using the Orient procedure.
2. Queen Athene approaches the problem by expressing it in terms of known parameters and procedures. This crucial initial assessment is a data analysis problem requiring the use of the Occident procedure.
3. Thorough indexing enables Queen Athene to list pets by their owners, instead of the laborious and irrelevant task of listing every breed of dog. Indexing is an internal function of the IDEAL log component **L**.
4. Having obtained an initial list, Queen Athene is able to reduce it to a manageable size by judiciously implementing various selection criteria. These criteria weed out occurrences that are unsuited to the context, duplicates, or represented by another entry. This is an iterative application of the Orient procedure.
5. The final list is a manageable set of representative cases that span the range of possible options. This 'concept set' (or 'conset' for short) is a robust foundation for rapid decision-making and as such it is the useful product of the data refinement process. That is, once data refinement has taken place then its results will be expressed as a small conset of representative cases (or 'particular instances', to use terminology introduced earlier). The conset is retained in **L**, while data culled from the conset may be demoted or deleted. When this has been done the data refinement is complete and control returns to **D**.
6. The problem is addressed by Queen Athene choosing between the alternatives in the conset. This tactical decision-making, undertaken by **D**, need not be very complicated. As shown in the example, it all depends on the quality of the conset that has been obtained through the process of data refinement.

Investigation. *Meaning and emotions.* Data prioritisation, as utilised in the previous example, would be impossible without a quick and simple means of assessing different items of data in relation to one another. In humans this is the process of assigning *meaning* to different sense perceptions. Carter suggests that the most important faculty of the frontal lobe

> ...is not the ability to plan, or choose, or follow through a strategy despite the insistent urgings of our unconscious brain to chase each

passing shadow. Rather it is the intuitive sense of meaning that binds our perceptions into a seamless whole and makes sense of our existence. Can that, too, be pinpointed? Astonishingly, it seems that it can. Meaningfulness is inextricably bound up with emotion.[16]

In other words, our emotional responses enable us to differentiate between items of data, and this is a necessary prerequisite for decision-making. Emotional responses have been discussed already, in the context of the five IDEAL learning styles:

IDEAL learning style	Positive emotion	Negative emotion
Empiricist	Attraction	Disgust
Idealist	Joy	Sorrow
Theorist	Inspiration	Fear
Activist	Excitement	Anger
Conformist	Love	Hate

In order to associate these archetypal positive and negative emotions with different items of data, it is convenient to quantify them by drawing up a graded scale for each pair, for example, a five-point scale where 1 represents 'Attraction' and 5 represents 'Disgust', and so on. Thus, for example:

Pet	Attraction / Disgust	Joy / Sorrow	Inspiration / Fear	Excitement / Anger	Love / Hate
Beagle	1	2	3	3	2
Chihuahua	5	3	4	3	4
Dobermann	5	4	5	3	5

"Oh dear!" thought Queen Athene…

Note that these response scores depend both on the individual item of data and on the characteristic learning style of the *observer*, that is, the 'owner' of these emotions. In IDEAL these emotional response scores may be stored in **L** and retrieved by data recognition. Their values may be adjusted through data refinement.

How does this implementation of 'emotional response scores' relate to the human emotional experience? In humans, emotional responses to sense perceptions are generated in the amygdala and other components of the limbic system and transmitted to the frontal lobe. In IDEAL,

[16] Rita Carter, *Mapping the Mind* (Phoenix 1998).

emotional response scores to input data (from **E**) are retrieved (from **L**) through data recognition (using **I**) and transmitted to the decision component **D**, which corresponds to the frontal lobe:

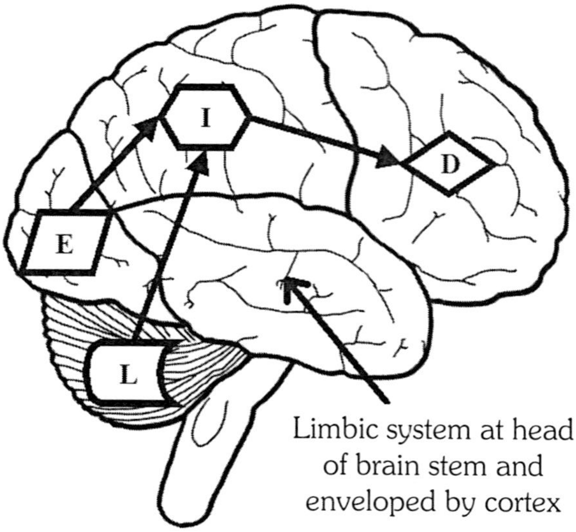

It is clear from this diagram that IDEAL has subsumed the emotion-generating role of the limbic system in the components **E**, **L** and **I**. Does this matter? Arguably *not*, as in both descriptions the procedure ends with the same faculty (the frontal lobe, **D**), which initiates the physical reactions that are the main measureable effects of emotions.

Investigation. *Refining code data.* The IDEAL model of learning specifies that "each IDEAL component stores and refines the codified descriptions of its own operations". However, 'refining code data' cannot be the same procedure as 'refining stored data', since **L** stores no code data other than its own. How, then, does each component develop its faculties? Three possible procedures come to mind:

1. Code data are sent to **L** where they may be treated as stored data. This procedure is open to **E**, **A** and **L** itself, with **E** and **A** retrieving their refined code data via **O**. That is, **E**'s power of observation depends on **L**'s power of expression, and **A**'s power of analysis depends on both. In particular, if **E** and **L** develop the ability to communicate via the written word then **A**'s ability to refine its deductive and arithmetical algorithms is transformed. This is because the written word is a unique medium for presenting multiple representations of the same thing, and this has great advantages for learning—as we shall see.

2. Code data are refined locally through trial-and-error testing of small, random adjustments to the code. This procedure is open to all IDEAL components and results in a gradual, cumulative development of capability.
3. Code data are refined locally through trial-and-error selection between a small number of self-contained alternatives. This procedure is open to all IDEAL components and results in discontinuous changes in capability, sometimes with spectacular success, at other times with disastrous failure. It presupposes the existence of 'self-contained alternatives', that is, functioning capabilities that have been learned by some other procedure.

In each of these cases, in order to test the effects of changing code data it is necessary to keep other data unchanged. For example, changes to **A**'s deduction algorithm should be tested by inputting the same premises both before and after the changes, and comparing the two conclusions. This *ceteris paribus*[17] clause also applies to the refinement of stored data, where it is assumed that operations such as **A**'s deduction algorithm do not change mid-way through an analysis. By alternating frequently between refining code data *ceteris paribus* and refining stored data *ceteris paribus*, it is possible to refine *all* the information in IDEAL. For instance, when discussing learning style development in humans, an example was given of changing a 'conceptual framework' while 'ordinary learning' was put on hold. Give Archimedes a place to stand, and he can move the world; then stand him on the world, and he can move his earlier standing-place; and so on, across the universe of knowledge. This method of alternating between *refining specific information* and *refining the means of analysing specific information* is the basis of 'self-learning', in that it leads to a general development of knowledge while being both self-regulating and self-sufficient.

Human learning skills

Investigation. *Consets and common data tags.* Data recognition relies upon the presence of common elements in compared datasets. Indeed, although they have not been explicitly identified in the earlier investigations, these 'common elements' play a central part, as can be seen from the following example.

---

[17] "All other things being equal."

Suppose that we want to be able to recognise a dog when we see one. Let our stored data comprise names, breeds and images of a number of dogs, for example:

Animal	Name	Breed	Image
Dog	Buddy	Beagle	
Dog	Charlie	Chihuahua	
Dog	Desmond	Dobermann	

Note that these items of data have been identified as particular instances of a type of animal called a 'dog'. This 'common data tagging' enables the selection of these items of data and no others (cats, rabbits and so on), thereby greatly simplifying the task of data recognition. By comparing these images it is possible to detect common elements—four legs, tail, black nose and so on—that may be included in a new conset defining the essential characteristics of a dog:

Animal	Common elements	Particular instance 1	Particular instance 2	Particular instance 3
Dog				

Similarly, we can identify consets for other animals:

Animal	Common elements	Particular instance 1	Particular instance 2	Particular instance 3
Cat				
Rabbit				

Now we introduce a new item of data relating to an unknown type of animal:

Animal	Name	Breed	Image
?	Andy	Airedale	

By inputting Andy's image and comparing it with the conset images for dog, cat and rabbit, one can identify Andy as a dog with little ambiguity. All conset images may be used for this comparison, perhaps using the common elements for the initial identification and the particular instances for a validation check.

From this example we see that common data tagging enables the definition of consets that are the basis of data recognition. In addition, since these consets are uniquely identified by their data tags, we see that data recognition is simply a matter of finding the correct data tag for a new item of data:

Teacher : What type of animal is Andy?

Pupil : Andy is a *dog*.

As this exchange suggests, common data tagging is *also* the basis of our acquisition of abstract concepts such as our 'idea' of a dog. And common data tagging is implicit in the way we teach children to read:

Teacher	:	"Andy the dog came out to play." Which one is Andy?
Pupil	:	That one. *Points to picture of dog.*
Teacher	:	Very good! What is Andy doing?
Pupil	:	Chasing Sybil. *Points to picture of cat.*
Teacher	:	Yes! "Sybil the cat ran up the tree." Where is Andy now?
Pupil	:	There. *Points to picture of dog.*
Teacher	:	That's right. "Andy the dog sat by the tree." Where is the tree?
Pupil	:	*Points to picture of tree.*
Teacher	:	And where is the dog?
Pupil	:	"Andy!" *Points to picture of dog.*
Teacher	:	Very good! Now, follow my finger. "Andy the dog sat by the tree." This word here says "Andy". Which word says "dog", do you think?
Pupil	:	That one. *Points to the word "dog".*

This is not a contrived example; my own son was already reading by his third birthday, having been taught in this style. The key feature of this approach is to have several representations of the same thing, all linked by a common data tag. Thus in this example we have the sounds "Andy" and "dog", the written words "Andy" and "dog", and the image of Andy the dog, all related by means of the common data tag 'dog'. In brief: *consets*, uniquely identified by *common data tags*, are the basis of the human faculty of language comprehension.

Investigation. *Data output.* Comprehension is not sufficient to learn the full set of language skills; participation is also required. A key determinant in language participation is the ability to impart information to the outside world. We have seen that IDEAL sends information to the 'outside world' **O** via its log component **L**. Also, we have seen that IDEAL initiates physical reactions (including, we suppose, gesturing, speaking and writing) via its decision component **D**. That is, both **L** and **D** appear to be in charge of imparting information to the outside world, which sounds like a recipe for conflict. How can this be resolved?

In the human brain, actions are initiated by the frontal lobe, or, more accurately, by a part of the frontal lobe called the motor cortex. However, the procedural memories detailing how specific actions are to be performed are stored in the cerebellum. That is, although actions are initiated by the frontal lobe, they are 'made flesh' by the cerebellum. The frontal lobe and cerebellum correspond to **D** and **L** respectively:

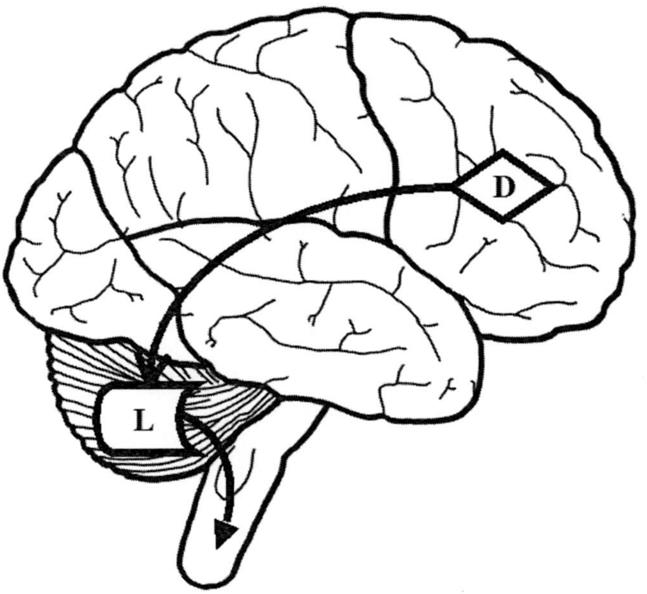

Thus **D** determines whether an action takes place, and **L** determines the precise nature of the action. We see that **D** and **L** are working together and not in competition, as befits the IDEAL model of learning that is based on the interdependence of components.

This description raises an interesting question concerning the nature of the information that can be imparted to the outside world. As we have seen, the IDEAL model of learning is formulated such that not all data information can be stored in **L**. The decision component **D** *can* access all data, but **D** has no direct means of communicating data to the outside world, or even to **L**. Although **D** can command **L** to output data, **L** cannot output data that it is not privy to. **L** can output a *representation* of **D**'s data—an example or a model, perhaps—but it cannot output the real thing. Always there will be a difference between the internal and external representations of information. As it is written: "We see through a glass, darkly".

Investigation. *Synchronous coordination*. In the last investigation the notion of 'output data' was broadened to include all physical reactions, including gesturing, speaking and writing. Since these responses are imparted by **L** to **O**, their effects in **O** may be detected by **E**. **D** can then monitor these effects by using the Orient procedure to compare **E**'s new input data with stored data retrieved from **L** by means of a 'predictive conset'. A good match for this data comparison shows that the comparator dataset from **L** was well-chosen, that is, IDEAL has made a good prediction of the effects of its output responses. In this case **D** may follow up with further commands to **L** for continued output, either in an attempt to perpetuate the good match between output and input, or in an attempt to discover its limits. If at any time there is a poor match for the data comparison then **D** can fall back on the results of a deeper Occident analysis that may be conducted in parallel with the Orient temporal matching. The Occident analysis identifies the implications of the changed circumstances represented by **E**'s new input data. The results of this procedure constitute revised predictions that may be made the basis of further commands from **D** to **L** for revised output responses. Alternatively, **D** is free to call a halt to the proceedings.

What has been described here is *synchronous coordination*, that is, the stable management of an interaction between input and output that develops iteratively through time. In IDEAL this is achieved through *predictive consets* that establish temporal sequences of particular sensations or events. These consets may come about through trial-and-error improvement or they may be adopted as complete entities from the environment **O**, comprising anything from simple rhythms and sayings through popular tunes and familiar tales to complete symphonies and histories. Whatever their origin, predictive consets act as distinctive temporal patterns against which sequences of specific physical responses may be attached (memorised) and detached (reproduced), in the manner described above.

Synchronous coordination is the basic skill that we use when learning how to interact with our environment. That is, synchronous coordination is the common basis of hand-eye coordination, eating, walking, gymnastics, speaking, singing, dancing, playing a musical instrument, controlling a machine, writing; the list goes on. It is claimed, therefore, that through this mechanism IDEAL is capable of exercising a degree of automotive control that is no less versatile and sophisticated than that enjoyed by humans.

Investigation. *Focussing and awareness.* Descartes, the 'Father of Modern Philosophy', famously began his philosophical investigations by calling into question everything he knew. The opinions of others, the evidence of his senses, proofs based on reasoning, and thoughts which "can also come to us when we are asleep" were all discarded in Descartes' ruthless application of his 'method of doubt'. Then came his great discovery:

> But immediately afterwards I became aware that, while I decided thus to think that everything was false, it followed necessarily that I who thought thus must be something; and observing that this truth: *I think,*

therefore I am, was so certain and so evident that all the most extravagant suppositions of the sceptics were not capable of shaking it, I judged that I could accept it without scruple as the first principle of the philosophy I was seeking.[18]

As support for his method of doubt Descartes describes his (frequently wayward) train of thought as he sits before the fire ruminating. Indeed it is clear from his account that he has strong grounds to doubt the veracity of his thoughts. It is also clear that he is prone to distraction, with a multitude of apparently unconnected thoughts competing for his attention. *I think, therefore I am*, concludes the philosopher, a thought that sets him on an ambitious course to prove that God exists and all's right with the world. So keen is he to follow this course that he misses a different conclusion that is more useful and (in retrospect) more obvious: *I am distracted, therefore I am aware*. That is, the occurrence of distraction implies a sense of shifting between competing thoughts, and it is this sense which we call 'awareness'. Thus we can advance a minimalist definition of 'awareness' as the sense of shifting between competing thoughts, and sufficient control over this shifting that one can (at least) monitor its progress.

By this definition, IDEAL can do awareness. For example, in the last investigation we saw **D** initiating the Orient and Occident procedures in parallel. These procedures use **I** and **A** respectively, components that can operate simultaneously as they have no direct connection. **D** can monitor **I** and see one 'train of thought', or **D** can monitor **A** and see another. Thus **D** can shift between different 'thoughts' and as such it experiences 'awareness'. We recall that **D** corresponds to the frontal lobe (or lobes):

The frontal lobes are where ideas are created; plans constructed; thoughts joined with their associations to form new memories; and fleeting perceptions held in mind until they are dispatched to long-term memory or to oblivion. This brain region is the home of consciousness—the high-lit land where the products of the brain's subterranean assembly lines emerge for scrutiny. Self-awareness arises here, and emotions are transformed in this place from physical survival systems to subjective feelings. If we were to draw a 'you are here' sign on our map of the mind, it is to the frontal lobes that the arrow would point. In this our new view of the brain echoes an ancient knowledge—for it is here, too, that mystics have traditionally placed the Third Eye—the gateway to highest point of awareness.[19]

---

[18] René Descartes, *Discourse on Method and The Meditations* (1637-41), tr. F.E. Sutcliffe (Penguin 1968).

[19] Rita Carter, *ibid.*

Why can IDEAL do awareness? As we have seen, learning works best when all parts of the learning cycle are fully engaged: *Omnis extremus, sed non in extremis*. There is a virtue, too, in maintaining an agile awareness by switching the focus of attention between processes at frequent intervals[20]. Bogged down with **A**'s intricate analysis? Then take a look at **I**'s bigger picture. Tired of abstract generalities? Then stimulate **E** by going for a walk and finding new data. Overwhelmed by new information? Then go to sleep by putting **E** and **D** on standby, meanwhile **L** can use your down-time to organise its archive. These learning strategies work by restoring the balance between the different components, to the greater good of all. In each case the necessary feature is the ability to switch the focus of attention—or, in a word, 'awareness'.

Investigation. *Abstract thought.* When discussing the refinement of code data, it was found that the ability to read and write transforms **A**'s ability to refine its algorithms. What is the effect of this on "the home of consciousness", **D**? From **D**'s perspective **A**'s algorithms are undifferentiated 'black boxes', but when associated with specific applications and represented to **D** as different consets, these model-data associations may be treated as specific coherent entities: we call them 'thoughts', 'ideas' or 'concepts'. That is, in transforming **A**'s ability to refine its algorithms, the ability to read and write also transforms **D**'s ability to refine its thoughts. A case in point is right in front of you: none of the key ideas in *Principia Intellegentia* would have been formulated if I had not spent the last 25 years committing my thoughts to paper.

Abstract thought requires the ability to read and write. In humans these skills are well-developed, having co-evolved over thousands of years[21]. In IDEAL, as we have seen, **E** and **L**'s capacities to input and output data are required to be human-like. It follows that IDEAL fulfils the essential prerequisites for abstract thought.

The quest for artificial intelligence

Definition. The phrase 'artificial intelligence' or 'AI' has come to mean many things, including: (i) The design and operation of robots and their components; (ii) The design and operation of artificial neural networks;

---

[20] The contribution to learning of actively switching the focus of attention is also discussed in **2. Where and When?**

[21] This is a special case of Deacon's notion that symbolic representation co-evolved with language. See Terrence Deacon, *The Symbolic Species* (Penguin 1997), and **3. How?**

(iii) The design and operation of specialised problem-solvers, for example, games programs; (iv) The application of specialised computing techniques, for example, expert systems; (v) A science-fiction world in which humans and computers are virtually indistinguishable[22]. Vast resources have been expended in the pursuit of these different agendas. Nevertheless, it remains the case that, as the saying goes, "artificial intelligence is no match for natural stupidity". Perhaps there has not been sufficient emphasis on understanding *human* intelligence, as this definition seems to suggest:

> **artificial intelligence** (or *machine intelligence*). A new, computer-based science aimed partly at understanding the nature of human and animal intelligence and specifically at creating machines capable of intelligent problem-solving, by any means open to the logician and the engineer.[23]

Proposition. The goals of AI research will not be achieved without addressing similar goals in human intelligence research.

Proposition. It has been shown that IDEAL has the capacity to simulate the key human learning skills of language, physical coordination, awareness, and abstract thought. These conclusions are based on applications of the computable procedures permitted by the flowchart diagram defining IDEAL. It follows that IDEAL may be applied to the design of learning algorithms for automated computing machines.

Proposition. It has been shown that the phenomenon of intelligence in humans is entirely bound up with their individual ability to learn—using IDEAL. It follows that IDEAL also addresses the goals of AI research.

---

[22] If computers were *entirely* indistinguishable from humans then there would be little point portraying them as fictional characters. Thus science-fiction plotlines typically turn on a key distinction between the species, an 'Achilles heel' for one or the other. See, for example: *2001—A Space Odyssey*; *Alien*; *Artificial Intelligence—AI*; *Blade Runner*; *I, Robot*; *The Matrix*; *Metropolis*; *The Terminator*; *Wargames*. Some of these films are discussed in **5. Who?**

[23] Alan Bullock and Oliver Stallybrass (eds.), *The Fontana Dictionary of Modern Thought* (Fontana 1977).

2. Where and When?

How that which is proposed fits in with its frame of reference; IDEAL; Scientific method in practice; General principles and particular instances; Normal science and scientific revolutions; The toolkit expert; The development of computing; Rules of thumb; Scientific method in theory; Falsification; Deductive-nomological explanation; Dialectic reasoning; Probabilistic inference; Truth criteria; Theory acceptance criteria.

How that which is proposed fits in with its frame of reference

By means of 'IDEAL', a high-level description of how humans learn, *Principia Intellegentia* establishes the principles governing human and machine intelligence. In the following, 'that which is proposed'—IDEAL—is critically assessed using the observations and rules of its 'frame of reference'—the philosophy of science. Why philosophy of science? Because it is the means by which we judge theories like IDEAL that claim to "reveal the truth about a hidden objective reality":

> **science, philosophy of.** Organized empirical science provides the most impressive result of human rationality and is one of the best accredited candidates for knowledge. The philosophy of science seeks to show wherein this rationality lies; what is distinctive about its explanations and theoretical constructions; what marks it off from guesswork and pseudo-science and makes its predictions and technologies worthy of confidence; above all whether its theories can be taken to reveal the truth about a hidden objective reality.[1]

Investigation. The topics to be covered have been arranged in two groups:

1. What scientists do. *Scientific method in practice; General principles and particular instances; Normal science and scientific revolutions; The toolkit expert; The development of computing; Rules of thumb.*
2. Philosophers' reasons for what scientists do. *Scientific method in theory; Falsification; Deductive-nomological explanation; Dialectic reasoning; Probabilistic inference; Truth criteria; Theory acceptance criteria.*

Between them, these topics address much of what is considered to be the 'philosophy of science'. However, the purpose is not to recapitulate known findings, nor to rewrite the field. The object of the exercise is to test IDEAL with what is known in the philosophy of science—*and vice versa.*

---

[1] Antony Flew (ed.), *A Dictionary of Philosophy* (Pan 1979).

Proposition. It will be shown that the key observations and rules in the philosophy of science guide the interpretation and implementation of IDEAL. At the same time, it will be shown that IDEAL explains the key observations and rules in the philosophy of science. Specifically, it is claimed that IDEAL implements an 'iterative dialectic' methodology; and it is claimed that this implementation contributes positively to our understanding of the philosophy of science.

The investigation commences with a summary of the relevant properties of IDEAL.

IDEAL

Definition. 'IDEAL' is an acronym for 'Iterative Dialectic Engine for Automated Learning'. It also stands for the five operational components in this flow diagram:

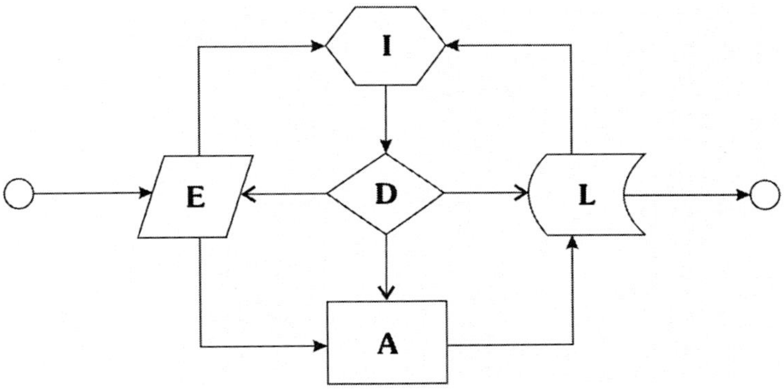

Observations and derivations setting out IDEAL's detailed properties are given elsewhere[2]. The properties that are of particular relevance here are as follows:

1. IDEAL has five components, each of which has a specific and distinct function by which it may be associated with a characteristic 'learning style': 'Empiricists' have a preference for learning through observation, which is closely related to the data-gathering function of the Evidence component **E**; 'Idealists' have a preference for learning through comparing and correlating information within a pre-existing framework, which is closely related to the data comparison function of the Iteration component **I**; 'Theorists' have a preference for learning through constructing and operating representative models, which is closely related to the analytical function of the Algorithm component **A**;

[2] See **1. What?** and **3. How?**

'Activists' have a preference for learning through action and reaction, which is closely related to the control function of the Decision component **D**; and 'Conformists' have a preference for learning through reference to an established authority, which is closely related to the data storage function of the Log component **L**.

2. *Omnis extremus, sed non in extremis.*[3] There are significant learning benefits in engaging with all five IDEAL learning styles in a balanced fashion. There is a benefit, too, in switching between different styles or operational procedures at frequent intervals.
3. IDEAL establishes a fundamental distinction between 'data' and 'control'. In the IDEAL flow diagram, items of data are transmitted by means of data connectors (solid arrows), while control commands are transmitted by means of control connectors (barbed arrows). This distinction underpins the derivation of IDEAL and determines its key characteristics.
4. At the simplest level, IDEAL's operation can be described in terms of two procedures known as the 'Orient' and the 'Occident'. The Orient procedure comprises the upper part of IDEAL and is responsible for orienting a dataset by comparing it with other datasets. The Occident procedure comprises the lower part of IDEAL and is responsible for analysing a dataset by treating it as input to a computational algorithm.
5. IDEAL stores its information in two forms, 'concept sets' (or 'consets') and 'code data'. A conset comprises sufficient information that it can describe the origin and composition of its constituents with some fidelity. For example, if a conset has been established through an analytical process then it will include an identifier for the generating algorithm as well as particular instances of data inputs and outputs for this algorithm, all associated with one another by means of a 'common data tag'. Expressed using a cipher equivalent to a human or computer language, 'code data' define the different operations undertaken by each of IDEAL's five components. On its own, a sequence of code data defining an algorithm has little meaning, but it acquires meaning when identified in a conset together with associated input and output data. For this reason the 'common data tag' identifying a specific coherent conset can be interpreted as a 'thought', 'idea' or 'concept'.
6. Consets are refined by the pairwise comparison of set members using the Orient procedure, once a suitable comparator set has been identified using the Occident procedure. The refinement or learning process is significantly enhanced if there are several different representations of

---

[3] "To be every extremist—but none too much."

the subject, for example: an image; a written word labelling the image; and a sound pronouncing the written word. The written word is a unique medium for this purpose.

7. Code data associated with the Algorithm component **A** can be included in consets and refined in the same way. With the ability to read and write, this approach can generate coherent sets of information that are the raw materials of complex abstract thought.
8. Code data associated with the Iteration component **I** and the Decision component **D** cannot be included in consets. These code data can only be refined by trial-and-error testing of small, random adjustments to the code (resulting in a gradual, cumulative development of capability) or by trial-and-error selection between a small number of self-contained alternatives (resulting in discontinuous changes in capability).
9. By alternating frequently between refining particular instances of input data *ceteris paribus*[4] and refining operational code data *ceteris paribus*, it is possible to refine all the information in IDEAL. This method is regarded as the basis of self-learning, in that it leads to the parallel development of knowledge and the means of acquiring that knowledge.

Scientific method in practice

One of the first things learnt by science students is how to write a report of an experiment. By tradition, this report should have the following sections:

1. *Aim*. A definition of the purpose of the experiment. Typically the aim is to measure certain parameter values for comparison with theory.
2. *Introduction*. A brief review of the field, setting the experiment in context.
3. *Theory*. A definition of the key parameters and equations that are expected to determine the outcome of the experiment, and a derivation of predicted parameter values for comparison with experimental measurements.
4. *Experiment*. A description of the experiment, detailing resources used and procedures followed.
5. *Results*. A tabulation of the actual parameter values measured during the experiment, and a comparison with the values predicted theoretically.
6. *Conclusion*. An assessment of whether or not the experiment has achieved its aim, and the implications of this judgement for further work.

Proposition. The 'Results' section divides naturally into two parts: (i) A tabulation of parameter values measured experimentally; (ii) A comparison

[4] "All other things being equal."

between parameter values measured experimentally and predicted theoretically. With no loss of information these two parts may be assigned to the 'Experiment' and 'Conclusion' sections respectively. Thus we have five sections that have an obvious correspondence with the five IDEAL learning styles:

IDEAL learning style	Report heading
Empiricist	Experiment
Idealist	Conclusion
Theorist	Theory
Activist	Aim
Conformist	Introduction

Proposition. Many of the questions that scientists ask, and many of their everyday lines of enquiry, derive from this traditional format for the reporting of experiments.

Example. When preparing to present her work at a seminar, a research student would do well to know the answers to these questions:

1. From the Empiricist: "What's the application?"; "What are you measuring?".
2. From the Idealist: "What's your conclusion?"; "How does this fit in with what is known in the field?".
3. From the Theorist: "What's your units?"; "What equations are you solving?".
4. From the Activist: "What's your objective?"; "What are your recommendations?".
5. From the Conformist: "What's your reference?"; "Have you taken into account the recent work of such-and-such?".

Example. Much of routine science research is focussed on gathering information in preparation for writing a dissertation or a paper to be submitted to a peer-reviewed journal. In the vast majority of cases, these publications are expected to manifest the *content* (and, often, the *form*) of the traditional report format identified above. This requirement translates directly into the lines of enquiry followed by most of the scientists most of the time.

Proposition. This account of the traditional approach to reporting experiments emphasises, as an essential element, the comparison of the results of theory and experiment. This *data comparison* feature is often overlooked in descriptions of 'scientific method'. Accordingly, it is instructive to formulate a working definition of empirical scientific method, using the framework of the traditional structure of a scientific report, and emphasising the role played by data comparison.

Definition. Empirical scientific method:

1. Empirical scientific investigation commences with an physical problem, that is, a question or puzzle relating to a measurable phenomenon.
2. Faced with this problem, the scientist first looks for recorded instances of similar problems in related application areas. These are down-selected to a manageable number having the greatest correspondence with the problem under consideration.
3. For each of the down-selected recorded instances, the principles determining their theoretical solution are identified. Typically these principles are formulated as a set of equations requiring values of input parameters conforming to a precise specification. The problem under consideration is analysed to extract appropriate parameter values that are input to the set of equations, yielding a theoretical prediction of the solution to the problem.
4. For each of the down-selected recorded instances, the principles determining their experimental analysis are identified. Typically these principles are formulated as a set of procedures involving the application of specific resources in a precise way. These procedures are applied to the problem under consideration, yielding the required experimental measurements of the physical phenomenon.
5. The experimental measurements are compared with the theoretical predictions, thereby either confirming or calling into question the applicability of the selected theoretical and experimental principles. Accordingly the scientist comes to a judgement as to whether the original problem has been solved.

Proposition. The above definition applies to empirical scientific method. A similar definition can be formulated for 'theoretical' scientific method, that is, where the problem to be solved is a thought-experiment. In this case, instead of comparing the results of theory and experiment, the scientist is comparing the results of two or more different theories, and steps 3 and 4 in the above definition may be combined.

Definition. Theoretical scientific method:

1. Theoretical scientific investigation commences with a theoretical problem, that is, a question or puzzle requiring a solution.

2. Faced with this problem, the scientist first looks for recorded instances of similar problems in related application areas. These are down-selected to a manageable number having the greatest correspondence with the problem under consideration.
3. For each of the down-selected recorded instances, the principles determining their theoretical solution are identified. Typically these principles are formulated as several sets of equations requiring values of input parameters conforming to a precise specification. The problem under consideration is analysed to extract appropriate parameter values that are input to the sets of equations, yielding theoretical predictions of the solution to the problem.
4. The theoretical predictions are compared with one another, thereby either confirming or calling into question the applicability of the selected theoretical principles. Accordingly the scientist comes to a judgement as to whether the original problem has been solved.

Proposition. These working definitions of scientific method implement known IDEAL procedures, in particular, the Orient and Occident procedures for data comparison and data analysis respectively. Drawing on these definitions and on IDEAL, it is possible to formulate a working definition of a general method for practical problem-solving.

Definition. Practical problem-solving method:

1. Practical problem-solving commences with a practical problem, that is, a novel situation or dilemma requiring a response.
2. Faced with this problem, the problem-solver first looks for recorded instances of similar experiences. These are down-selected to a manageable number having the greatest correspondence with the problem under consideration.
3. For each of the down-selected recorded instances, the principles governing their associated responses are identified. Typically these principles are formulated as general rules that acquire meaning when identified in a conset together with associated input and output data (that is, 'recorded instances of similar experiences' and 'associated responses' respectively). These general rules are applied to the new situation, yielding a proposed response.
4. The proposed response is compared with the responses associated with the recorded instances, thereby either confirming or calling into question the applicability of the selected general rules. Accordingly the problem-solver comes to a judgement as to whether the original problem has been addressed.

Proposition. This problem-solving method can be extended to allow learning from experience:

5. If, on comparison with recorded instances and associated responses, the new situation and/or its proposed response prove to be particularly unusual, then the problem-solver may commit both to memory for future use in step 2. This involves constructing a new conset comprising descriptions of the situation and response, and an identifier for the general rules governing the response.

Proposition. It has been shown that a traditional format for the reporting of experiments corresponds with the five IDEAL learning styles. Following this format, working definitions of the methods for empirical and theoretical scientific investigation have been identified. These definitions implement known IDEAL procedures, and in combination they lead to a working definition of a general method for practical problem-solving, which can be extended to allow learning from experience. This deepens our understanding of both scientific method and IDEAL.

General principles and particular instances

Implicit in the above analysis of practical scientific method is the assumption that all scientific knowledge can be divided into two categories. Conventionally termed 'general principles' (GPs) and 'particular instances' (PIs), these categories clearly relate to theoretical or experimental 'principles' and 'recorded instances', respectively; however, the philosophy of science literature often uses these terms for 'theory' and 'experiment' as well. From here it takes only a few small steps to include other familiar dualisms, rapidly leading to utter confusion.

Example. At what point in the following sequence do we draw the line at what constitutes a GP/PI pair?

1. Theoretical or experimental principles and recorded instances.
2. Theory and experiment.
3. Laws and examples.
4. Equations and data.
5. Data analysis and data comparison.
6. Propositions and sets.
7. Arithmetic and relations.
8. Algebra and geometry.
9. Calculus and graphs.
10. Variables and fields.

11. Particles and waves.
12. Matter and space-time.
13. Conservation laws and symmetries.
14. Equations of motion and calculus of variations.
15. Analytic and dialectic.
16. Words and pictures.
17. Science and art.
18. Rationality and inspiration.
19. Left hemisphere and right hemisphere.
20. Yang and Yin.
21. Material and spiritual.

Investigation. Some of these dualisms appear contrived—'words and pictures', for instance—but others are more deep, and these present a considerable challenge to any theory (such as IDEAL) that claims to explain learning behaviour in humans. For example, can our theory explain the following observations?

1. By leafing through any science or mathematics textbook, one quickly sees that these subjects are best learnt by alternating between defining fundamental principles and working through example applications.
2. The differential of a function is its gradient when plotted as a curve on a graph; its integral is the area under the curve. Calculus may not have developed at all without the preceding invention of coordinate geometry. For that matter, did algebra and geometry co-evolve?
3. It is impossible to think of coherent objects—particles—without at the same time thinking of the space inhabited by those objects—a 'field'. Consequently it is often feasible (and occasionally essential) to formulate two complementary descriptions of a dynamical system, one using equations of motion and the other using field equations.
4. Where there is more than one theoretical description of the same physical domain it is possible to construct a 'metatheory' or 'theory of theories' that relates these theoretical descriptions (as in the previous example). It is as if these theoretical descriptions, which are GPs in their own right, are also PIs in relation to the metatheory GP. That is, GPs may also be PIs with respect to a 'higher level' GP.

In order to 'explain' these and other observations, it is tempting to extend the basic GP/PI description by adding appropriate *ad hoc* hypotheses[5].

---

[5] The role of *ad hoc* hypotheses is discussed in Imre Lakatos, 'Falsification and the Methodology of Scientific Research Programmes', in Imre Lakatos and Alan Musgrave (eds.), *Criticism and the Growth of Knowledge* (Cambridge 1970).

Example. An *ad hoc* hypothesis that appears to relate to the question of 'metatheories' is Popper's notion of 'levels of universality':

> We may distinguish, within a theoretical system, statements belonging to various levels of universality. The statements on the highest level of universality are the axioms; statements on the lower levels can be deduced from them. Higher level empirical statements have always the character of hypotheses relative to the lower level statements deducible from them: they can be falsified by the falsification of these less universal statements. But in any hypothetical deductive system, these less universal statements are themselves still strictly universal statements, in the sense here understood. Thus they too must have the character of *hypotheses*—a fact which has often been overlooked in the case of lower-level universal statements. Mach, for example, calls Fourier's theory of heat conduction a 'model theory of physics' for the curious reason that 'this theory is founded not on a *hypothesis* but on an *observable fact*'. However, this 'observable fact' to which Mach refers is described by him by the statement '... the velocity of the levelling out of temperature differences, provided these differences of temperature are small, is proportional to these differences themselves'—an all-statement whose hypothetical character should be sufficiently conspicuous.[6]

This is incomprehensible metaphysics and a damning indictment of '*ad hoc* hypotheses'.

Proposition. All of these dualisms can be explained using IDEAL—without elaboration. The key principles are as follows:

1. All dualisms exist because humans are instinctive pattern-seekers. Given any piece of information, we are genetically predisposed to seek out recognisable features, and this involves comparing this new information with information retrieved from memory. This is simulated in IDEAL through repeated bilateral comparison of input data and stored data using the Iteration component **I**, whose *dyadic* mode of operation necessarily results in a dualistic interpretation of the compared datasets.
2. Abstract concepts have little meaning except when 'explained' by means of examples. *For example*, the concept of evolution by natural selection has been explained through a close examination of the different Galapagos finches, and the concepts of repentance and redemption have been explained through the parable of the prodigal son. Thus in IDEAL a GP acquires meaning only when identified in a conset together with associated PIs.
3. Persistent dualisms can co-evolve. This is simulated by IDEAL's self-learning mechanism which involves alternating frequently between refining GPs *ceteris paribus* and refining PIs *ceteris paribus*.

---

[6] Karl Popper, *The Logic of Scientific Discovery* (Hutchinson 1959).

4. Algebra and geometry is an example of a 'special' dualism that appears to benefit from having both algorithmic and pictorial representations. This feature is captured in IDEAL in two ways. First, IDEAL has no temporary internal memory space and therefore it must be able to read and write in order to recycle stored data. With these faculties, however, IDEAL can generate the complex consets that we interpret as abstract thoughts. Secondly, the complementary Occident and Orient procedures specialise in handling algorithmic and pictorial data respectively.
5. "GPs may also be PIs with respect to a 'higher level' GP." This is possible in IDEAL because "code data associated with the Algorithm component **A** can be included in consets": that is, code data definitions *of GPs* can be included *as PIs* in consets, where they will be associated with other GPs. Sometimes it helps to think of these latter GPs as residing on a 'higher level' and the resulting linked chain of GP/PI pairs as 'levels of universality'. However, for any GP/PI pair in this hierarchy, the GP is 'general' not in an absolute sense but relative to the PI, while the PI is 'particular' not in an absolute sense but relative to the GP, therefore it cannot be inferred that a 'higher level' GP is 'more universal' than a 'lower level' GP. That is, even though the 'levels of universality' model has inspired much *metaphysical* speculation (as philosophers from Plato to Popper have shown), it offers little or no *practical* insight: and these are two good reasons why we can do without it.

Proposition. IDEAL's ability to explain GP/PI and other dualisms without an increase in theoretical complexity is an 'emergent phenomenon' not anticipated in the original design. It means that we can refer to all such dualisms in the same way, that is, using the GP/PI terminology. Of the five 'principles' identified above, the first is probably the most important. This emphasises the role of IDEAL's **I** component whose mode of operation is both 'iterative'[7] and 'dialectic'[8]. Accordingly, these words feature in the definition of 'IDEAL'.

Definition. 'IDEAL' is an acronym for 'Iterative Dialectic Engine for Automated Learning'.

---

[7] That is, executing the same procedure in a stable, repeated sequence.

[8] That is, implementing a dyadic mode of operation. This usage of the word 'dialectic' is new but not inconsistent with previous definitions.

Normal science and scientific revolutions

The classic account of 'what scientists do' is Kuhn's *The Structure of Scientific Revolutions*[9], which sets out the historical evidence for the hypothesis that science proceeds by alternating between periods of normalcy and upheaval:

> Normal science, the activity in which most scientists inevitably spend almost all their time, is predicated on the assumption that the scientific community knows what the world is like. Much of the success of the enterprise derives from the community's willingness to defend that assumption, if necessary at considerable cost. Normal science, for example, often suppresses fundamental novelties because they are necessarily subversive of its basic commitments. Nevertheless, so long as those commitments retain an element of the arbitrary, the very nature of normal research ensures that novelty shall not be suppressed for very long. Sometimes a normal problem, one that ought to be solvable by known rules and procedures, resists the reiterated onslaught of the ablest members of the group within whose competence it falls. On other occasions a piece of equipment designed and constructed for the purpose of normal research fails to perform in the anticipated manner, revealing an anomaly that cannot, despite repeated effort, be aligned with professional expectation. In these and other ways besides, normal science repeatedly goes astray. And when it does—when, that is, the profession can no longer evade anomalies that subvert the existing tradition of scientific practice—then begins the extraordinary investigations that lead the profession at last to a new set of commitments, a new basis for the practice of science. The extraordinary episodes in which the shift of professional commitments occurs are the ones known in this essay as scientific revolutions. They are the tradition-shattering complements to the tradition-bound activity of normal science.

A scientific revolution, Kuhn explains, is the result of a collective shift from one 'paradigm' to another. Kuhn does not define what he means by 'paradigm', but—intending to help—one of his supporters has identified 21 different senses[10]:

1. "A universally recognized scientific achievement."
2. "A myth."
3. "A 'philosophy', or constellation of questions."
4. "A textbook, or classic work."
5. "A whole tradition."

---

[9] Thomas Kuhn, *The Structure of Scientific Revolutions* (second edition, Chicago 1970).

[10] Margaret Masterman, 'The Nature of a Paradigm', in Imre Lakatos and Alan Musgrave (eds.), *Criticism and the Growth of Knowledge* (Cambridge 1970).

6. "A scientific achievement."
7. "An analogy."
8. "A successful metaphysical speculation."
9. "An accepted device in common law."
10. "A source of tools."
11. "A standard illustration."
12. "A device, or type of instrumentation."
13. "An anomalous pack of cards."
14. "A machine-tool factory."
15. "A gestalt figure."
16. "A set of political institutions."
17. "A 'standard' applied to quasi-metaphysics."
18. "An organizing principle which can govern perception itself."
19. "A general epistemological viewpoint."
20. "A new way of seeing."
21. "Something which defines a broad sweep of reality."

Investigation. There are two main problems with Kuhn's hypothesis. First, while it appears that normal science and scientific revolutions are the result of collective behaviour in the scientific community, this description cannot be inferred from Kuhn's many examples of scientific practice, all of which feature the thoughts and actions of *individuals*. For instance:

> The success of a paradigm—whether Aristotle's analysis of motion, Ptolemy's computations of planetary position, Laviosier's application of the balance, or Maxwell's mathematization of the electromagnetic field—is at the start largely a promise of success discoverable in selected and still incomplete examples. Normal science consists in the actualization of that promise...[11]

Secondly, using 21 different definitions of 'paradigm' is wholly unscientific, as the following example illustrates.

Example. I once attended a talk on 'crop circles' which largely comprised a slide show of dozens of panoramic photographs of flattened wheat. The presenter derived great significance from the fact that no two flattened designs were the same. My reaction was the exact opposite: I would have been more impressed if all the shapes had been identical (circular, for instance), then one might have been justified in looking for a common cause.

---

[11] Thomas Kuhn, *ibid*.

Proposition. Like a field of wheat, Kuhn's use of the word 'paradigm' bends with the wind. This flexibility means that it appears to explain every casual observation—whereas in fact it explains nothing at all. 21 different definitions of 'paradigm' do not add to our understanding of the word, rather they render it meaningless.

Investigation. Despite these objections, Kuhn's epic depiction of science as a series of lab-coat revolutions is extremely attractive. Successful, too: *The Structure of Scientific Revolutions* is the only philosophy of science book to have sold over a million copies, and Kuhn has been hailed as "one of the outstanding philosophers of science of our time"[12]. Can nothing be salvaged from his grand vision?

Proposition. Kuhn's conflation of the behaviour of individual scientists and the behaviour of the scientific community as a whole is clearly inadmissible. However, if we are able to demonstrate that beneath their physical, intellectual and ideological differences all scientists are fundamentally the same, then it might be possible to argue that there is a simple link between individual behaviour and collective behaviour, thereby redeeming part or all of Kuhn's hypothesis. The premise of *Principia Intellegentia* is that all humans (including scientists) *are* fundamentally the same, the common feature being that they learn about the world using the same mechanism: IDEAL.

Proposition. Is it a coincidence that we have 21 different definitions of 'paradigm' and 21 examples of GP/PI pairs? No: the GP/PI list stops at 21 precisely in order to suggest an equivalence with paradigms. That is, a paradigm *is* a GP/PI pair, or (in IDEAL's terminology) a conset. It is of interest to explore the implications of this statement.

Investigation. An IDEAL conset may be refined by the pairwise comparison of set members or (indirectly) by the refinement of code data defining GPs belonging to the conset. There are three mechanisms for refining code data:

1. Code data associated with data analysis can be included in consets and refined in the same way.
2. Code data associated with data comparison and with decision-making can be refined by trial-and-error testing of small, random adjustments to the code.
3. Code data associated with data comparison and with decision-making can be refined by trial-and-error selection between a small number of self-contained alternatives.

---

[12] Margaret Masterman, *ibid.*

The first two mechanisms result in a gradual, cumulative development of capability, identifying these as the basis of 'normal science'. The third mechanism results in discontinuous changes in capability, identifying this with the shift between incommensurate paradigms that is the basis of a 'scientific revolution'. Thus normal science is mechanistic, routine, comforting and 'rational', while a scientific revolution is mysterious, unpredictable, disturbing and 'revelatory', like a religious conversion.

Proposition. IDEAL explains the key features of Kuhn's hypothesis that science proceeds by alternating between periods of normalcy and upheaval.

The toolkit expert

Empirical scientists use laboratory equipment to take measurements of physical phenomena. Theoretical scientists use analytical and computational models to predict the values of these measurements. In both cases, scientists are using 'tools' to investigate the nature of physical reality. If—as is usually the case—there is a choice of tools, then there is a need for a person who knows which tool to use and how to use it. Such a person might be termed a 'toolkit expert'.

Example. As part of my day job I have been called upon to advise on the choice and use of different atmospheric dispersion models. For example, the following extended extract from a recent book[13] on chemical warfare agents (CWAs) suggests a toolkit approach to atmospheric dispersion modelling:

> Through the preceding discussion it is apparent that atmospheric dispersion is a complex phenomenon involving a wide variety of physical processes. It is apparent also that there are a wide variety of approaches to modelling atmospheric dispersion. With this in mind, it is possible to formulate a number of key requirements for the present application, *viz.* modelling the dispersion of CWAs:
>
> - Atmospheric dispersion modelling requires an accurate and reliable description of the weather, including descriptions of the prevailing airflow, the atmospheric stability, and the effects of flow structures at the spatial and temporal scales of interest.
> - Spatial scales range from metres to a few kilometres.
> - Temporal scales range from seconds (for the estimation of incapacitation) to hours.

[13] Roger Kingdon and Steven Walker, 'Dispersion and Modelling of the Spread of Chemical Warfare Agents', in Timothy Marrs, Robert Maynard and Frederick Sidell (eds.), *Chemical Warfare Agents—Toxicology and Treatment* (second edition, Wiley 2007).

- It must be possible to model the effects of dense gases, buoyancy and terrain structures, such as hills, buildings and trees.
- It must be possible to characterize the CWA source term, taking into account the features of the delivery system.
- To be of any use in an emergency situation, the initial modelling response must be prompt, *e.g.* within 10 minutes of a reported release of a CWA.
- In a continuing (or anticipated) emergency situation, there is the opportunity to amend or elaborate advice based on modelling, but this further advice must be consistent with the initial response and it must lead to an improved understanding of the situation (and not merely add to the confusion through 'information overload').
- Modelling in support of CWA hazard assessments must be able to demonstrate compliance with statutory limits and procedures, which may involve assessments of health effects and other impacts.
- All modelling must be 'verifiable', *i.e.* amenable to checking and re-running if required.
- All modelling must be 'robust', *i.e.* conclusions drawn from model simulations must be qualified by statements (i) setting out the underlying modelling assumptions and their possible pitfalls, and (ii) defining the range of applicability of the conclusions.

In addition, it is possible to identify a number of features that are not 'key requirements' but would be 'nice to have':

- Modelling dispersion source term processes, *e.g.* combustion, explosions.
- Modelling the incapacitation effects of concentration fluctuations.
- Modelling aerosol and particle processes.
- Modelling chemical reactions.
- CWA atmospheric dispersion modelling should be consistent with similar studies for biological and radiological agents. The easiest way to implement this consistency is to use the same dispersion models and the same datasets for weather, terrain, assets *etc.*

How are these diverse and challenging requirements to be met? There is a growing acceptance that no one model can fulfil all of these requirements, and that what is needed is a 'general-purpose' dispersion modelling 'toolkit' comprising a variety of models and datasets that between them cover the required range of applicability. Thus the toolkit might include pre-calculated dispersion templates for prompt response, a Gaussian plume model for continuing response and hazard assessment, a Gaussian puff model for dispersion in urban environments, an adapted indoor dispersion model for simulating dispersion in semi-confined spaces and so on. The differing requirements of these models for meteorological data might be met by including several datasets, each at the appropriate scale of resolution.

The toolkit approach has major implications for the *modus operandi* or 'concept of use' for atmospheric dispersion modelling. Whereas expertise in the operation of a single model requires a deep understanding of its underlying algorithms, expertise in the operation of a toolkit of models requires a deep understanding of the range of applicability of each model. In practical situations, the role of the single-model expert is little more than that of a glorified data-entry clerk, while the role of the toolkit expert is that of a skilled artisan, selecting and applying the right tool for the job. This change of role affects the concept of use for CWA dispersion modelling in a number of ways:

- *Model development.* Whilst single-model experts rarely admit that their models are complete, toolkit experts must be able to use whatever models are available, regardless of their state of development. Thus the toolkit approach changes the focus of research from model development to model acquisition, integration and use.
- *Data handling.* The toolkit approach depends upon the existence of a database of common parameter values, defining CWA source terms, meteorology, terrain, operational scenarios and so on. This database must be in a standard format (*e.g.* a relational database) so that different toolkit models can be applied interchangeably at short notice.
- *Training.* Emergency exercises and the development of a database of operational scenarios provide the best means for honing the toolkit expert's understanding of the applicability of models.
- *Uncertainty handling.* Situations will arise in which equally applicable models predict different outcomes. The toolkit expert can use this spread in predictions to estimate the margin of error in the advice to decision-makers.
- *Control and reporting.* Toolkit experts need to be able to reconcile the outputs from different models. Typically, this is carried out by a variety of informal methods ranging from automated information fusion to open debate. In an operational situation, such 'methods' would be deeply worrying to the decision-makers, who prefer to receive advice that is coherent, consistent and, above all, uncontested. The legitimate needs of experts and decision-makers can be satisfied by providing each with a separate environment—the 'expert panel' and the 'operations room', respectively—and restricting official communications between these environments to a standard reporting format that forces the experts to come to a consensus. Equally, this mechanism forces decision-makers to properly formulate their requests for advice from the experts, and to ensure the adequate provision of appropriate information. This mechanism has the additional advantage that it is 'self-documenting' and assists post-operation analysis and review.

These measures are recommended to the CWA dispersion modelling community.

Investigation. In treating physical theories as models or tools, the toolkit approach is a direct challenge to the traditional 'absolutist' attitude (particularly common amongst mathematicians and theoretical physicists) that the goal of science is to discover the axioms of a 'theory of everything' that will encompass and explain all other theories. Such an attitude is simply not sustainable given the presence of a choice of equally-valid approaches, for example, a 'least time' solution to a dynamical problem based on the calculus of variations, in addition to a 'classical' solution based on the equations of motion. Even where overlapping theories have been 'unified' by means of a higher-level 'metatheory', the fact remains that every theory (and metatheory) is applicable in its own *finite* domain. For example, Newton's law of gravitation does not help our understanding of the evolution of species, and Darwin's theory of the evolution of species by natural selection does not help our understanding of the revolution of planets. Neither is it clear that there is any metatheory that can encompass and explain both of these physical theories. The job of the toolkit expert is to develop and exercise a clear understanding of the limits of applicability of different experimental observations and theoretical models.

Maxim. "Use the right tool for the job."

Proposition. IDEAL is designed to store and refine 'knowledge' (PIs, the results of experiments) and the 'means of acquiring that knowledge' (GPs, theories). It can do this on any number of 'levels' through identifying GP/PI pairs in consets. In particular, 'higher level' theory-choice methodologies such as the toolkit approach may be implemented by IDEAL in precisely the same way as 'lower level' theories describing the nature of physical reality. It follows that IDEAL is well-suited to being a 'toolkit expert'.

The development of computing

The development of computing has been included here for two reasons: first, as an example of 'what scientists do'; and secondly, because IDEAL may be applied to the design of learning algorithms for automated computing machines. The following investigation focusses on a single piece of research of great importance, von Neumann's 'First Draft of a Report on the EDVAC'[14]. In doing this, the intention is not to belittle the contributions of Babbage, Turing and others, nor to revise history with

[14] John von Neumann, 'First Draft of a Report on the EDVAC' (1945), published in *IEEE Annals of the History of Computing*, vol. 15, no. 4, pp. 27-75 (1993).

the benefit of hindsight. Indeed, it appears to be the case that von Neumann's EDVAC report has acquired a high stature more through the reputation of its author and the timeliness of its release, rather than from any direct contribution it has made to a productive research programme. Even so, it remains a "brilliant piece of work" that made a "key contribution"[15] at a critical time in the development of computing, and for this reason it is worthy of close scrutiny.

Investigation. The following quotations from von Neumann's EDVAC report summarise its key points.

1. "An *automatic computing system* is a (usually highly composite) device, which can carry out instructions to perform calculations of a considerable order of complexity—e.g. to solve a non-linear partial differential equation in 2 or 3 independent variables numerically."
2. "In analyzing the functioning of the contemplated device, certain classificatory distinctions suggest themselves immediately." "First: Since the device is primarily a computer, it will have to perform the elementary operations of arithmetics most frequently. These are addition, subtraction, multiplication and division: +, −, ×, ÷. It is therefore reasonable that it should contain specialized organs for just these operations." "At any rate a *central arithmetical* part of the device will probably have to exist, and this constitutes *the first specific part: CA*." "Second: The logical control of the device, that is the proper sequencing of its operations can be most efficiently carried out by a central control organ. If the device is to be *elastic*, that is as nearly as possible *all purpose*, then a distinction must be made between the specific instructions given for and defining a particular problem, and the general control organs which see to it that these instructions—no matter what they are—are carried out." "By the *central control* we mean the latter function only, and the organs which perform it form *the second specific part: CC*." "Third: Any device which is to carry out long and complicated sequences of operations (specifically of calculations) must have a considerable memory." "At any rate the total *memory* constitutes *the third specific part of the device: M*." "The three specific parts CA, CC (together C) and M correspond to the *associative* neurons in the human nervous system. It remains to discuss the equivalents of the *sensory* or *afferent* and the *motor* or *efferent* neurons. These are the *input* and the *output* organs of the

[15] Michael Godfrey and David Hendry, 'The Computer as von Neumann Planned It', *IEEE Annals of the History of Computing*, vol. 15, no. 1, pp. 11-21 (1993).

device, and we shall now consider them briefly." "The device must be endowed with the ability to maintain the input and output (sensory and motor) contact with some specific medium... That medium will be called the *outside recording medium of the device: R*." "Fourth: The device must have organs to transfer (numerical or other) information from R into its specific parts, C and M. These organs form its *input*, the *fourth specific part: I*. It will be seen that it is best to make all transfers from R (by I) into M, and never directly into C." "Fifth: The device must have organs to transfer (presumably only numerical information) from its specific parts C and M into R. These organs form its *output*, the *fifth specific part: O*. It will be seen that it is again best to make all transfers from M (by O) into R, and never directly from C."

3. "The classification of 2.0 [above] being completed, it is now possible to take up the five specific parts into which the device was seen to be subdivided, and to discuss them one by one. Such a discussion must bring out the features required for each one of these parts in itself, as well as in their relations to each other." "Every digital computing device contains certain relay like *elements*, with discrete equilibria." "It is worth mentioning, that the neurons of the higher animals are definitely elements in the above sense. They have all-or-none character, that is two states: Quiescent and excited." "Following W.S. MacCulloch and W. Pitts ("A logical calculus of the ideas immanent in nervous activity," *Bull. Math. Biophysics*, Vol 5 (1943), pp. 115-133) we ignore the more complicated aspects of neuron functioning: Thresholds, temporal summation, relative inhibition, changes of the threshold by after-effects of stimulation beyond the synaptic delay, etc. It is, however, convenient to consider occasionally neurons with fixed thresholds 2 and 3, that is, neurons which can be excited only by (simultaneous) stimuli on 2 or 3 excitatory synapes (and none on an inhibitory synapse)." "It is easily seen that these simplified neuron functions can be imitated by telegraph relays or by vacuum tubes." "Thus, whether the tubes are used as gates or as triggers, the all-or-none, two equilibrium, arrangements are the simplest ones. Since these tube arrangements are to handle numbers by means of their digits, it is natural to use a system of arithmetic in which the digits are also two valued. This suggests the use of the binary system."
4. "The device should be as simple as possible, that is, contain as few elements as possible. This can be achieved by never performing two operations simultaneously, if this would cause a significant increase in the number of elements required. The result will be that the device

will work more reliably and the vacuum tubes can be driven to shorter reaction times than otherwise." "It is also worth emphasizing that up to now all thinking about high speed digital computing devices has tended in the opposite direction."

5. "**6.1** The considerations of 5.0 [above] have defined the main principles for the treatment of CA. We continue now on this basis, with somewhat more specific and technical detail. In order to do this it is necessary to use some schematic picture for the functioning of the standard element of the device: Indeed, the decisions regarding the arithmetical and the logical control procedures of the device, as well as its other functions, can only be made on the basis of some assumptions about the functioning of the elements." "...we will base our considerations on a hypothetical element, which functions essentially like a vacuum tube—e.g. like a triode with an appropriate associated RLC-circuit..." "The analogs of human neurons... seem to provide elements of just the kind postulated at the end of 6.1. We propose to use them accordingly for the purpose described there: As the constituent elements of the device, for the duration of the preliminary discussion. We must therefore give a precise account of the properties which we postulate for these elements. The element which we will discuss, to be called an E-element..."
6. The remainder of the report comprises detailed representations of the functions of the computer, that is, arithmetical operations and so on, all based on E-elements. The penultimate section calls for the use of 'code', that is, what we now call a computing language: "Our next aim is to go deeper into the analysis of CC. Such an analysis, however, is dependent upon a precise knowledge of the system of orders used in controlling the device, since the function of CC is to receive these orders, to interpret them, and then either to carry them out, or to stimulate properly those organs which will carry them out. It is therefore our immediate task to provide a list of the orders which control the device, i.e. to describe the *code* to be used in the device, and to define the mathematical and logical meaning and the operational significance of its *code words*."

Investigation. It is of interest to assess EDVAC and IDEAL in relation to one another. For ease of reference, the numerical sequence established above is repeated in the following.

1. Like Turing before him, von Neumann is interested not in 'computing' but in 'calculating' (in the current senses of these words). However,

there is more to computing than calculating: specifically, as well as EDVAC-style *algorithmic programming* there is a need for *relational programming*. It is quite possible that these two approaches would not have developed separately if EDVAC had included both in its design. As it is, to this day physical scientists prefer to use algorithmic code languages such as Fortran and C, while social scientists prefer to use relational databases, with both groups largely unaware of the enormous benefits of a combined approach. IDEAL is constructed on the understanding that both of these approaches are necessary for general-purpose computing. This is the basis of the complementary Occident and Orient procedures which implement algorithmic programming and relational programming respectively.

2. EDVAC's components correspond to IDEAL's components as follows:

IDEAL component	EDVAC component
Evidence **E**	Input I
Iteration **I**	—
Algorithm **A**	Central Arithmetic CA
Decision **D**	Central Control CC
Log **L**	Memory M and Output O

The absence of an equivalent of **I** means that EDVAC cannot compare datasets in the manner envisaged for IDEAL. By holding data in M, EDVAC can undertake simple data comparisons sufficient for basic arithmetic (for example, determining the greater of two numbers), but this mechanism is inadequate for more complex assessments (for example, detecting the similarities between two spatial patterns). Thus "A prominent feature of the report is von Neumann's recognition that his computer would not perform relatively efficiently on sorting problems. This remains, substantially, an unsolved problem to this day."[16] Sorting and other data comparison operations can be executed very efficiently using a relational database, however.

It is arguable that even for simple two-valued relations, data comparison is sufficiently important that it merits its own component. For example, the 'B-APT' Berger aptitude test, which is based on a reduced set of commands that nevertheless is sufficient for algorithmic programming, includes 'COM' for comparing the values of two numbers. The full mapping of B-APT commands to IDEAL components is as follows:

---

[16] Michael Godfrey and David Hendry, *ibid.*

IDEAL component	B-APT command
Evidence **E**	WRT
Iteration **I**	COM, INC
Algorithm **A**	ADD, SUB, MUL, DIV
Decision **D**	GOTO, STP
Log **L**	STO

IDEAL's conflation of EDVAC's M and O components means that its equivalent of M has a direct connection with the 'outside recording medium' R, contrary to von Neumann's intention. This does not appear to be of critical importance, however. In any case, IDEAL's components **I**, **A** and **D** fulfil this requirement.

In other respects, these two sets of components are remarkably similar.

3. The analysis of EDVAC's components in terms of the discrete-state operation of vacuum tubes and neurons is von Neumann's major theoretical contribution in this paper. Whilst his analytical approach follows that of MacCulloch and Pitts, von Neumann's application of this approach is entirely original. Can this same approach be applied to IDEAL? There are several grounds for thinking that such an application might be fruitful: (i) The input and output connectors of IDEAL's **E**, **A** and **L** components are similar in number and function to the connectors of a triode; (ii) The role of IDEAL's data connectors is similar to that of excitatory synapses, and likewise for control connectors and inhibitory synapses; (iii) Although the dyadic operation of IDEAL's **I** component has no obvious counterpart in EDVAC, equivalent configurations have been constructed by MacCulloch and Pitts. These positive indications notwithstanding, an EDVAC-style analysis has *not* been used in the derivation of IDEAL, as an alternative approach using flow charts is simpler to explain and its assumptions easier to defend[17].
4. Taken out of context, von Neumann's call for simplicity *and* as few elements as possible might be seen as self-contradictory. His target was the use (at that time) of "telescoping procedures" that maximised the number of operations carried out simultaneously. Did von Neumann also predict the failure of complex systems such as analogue computers and transputers? Or did he fail to see the need for a massive number of transistor switches on an integrated circuit? It can be argued both ways. Accordingly, it would not be meaningful to assess IDEAL using these criteria.

[17] See **3. How?** for this derivation.

5. "This is, as far as I am aware, the first substantial work (since Babbage) which clearly separated logic design from implementation, and gave a formal scheme for logic representation. It is a curious fact that the notation which was fully established and extensively used here was totally absent from subsequent works"[18]. These "subsequent works" include publications by von Neumann himself. Did he perceive a weakness in the approach? Perhaps, having developed this analysis to justify the use of components that he had already selected, and finding that it did not uncover alternative components or combinations thereof, von Neumann discarded it as 'spent'. Arguably, von Neumann's analysis is just one amongst many attempts to formulate a 'universal' logic. If so, it is critically handicapped by focussing on algorithmic programming only. However, even if relational programming had been included by some means, it is not clear that the outcome would have been any different. For example, Gillies[19] attempts just such a 'unification' through the formulation of a "new framework for logic" based on the Prolog logic programming system (which includes key elements of relational programming). Gillies' analysis is quite interesting because he makes a number of observations that *might* be relevant to IDEAL, but he does not succeed in establishing a convincing, rigorous, 'universal' logic. The same might be said of other systems such as modal logic, fuzzy logic and so on. It appears that the fault lies not in the choice of logic system but in the choice of logic itself, as the sole means by which we might arrive at a system such as EDVAC or IDEAL. As indicated above, it appears from his report that von Neumann arrived at EDVAC by a variety of means, not all connected with his analysis based on E-elements. It is certainly the case that IDEAL was devised before it was derived. In both cases, having been devised, it is possible to derive them 'properly', that is, showing that they conform to the usual norms of first order predicate calculus; but such an approach is simply a '*post hoc* rationalisation', adding little to the original model. This is the most likely explanation for the early abandonment of von Neumann's analysis.
6. The proposed use of 'code' is von Neumann's major practical contribution in this paper. Its obvious equivalent in IDEAL is the use of 'code data'.

Proposition. IDEAL revitalises, realigns and fulfils the EDVAC research programme.

---

[18] Michael Godfrey and David Hendry, *ibid*.

[19] Donald Gillies, *Artificial Intelligence and Scientific Method* (Oxford 1996).

Rules of thumb

Scientists often act on the basis of simple 'rules of thumb' that appear to have no rationale other than 'tradition'. Chief among these are the following:

1. Explanations invoking non-physical agents have no place in science.
2. It is better to say something small and specific than something grand and general.
3. A theory that explains everything, explains nothing.
4. "Make everything as simple as possible, but not simpler."[20]
5. Only trust a calculated or measured value if you can reach it by two entirely different routes.

These are discussed in turn.

Investigation. *Explanations invoking non-physical agents have no place in science.* On the face of it, this principle is obvious and straightforward. Science is founded on measurements of physical phenomena, but non-physical agents cannot be measured, therefore they have no place in science. But what do we mean by 'measurement'? Nothing, physical or otherwise, can be measured *directly*, in the sense of affirming the existence of Kant's *ding-an-sich*, the 'thing-in-itself'. Rather, every measurement affirms the existence of *something*, by quantifying its influence on a scale that has been delineated through subjecting other things to the same measuring procedure. If the measurement is repeatable and persistent then we give the *something* a name—'big bang' or 'hypnotism', for example—but naming it doesn't necessarily mean that the *something* exists as a coherent physical agent. Indeed, there are many things which *on the basis of measurements* were once thought to exist but which now are thought not to exist, for example, 'aether' and 'telepathy'. So how can we classify some agents as 'physical' and others as 'non-physical'?

In IDEAL, an observation is a PI that can be raised to the level of an 'idea' or 'concept' by pairing it with a GP to form a conset. This conset—call it 'X'—can then collaborate or compete with others in a variety of ways:

1. X can acquire further PIs, depending on the generality and simplicity of X's GP. Likewise, X can acquire further GPs, depending on the clarity and distinctness of X's PI. This can be used as evidence of X's applicability in describing objective reality.
2. X's GP can be included as a PI in another conset, relating it to a 'higher level' GP. Likewise, X's PI can be included as a GP in another

[20] Attributed to Albert Einstein.

conset, relating it to a 'lower level' PI. This can be used as evidence of X's relevance to other concepts.

3. X's GP and PI can be refined in a variety of ways, thereby enhancing X's ability to undertake processes 1 and 2.

IDEAL is a dynamic system in which the fate of an individual conset lies in its relative propensity to collaborate or compete with other consets. To survive in this system, non-physical agents must participate with and compete against their physical counterparts, comprising well-defined GPs of relevance to many different PIs that themselves are highly-specific and measurable. In today's *information environment* such physical agents exist in abundance, therefore it is reasonable to suppose that in any competition non-physical agents will be marginalised and eliminated in a very short time. They are not *necessarily* doomed, but neither do they have any foreseeable future. In other words, it is reasonable to suppose that non-physical agents have no place in science.

Maxim. "As nature abhors a vacuum, so science abhors a ghost."

Investigation. *It is better to say something small and specific than something grand and general.* A natural corollary of the concept of induction, this rule of thumb is implicit in virtually every aspect of 'normal science'. Quite rightly, it emphasises the importance of detailed observation over generalised theorising. There is a rejoinder, however. Yes, it is better to say something small and specific than something grand and general; but it is best of all to say both, each in relation to the other. The 'small and specific' observations are PIs: they guide the application of GPs. The 'grand and general' theories are GPs: they tell us where to look for PIs. Learning takes place when we alternate between refining GPs *ceteris paribus* and refining PIs *ceteris paribus*. If this process is undertaken rapidly then in a short time we observe the 'co-evolution' of GP/PI pairs, the end result being precise, well-defined GPs and PIs that bear little relation to their earlier incarnations. PIs are the water of knowledge, and GPs are the pots to carry the water. For a journey across the desert of ignorance, neither is much use without the other.

Maxim. "Particular instances without general principles are wasted; general principles without particular instances are empty."

This is quite different from the traditional view, represented by Newton's statement that his theory of gravitation was obtained by a one-off process in which "particular propositions are inferred from the phenomena, and afterwards rendered general by induction" [21]. Newton considered this to be a deductive process, but beyond this statement he does not set down the underlying logic, and today, 280 years later, it remains the case that no-one has been able to give a satisfactory explanation of 'induction'[22]. As with IDEAL (and EDVAC, for that matter), it is likely that Newton's theory of gravitation came about through a rapid iteration between GPs and PIs, rather than a one-off inductive process. Why, then, does Newton endorse induction? Because it was the only physical explanation extant at that time.

This account gives further support to the GP/PI model which, as we have seen, can be explained in terms of the operation of IDEAL's procedures.

Investigation. *A theory that explains everything, explains nothing.* This holds for the following reason. A theory that explains everything is essentially a metatheory GP for which every other theory is a PI. That is, the conset referring to this 'universal' GP also itemises a vast set of PIs, each one corresponding to a 'lower level' GP. However, this vast all-encompassing set of PIs completely wrecks our 'practical problem-solving method', which operates on the assumption that there are several small, distinct, representative sets of PIs that are amenable to further down-selection, giving a manageable number of PIs having the greatest correspondence with the problem under consideration. Thus deprived of this method, the only alternative is to guess; an approach which sometimes 'works' (in the sense of solving the problem), but which explains nothing.

The obvious alternative to the universal 'theory of everything' is the toolkit approach, discussed earlier. This introduces several new rules of thumb, including:

Maxim. "Everything has its limits."

Maxim. "Never introduce a new parameter to a calculation without at the same time stating its limiting values."[23]

Maxim. "A bad workman blames his tools, and a good workman blames himself for not using the right tool."

---

[21] Isaac Newton, *Philosophiae Naturalis Principia Mathematica* (third edition, 1726), tr. I. Bernard Cohen and Anne Whitman (California 1999).

[22] See 'Scientific method in theory' for a discussion of induction.

[23] This maxim has many variants, for example, "Never introduce a new weapon to a streetfight without at the same time knowing how to use it", "Never ask a question without having a good idea of the answer", "Look before you leap", and so on.

Following this approach to its logical conclusion, metatheories (including induction and IDEAL[24]) must show that they conform to their *own* limits:

Maxim. "Law, judge thyself."

Every GP has its range of applicability, and associated with that range are PIs that are best explained using that GP *alone*. This principle is most apparent where different physical scales are involved, for example:

1. The phenomenon of lightning is best explained in terms of the interaction of clouds, which (for the purpose of the explanation) are assumed to be coherent physical entities. By comparison, it might be possible to explain lightning in terms of the interaction of individual water molecules, but any such explanation is unlikely to be convincing.
2. The operation of a syphon can be explained using the concept of atmospheric pressure. By comparison, it might be possible to explain the operation of a syphon in terms of the interaction of individual water molecules, but any such explanation is unlikely to be convincing.
3. The field of thermodynamics concerns the thermal properties of gases, measured in terms of pressure, volume, temperature, enthalpy and entropy. A major scientific achievement of the 19th Century was the development of the theory of statistical mechanics, which derived expressions for these thermodynamic parameters in terms of the 'lower level' dynamics of ensembles of 'classical' particles. However, to this day, engineers continue to use the old theory of thermodynamics, as if the new theory of statistical mechanics never existed. This is because the old theory was developed for a practical purpose, and the existence of the new theory does not alter the established applicability of the old. Indeed, from a thermodynamics perspective, the development of statistical mechanics appears nothing more than a '*post hoc* rationalisation': a new reason for doing something that has already been done perfectly well for many years. Of course, statistical mechanics is a rich theory that describes and predicts many novel phenomena beyond the scope of thermodynamics; but, for precisely this reason, this does not concern the thermodynamicist.
4. A similar argument applies to the development of the theory of relativity, which *for the classical domain* simply validates the existing expressions of classical mechanics. It is noted, however, that new and old theories such as relativity and classical mechanics are not entirely indifferent to one another, because each performs the vital function of setting the others limits of applicability.

[24] See 'Theory acceptance criteria' for this analysis of IDEAL.

5. Zeno's paradoxes arise because of a (deliberate) confusion of scales and consequent misapplication of modelling principles. For example: "In the stadium paradox (also known as the dichotomy paradox) Zeno argues that it is impossible to complete the course. Before you reach the far end, you must reach the halfway point. Before you reach that, you must reach the halfway point to it. And so on indefinitely. If space is infinitely divisible any finite distance must, allegedly, consist in an infinite number of points; and it is, it is also said, impossible to reach the end of an infinite series of operations in a finite time."[25] Here the contrasting scales are $1/\infty$ metres (for infinitely divisible space) and of order 100 metres (for the stadium). The first leads to paradox, while the second leads to the use of equations describing linear motion on 'human scales', that is, spatial and temporal scales within direct human experience. These equations are expressed in terms of distance, time, velocity and acceleration, parameters that will not lead to paradox when applied on human scales.

Thus the toolkit expert is likely to support the *practical* implications of anti-reductionism:

> **reduction.** In philosophy and related subjects, the process whereby concepts or statements that apply to one type of entity are redefined in terms of concepts, or analysed in terms of statements, of another kind, normally one regarded as more elementary or epistemologically more basic... The reductionist sometimes justifies his activity as a principle of economy in explanation, a principle that has obviously paid off in science; the anti-reductionist argues the existence of irreducible or emergent properties.[26]

In contrast, dogmatic reductionism introduces absurdities such as Dawkins' *The Selfish Gene*, which (both in its title and in its contents) demonstrates its author's irrational reluctance to set limits on what his theory can explain.

Maxim. "Reduction. You can do it. But what's the point?"

This account gives further support to the toolkit approach which, as we have seen, is an integral part of the IDEAL model.

Investigation. *Make everything as simple as possible, but not simpler.* This is a development of Ockham's razor:

> **Ockham's razor.** The principle of ontological economy, usually formulated as 'Entities are not to be multiplied beyond necessity' (*Entia*

---

[25] Antony Flew (ed.), *ibid.*

[26] Alan Bullock and Oliver Stallybrass (eds.), *The Fontana Dictionary of Modern Thought* (Fontana 1977).

non sunt multiplicanda praeter necessitatem). These actual words are not in fact to be found in the extant works of William of Ockham.[27]

Every skilled craftsman knows that if a job is difficult, then he's probably using the wrong tool. Even if the job is of a new kind, such that the craftsman has never come across the appropriate tool, he still knows how to go about acquiring it. The same applies in science. If the application of a theory to a particular problem appears *to a skilled theoretician* to be 'complicated' and 'unconvincing', then it's probably the wrong theory, and there's likely to be a more appropriate theory somewhere else. This compulsion to move away from difficulty and towards simplicity is the same for the skilled craftsman and the skilled theoretician, the reason being that they are both toolkit experts.

Maxim. "Keep it simple."

In relation to this maxim, we should not be surprised if our key physical theories can be expressed using simple linear equations, for the following reasons:

1. The purpose of equations expressing physical theories is to predict parameter values for comparison with experimental measurements.
2. Linear equations predict simple and regular sets of parameter values for comparison with measurements of observed phenomena that are also simple and regular.
3. Measurements of observed phenomena are simple and regular because, if otherwise, we would not have discerned any persistent or repeating patterns that we felt needed explaining through the development of a predictive theory.

As for nonlinear equations, these tell us about complex phenomena such as phase transitions and other 'inter-level' behaviour. Thus, while novel 'complexity' theories help us to understand the limits of linear theories, they do not replace or rewrite the established knowledge.

Maxim. "Physical reality may be described as a complexity of linearities."

This last maxim appears to capture the subtle ambivalence of Einstein's phrase: "Make everything as simple as possible, *but not simpler*." Again we see the toolkit approach explaining the origins of scientific rules of thumb that until now had appeared to be no more than 'tradition'.

Investigation. *Only trust a calculated or measured value if you can reach it by two entirely different routes.* This is a well-established rule of

[27] Antony Flew (ed.), *ibid.*

thumb that is found in many fields ranging from elementary school mathematics to formal validation procedures in accountancy and other professions. An important feature of our practical problem-solving methodology, this principle expresses the fundamental necessity to always compare 'input data' and 'stored data', each comprising observations, theories and so on. As we have seen, this requirement for *data comparison* is at the very heart of IDEAL's design.

Proposition. Together with its associated concepts of GP/PI pairing and the toolkit approach, IDEAL provides the rationale for the key 'rules of thumb' used by scientists.

Scientific method in theory

So much for the practical considerations of 'what scientists do'. There are also a number of theoretical considerations that constitute the bedrock of the field of philosophy of science. First amongst these is the notion of scientific method.

> **scientific method.** The procedure by which, as a matter of definition, scientific laws, as contrasted with other kinds of general statement, are established. The orthodox view is that this procedure is inductive, but several philosophers of science have criticized inductivism as misrepresenting the actual procedure of scientists. Two phases of scientific activity need to be distinguished: the initial formulation of hypotheses, which seems mainly, as the anti-inductivists maintain, to be a business of inspired guessing that cannot be mechanized, and the confirmation of hypotheses thus formulated, which does appear to be a comparatively pedestrian and rule-governed undertaking.[28]

Investigation. Induction is defined as "A method of reasoning by which a general law or principle is inferred from observed particular instances"[29]. Diagrammatically this may be represented as follows:

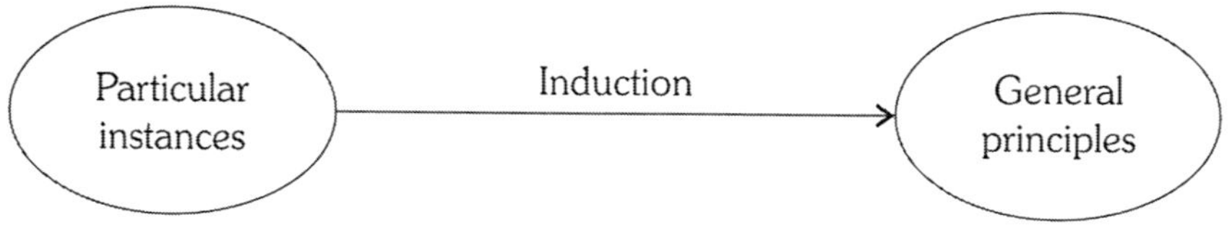

In setting out his theory of falsification, Popper (with characteristic *emphasis*) took the opposing view:

[28] Alan Bullock and Oliver Stallybrass (eds.), *ibid.*
[29] Antony Flew (ed.), *ibid.*

The theory to be developed in the following pages stands directly opposed to all attempts to operate with the ideas of inductive logic. It may be described as the theory of *the deductive method of testing*, or as the view that a hypothesis can only be empirically *tested*—and only *after* it has been advanced.[30]

Or, implementing a consistent notation:

These simple diagrams suggest that induction and falsification are two complementary parts of the same *iterative* process:

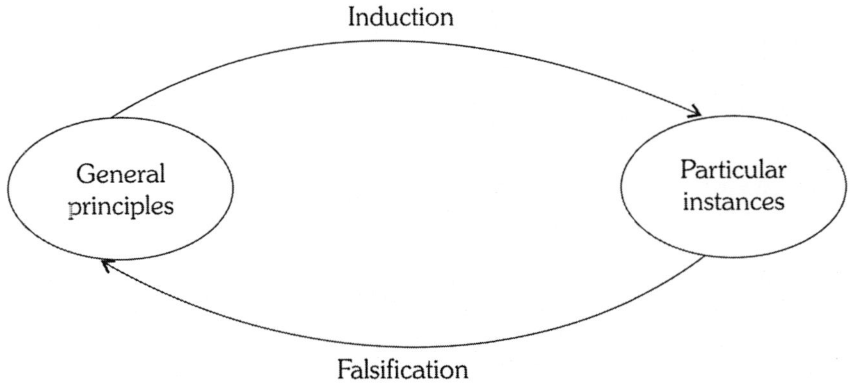

Supposing this visual interpretation of scientific method to be correct, we infer the following:

1. The important feature in this representation is *iteration* between GPs and PIs, and the processes of induction and falsification each tell only half the story.
2. Even then, it is not sufficient to simply repeat the same iterative cycle with the same GPs and the same PIs. To avoid stagnation, there must be continual efforts to consider new GPs and new PIs, the result being the *cumulation* of knowledge that led Newton to comment that "If I have seen a little further it is by standing on the shoulders of giants"[31].
3. It was suggested above that in developing his theory of gravitation Newton engaged in a process of rapid iteration between GPs and PIs (thereby standing on his own shoulders, metaphorically). Here the

[30] Karl Popper, *ibid.*

[31] Isaac Newton, letter to Robert Hooke (1676).

emphasis is on the *rapidity* of the process, alternating frequently between 'bottom up' and 'top down' views of the problem and not getting entrenched in any one part of the iterative cycle.

4. Attempts have been made to take parts of this theoretical description further by developing rigorous formulations for "inductive logic" and "the deductive method of testing". Such attempts have not succeeded, for the simple reason that the basis of scientific method is not logical inference but data comparison. This also explains why there is a difference between the present 'theoretical' description of scientific method and the 'practical' description set out earlier.

Example. Traditionally, computer programs have been written following the 'waterfall' methodology. This implements a logical series of steps that appears to originate from engineering practice: (i) Plan; (ii) Design; (iii) Create; (iv) Test; (v) Commission. In practice, however, a much better approach is the 'iterative' methodology: (i) Plan, design, create, test and commission a 'skeleton' system having the major features of the intended system but none of the fine detail; (ii) Flesh-out the skeleton in some detail, then test and commission this version of the system; (iii) Repeat the last step several times in quick succession, until all pre-defined stopping criteria have been fulfilled. This approach and its variants (such as 'extreme programming') now dominate the field.

Example. It has taken 25 years to accumulate and refine the key ideas presented in *Principia Intellegentia*. However, within this quarter-century period there have been long periods of apparent stagnation punctuated at infrequent intervals by dramatic bursts of activity. On a small scale, this is precisely the alternation between 'normal science' and 'scientific revolutions' that has been described by Kuhn. In the case of IDEAL, the record shows that most of the 'dramatic bursts of activity' were triggered by new ideas or puzzles that themselves came about by stepping back from the problem. 'Stepping back' involves leaving the problem for a while, then undertaking a rapid high-level review by skimming through all the past notes and picking out the salient points. Here, speed is of the essence, for it is almost always the case that a slow review will get lost in the detail and miss the overall picture. Rapid review; building on past work; the active investigation of new ideas: these are strong indicators that IDEAL has come about through the systematic iterative cumulation of knowledge.

Proposition. For a learning mechanism to be considered 'scientific', it must be both iterative and cumulative. These criteria are fulfilled by the IDEAL 'self-learning' procedure, which involves alternating frequently between refining GPs *ceteris paribus* and refining PIs *ceteris paribus*.

Falsification

Two important features of Popper's theory of falsification are (i) The use of *modus tollens*[32] and (ii) 'Scientific method' interpreted as a process of natural selection. These features are discussed in turn.

Investigation. In *The Logic of Scientific Discovery*, Popper establishes *modus tollens* as the logical basis of his "deductive method of testing":

> The falsifying mode of inference here referred to—the way in which the falsification of a conclusion entails the falsification of the system from which it is derived—is the *modus tollens* of classical logic. It may be described as follows:
>
> Let *p* be a conclusion of a system *t* of statements which may consist of theories and initial conditions (for the sake of simplicity I will not distinguish between them). We may then symbolize the relation of derivability (analytical implication) of *p* from *t* by '$t \rightarrow p$' which may be read: '*p* follows from *t*'. Assume *p* to be false, which we may write '$\bar{p}$', to be read 'not-*p*'. Given the relation of deducibility, $t \rightarrow p$, and the assumption $\bar{p}$, we can then infer $\bar{t}$ (read 'not-*t*'); that is, we regard *t* as falsified. If we denote the conjunction (simultaneous assertion) of two statements by putting a point between the symbols standing for them, we may write the falsifying inference thus: $((t \rightarrow p).\bar{p}) \rightarrow \bar{t}$, or in words: 'If *p* is derivable from *t*, and if *p* is false, then *t* also is false'.
>
> By means of this mode of inference we falsify *the whole system* (the theory as well as the initial conditions) which was required for the deduction of the statement *p*, *i.e.* of the falsified statement.

It is instructive to take a closer look at this use of classical logic. *Modus tollens* and other classical inferences may be demonstrated to be valid through the use of truth-tables[33]. This approach is based on the following tabular definitions of the basic operators of propositional logic: $\wedge$ ('AND', also called 'conjunction'), $\vee$ ('OR', also called 'disjunction'), $\neg$ ('NOT', also called 'negation'), $\rightarrow$ ('IF… THEN', also called 'logical implication', 'material implication' or simply 'implication'), and $\leftrightarrow$ ('IF AND ONLY IF', also called 'biconditional implication' or 'mutual implication'). 'T' and 'F' stand for the truth values 'True' and 'False', respectively.

A	B	$A \wedge B$	$A \vee B$	$\neg A$	$\neg B$	$A \rightarrow B$	$A \leftrightarrow B$
F	F	F	F	T	T	T	T
F	T	F	T	T	F	T	F
T	F	F	T	F	T	F	F
T	T	T	T	F	F	T	T

32 "The mood that denies." That is, denying the consequent.

33 See, for example, *Logic* by Nick Earle (Macmillan 1973) or *Logic with Trees* by Colin Howson (Routledge 1997).

The truth-table approach involves obtaining an algebraic expression for the inference to be tested, and calculating the truth value of that expression for every combination of truth values of its antecedents. If all the consequent truth values are 'True' then the inference is valid, but if one or more of the consequent truth values is 'False' then the inference is not valid. Taking *modus tollens* as an example:

If A is true then B is true
B is not true

A is not true

Using the notation of propositional logic:

$A \rightarrow B$
$\neg B$

$\neg A$

In algebraic form:

$$((A \rightarrow B) \wedge \neg B) \rightarrow \neg A$$

The antecedents in this expression are the truth-functional variables A and B, each of which can take two values, 'True' or 'False'. The validity of *modus tollens* is tested by stepping through each part of its algebraic expression in a truth-table, for each combination of antecedent values:

A	**B**	**A → B**	**¬B**	**(A → B) ∧ ¬B**	**¬A**	**((A → B) ∧ ¬B) → ¬A**
F	F	T	T	T	T	T
F	T	T	F	F	T	T
T	F	F	T	F	F	T
T	T	T	F	F	F	T

Since all the truth values in the final column are 'True', *modus tollens* is a valid inference.

Taking into account differences in notation ('.' in place of '∧' and '–' in place of '¬'), Popper's understanding of *modus tollens* is the same as given here. However, his use of *modus tollens* introduces the implicit assumption that $t \rightarrow p$ (that is, if "a system t of statements which may consist of theories and initial conditions" is true, then conclusion p is true). What if this assumption is incorrect? In particular, what if it is more likely to be the case that $p \rightarrow t$? This possibility is not as far-fetched as first appears. The above-quoted excerpt from *The Logic of Scientific Discovery* appears as part of Popper's discussion of 'levels of universality' that was considered earlier. From this discussion it is clear that Popper considers some statements to be 'more universal' than others. The word 'universal' also appears in set theory, the 'universal set' (U) referring to the set that contains all other sets. It can be shown that the operators of set theory correspond to the operators of propositional logic as follows:

Propositional logic	**Set theory**
AND ($\wedge$)	INTERSECTION ($\cap$)
OR ($\vee$)	UNION ($\cup$)
NOT ($\neg$)	COMPLEMENT (′)
IF… THEN ($\rightarrow$)	SUBSET OF ($\subset$)
IF AND ONLY IF ($\leftrightarrow$)	EQUALITY (=)

That is, $t \rightarrow p$ ('t implies p') corresponds to $t \subset p$ ('t is a subset of p'). Drawn on a Venn diagram, this suggests that t is 'less universal' than p (to use Popper's terminology):

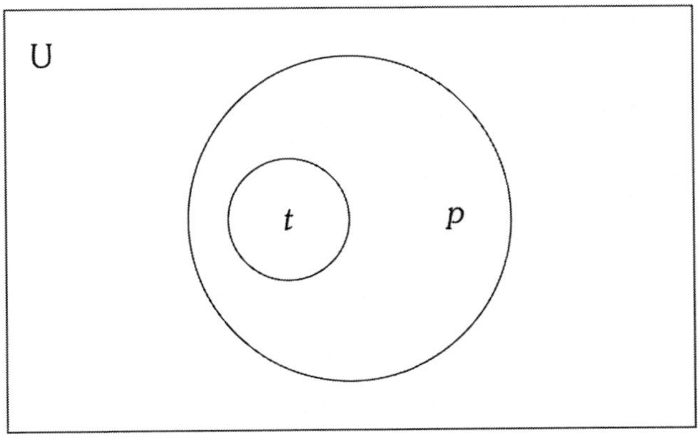

From Popper's point of view, this is the wrong way round: t is a system of theories and initial conditions (together comprising a GP, presumably[34]) and p is a conclusion (a PI), so t cannot be 'less universal' than p. But if t is to be 'more universal' than p then it must be a larger set on the Venn diagram, in which case the only possible relationship involving implication is $p \rightarrow t$.

---

34 This assignment may also be inferred from the earlier diagram of 'falsification' which showed GP $\rightarrow$ PI.

Popper's $t \rightarrow p$ and 'more universal' t can both be realised by unpicking his conflation of 'theories' and 'initial conditions' in t. Expressing these as t_{GP} and t_{PI} respectively, we reformulate $t \rightarrow p$ as $(t_{GP} \wedge t_{PI}) \rightarrow p$, which can be represented in a Venn diagram by supposing $(t_{GP} \cap t_{PI}) \subset p$ regardless of the 'universality' (size) of t_{GP} and t_{PI}:

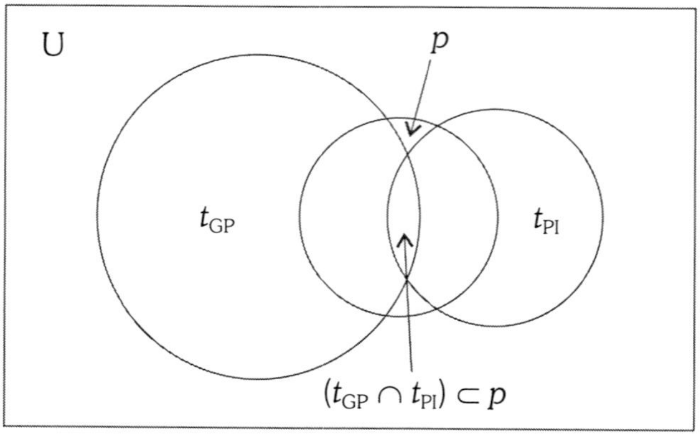

However, we see from this diagram and from the following truth-table[35] that $\neg p$ negates the conjunction $(t_{GP} \wedge t_{PI})$ but not the terms t_{GP} and t_{PI} taken separately. This result directly contradicts Popper's application of *modus tollens*, such that its significance in relation to the theory of falsification is no longer secure.

A	**B**	**C**	**D ↔ ((A ∧ B) → C)**	**(D ∧ ¬C) → ¬(A ∧ B)**	**(D ∧ ¬C) → ¬A**	**(D ∧ ¬C) → ¬B**
F	F	F	T	T	T	T
F	F	T	T	T	T	T
F	T	F	T	T	T	**F**
F	T	T	T	T	T	T
T	F	F	T	T	**F**	T
T	F	T	T	T	T	T
T	T	F	F	T	T	T
T	T	T	T	T	T	T
Validity of inference				**Valid**	**Invalid**	**Invalid**

[35] This is an application of the maxim, "Only trust a calculated or measured value if you can reach it by two entirely different routes".

Proposition. Popper cannot rely on *modus tollens* as the logical basis of his "deductive method of testing". This finding reinforces an earlier statement to the effect that attempts to develop logical formulations for 'scientific method' have not succeeded.

Investigation. In building on his theory of falsification, Popper implements a stark interpretation of Darwinian natural selection:

> If the method of trial and error is developed more and more consciously, then it begins to take on the characteristic features of 'scientific method'. This 'method' can briefly be described as follows. Faced with a certain problem, the scientist offers, tentatively, some sort of solution—a theory. This theory science accepts only provisionally, if at all; and it is most characteristic of the scientific method that scientists will spare no pains to criticize and test the theory in question. Criticizing and testing go hand in hand; the theory is criticized from very many different sides in order to bring out those points which may be vulnerable. And the testing of the theory proceeds by exposing these vulnerable points to as severe an examination as possible. This, of course, is again a variant of the method of trial and error. Theories are put forward tentatively and tried out. If the outcome of a test shows that the theory is erroneous, then it is eliminated; the method of trial and error is essentially a method of elimination. Its success depends mainly on three conditions, namely, that sufficiently numerous (and ingenious) theories should be offered, that the theories offered should be sufficiently varied, and that sufficiently severe tests should be made. In this way we may, if we are lucky, secure the survival of the fittest theory by the elimination of those which are less fit.[36]

Proposition. This is an uncompromising picture of science 'red in tooth and claw'. If Popper's "method of elimination" were applied rigorously, then no theory would survive and science would go back to Year Zero. In practice, theories are rarely (if ever) eliminated in the manner described in this passage. This is because scientists appreciate that *every* theory will fail if applied beyond its limits. Indeed, failed tests are the best means of discovering the range of applicability of a theory, and a theory proved "erroneous" in one application may turn out to be extremely useful in another. This is precisely the toolkit approach: theories are tools used for exploring the physical world, and the successful scientist is the one who uses the right tool for the job, regardless of convention or ideology.

---

[36] Karl Popper, *Conjectures and Refutations* (Routledge 1972).

Deductive-nomological explanation

Another attempt to formalise scientific method is Hempel's 'deductive-nomological' model (also known as the 'covering law' model):

> Scientific explanation, prediction, and postdiction all have the same logical character: they show that the fact under consideration can be inferred from certain other facts by means of specified general laws. In the simplest case, the type of argument may be schematized as a deductive inference of the following form:
>
> $$\frac{\begin{array}{l} C_1, C_2 \ldots C_k \\ L_1, L_2 \ldots L_r \end{array}}{E}$$
>
> Here, $C_1, C_2 \ldots C_k$ are statements of particular occurrences (e.g., of the positions and momenta of certain celestial bodies at a specified time), and $L_1, L_2 \ldots L_r$ are general laws (e.g., those of Newtonian mechanics); finally, E is a sentence stating whatever is being explained, predicted or postdicted. And the argument has its intended force only if its conclusion, E, follows deductively from the premises.[37]

Investigation. Hempel's C and L statements correspond to PIs and GPs respectively, and his conclusion E is another PI. Thus the deductive-nomological form may be written

$$\frac{\begin{array}{l} \mathrm{GP} \\ \mathrm{PI}_a \end{array}}{\mathrm{PI}_c}$$

where subscripts 'a' and 'c' denote 'antecedent' and 'consequent' respectively[38]. In this context, 'GP' (general principle) can be taken to mean any of the following:

1. The propositional logic statement 'If PI_a then PI_c'.
2. The predicate logic statement 'All PI_a are PI_c'.
3. The algorithmic operation **GP** such that $\mathrm{PI}_c = \mathbf{GP}(\mathrm{PI}_a)$.

---

[37] Carl Hempel, *Aspects of Scientific Explanation and other Essays in the Philosophy of Science* (The Free Press 1965).

[38] It follows that the expression $(t_{GP} \wedge t_{PI}) \rightarrow p$ introduced in the previous discussion is in deductive-nomological form.

For example, if GP ≡ 'If PI_a then PI_c' then we recover *modus ponens*[39]:

$$\frac{PI_a \rightarrow PI_c \quad PI_a}{PI_c}$$

Equivalently:

$$\frac{A \rightarrow B \quad A}{B}$$

In algebraic form:

$$((A \rightarrow B) \wedge A) \rightarrow B$$

The truth-table confirms the validity of this inference:

A	**B**	**A → B**	**A**	**(A → B) ∧ A**	**B**	**((A → B) ∧ A) → B**
F	F	T	F	F	F	T
F	T	T	F	F	T	T
T	F	F	T	F	F	T
T	T	T	T	T	T	T

In discussing the deductive-nomological model, Okasha[40] summarises its three conditions for an explanation to be considered 'scientific':

1. Its premises must include at least one GP.
2. Its premises must all be true.
3. Its conclusion must follow deductively from its premises.

On this basis, Okasha finds that the model fails to exclude inferences that are not 'explanations' in the conventional sense. For example, both of the following inferences are valid and permitted by the model, but the second should be excluded because the 'explanation' for the height of a flagpole is likely to be found in the relevant local requirements, customs and regulations, rather than in the length of its shadow at a particular time:

---

39 "The mood that affirms." That is, affirming the antecedent.

40 Samir Okasha, *Philosophy of Science—A Very Short Introduction* (Oxford 2002).

GP: The laws of trigonometry
PI_a: The elevation of the sun and the height of a flagpole

PI_c: The length of the shadow of the flagpole

GP: The laws of trigonometry
PI_a: The elevation of the sun and the length of a flagpole's shadow

---

PI_c: The height of the flagpole

It is possible that Okasha's counter-examples can be eliminated through *ad hoc* modifications to Hempel's model, but this would mean sacrificing its main advantage—simplicity.

Proposition. IDEAL is founded on the assumption that the basis of scientific method is not logical inference but data comparison. This does not mean that all logic is abandoned and false premises are acceptable. What it means is that (in the majority of situations that we would regard as applications of 'scientific method') the truth or falsity of statements is incidental to the way we evaluate them. Data comparison involves assessing two sets of data in relation to one another by looking at their similarities and differences. For the purpose of their comparison the datasets are 'given', that is, their truth-values are assumed to be equal but otherwise unknown. Thus they are not truth-functional and cannot be used as premises in a logical inference. As for deductive-nomological explanation, this is an attractive and plausible model, not because of its emphasis on logical inference (which is misplaced), but because it enforces the formulation of a GP/PI pair as antecedent to any argument; and this, as we have seen, is a vital element of scientific discourse.

Dialectic reasoning

Dialectic is a highly contentious subject, because it means different things to different people, and some of the people who derive meaning from it hold quite strange views. The following lines from *Apocalypse Now* are a clear expression of the more extreme mindset. Kurtz (Marlon Brando) is reading aloud Eliot's *The Hollow Men*, when the harlequin journalist (Dennis Hopper) chooses to enlighten Willard (Martin Sheen) on the meaning of the recitation:

> Do you know what the man's saying? Do you? This is dialectics. It's very simple dialectics, one through nine, no maybes, no supposes, no fractions, you can't travel in space, you can't go out into space, you know, without like, you know, with fractions, what are you going to land

on, one quarter, three eighths, what are you going to do when you go from here to Venus or something? That's dialectic, physics, OK? Dialectic logic is, there's only love or hate, you either love somebody or you hate them...

At this point the harlequin has to break off in order to evade a poetry book lobbed in his direction.

Investigation. Like Kurtz, Popper's reaction to dialectic was vigorous and expressed through the written word. Indeed, Popper's devastating attack on Hegelian dialectic remains unsurpassed as a refutation of woolly thinking. His main criticism is aimed at the acknowledged contradiction between the first two terms of Hegel's thesis/antithesis/synthesis triad:

> ...if a theory contains a contradiction, then it entails everything, and therefore, indeed, nothing. A theory which adds to every information which it asserts also the negation of this information can give us no information at all. A theory which involves a contradiction is therefore entirely useless *as a theory*.[41]

The logical basis of Popper's argument is as follows. Suppose we take as antecedent a simple contradiction, for example, $A \wedge \neg A$:

$$\begin{array}{l} A \\ \neg A \\ \hline B \end{array}$$

In algebraic form:

$$(A \wedge \neg A) \rightarrow B$$

The truth-table confirms the validity of this inference:

A	**B**	**¬A**	**A ∧ ¬A**	**B**	**(A ∧ ¬A) → B**
F	F	T	F	F	T
F	T	T	F	T	T
T	F	F	F	F	T
T	T	F	F	T	T

Since the antecedent $(A \wedge \neg A)$ is always false, the validity of the inference is assured regardless of the truth-value of the consequent (B). So B can be

[41] Karl Popper, *ibid*. This is an application of the maxim, "A theory that explains everything, explains nothing".

anything one likes and the inference remains valid. For example, both of the following are valid inferences:

Black is white	Black is white
God exists	God does not exist

The rejoinder to this argument is that it applies only where statements are truth-functional. In particular, it does not apply to data comparison operations where the truth-functionality of inputs is irrelevant. Thus IDEAL's Iteration **I** component, which deals with data comparison, has connectors for input data, stored data and evaluation data, equivalent to 'thesis', 'antithesis' and 'synthesis' respectively:

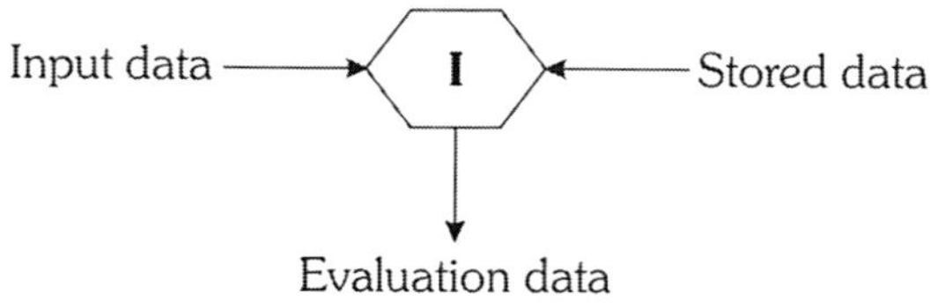

However, there is no IDEAL component having two input control connectors, as control commands are non-negotiable imperatives that can be ascribed truth-functionality. For example, two-value control commands such as {On, Off} or {Go, Stop} can be interpreted as {True, False} with no loss of meaning.

Proposition. Because it establishes a fundamental distinction between 'data' and 'control', IDEAL is able to retain the useful contribution of 'dialectic' (that is, the notion that there is something to be gained from considering two different views of the same phenomenon) while taking into account Popper's logical refutation of Hegelian dialectic. The result is an automatic 'iterative dialectic' system that is guaranteed to avoid contradictory premises in a fail-safe manner, and thereby forestall situations such as that experienced by HAL in *2001—A Space Odyssey*.

Probabilistic inference

According to Howson and Urbach[42], a 'rational' scientist is one who will not accept betting odds that do not appear to be fair. Fair betting quotients are determined by probability theory. Therefore "scientific

[42] Colin Howson and Peter Urbach, *Scientific Reasoning—The Bayesian Approach* (Open Court 1989). All quotations in this section are from this book.

reasoning is reasoning in accordance with the calculus of probabilities". Furthermore, the word 'appear' suggests a degree of subjectivism, and *subjective* betting quotients may be calculated using a part of probability theory known as Bayes' Theorem. Consequently, "the Bayesian approach gives a penetrating insight into the nature of scientific reasoning far superior to that afforded by any of its rivals".

Proposition. Probability theory is an important algorithmic tool for the analysis of collective trends in well-defined sets of data. However, one cannot conclude that 'scientific reasoning' in general is best served by following betting odds. On the contrary, it will be argued that the IDEAL model gives a penetrating insight into the nature of scientific reasoning far superior to that afforded by Bayes' Theorem or any other part of the theory of probability.

Investigation. Since it has been raised, it is only 'fair' to define Bayes' Theorem:

$$P(a|b) = \frac{P(a \,\&\, b)}{P(b)} = \frac{P(b|a)P(a)}{P(b)}$$

> This result which, as we have seen, is mathematically trivial, is nonetheless of central importance in the context of so-called Bayesian inference; there *a* is usually the hypothesis to be evaluated relative to empirical data *b*, and this form of Bayes's Theorem thus states that the probability of the hypothesis conditional on the data (or the *posterior probability* of the hypothesis) is equal to the probability of the data conditional on the hypothesis (or the *likelihood* of the hypothesis) times the probability (the so-called *prior probability*) of the hypothesis, all divided by the probability of the data.[43]

The 'Principle of Conditionalisation' states that, if empirical data *b* turn out to be true, then the unconditional ('prior') degree of belief in hypothesis *a* can be assigned the conditional ('posterior') value,

$$P(a_{t+1}) = P(a_t|b_t),$$

where subscripts t and $t+1$ indicate discrete relative timestep. This equation 'closes the loop' on Bayes' Theorem, raising the interesting possibility that it can be made the basis of an 'iterative learning' mechanism. Another application of the theorem is the development of the 'Bayesian Belief Network' formalism for discrete decision choice. However, the only

[43] Colin Howson and Peter Urbach, *ibid*. The left-hand equation (with the '&') is an axiom of the probability calculus, and the right-hand equation follows from the left. '&' is the authors' notation for the logical conjunction '$\wedge$'.

thing these specialised applications have in common is their reference to Bayes' Theorem itself, an indication that it is too simple to be made the basis of a unifying theoretical structure equivalent to IDEAL. But let us keep an open mind, at least until there is more specific evidence[44]. To whit, let us take a closer look at the stated application of Bayes' Theorem, that of probabilistic inference in relation to 'rational' choice.

It is beyond dispute that, for any *closed, well-defined* decision problem, probability theory in general and Bayes' Theorem in particular can be used to indicate the optimal or 'rational' course of action. The difficulty is that very few problems in science (or anywhere else) are as well-behaved as this. Probability would be unnecessary without the presence of 'uncertainty', which comes in at least four variants:

1. *Reliability/Failure* of physical components, expressed as 'objective probability'.
2. *Safety/Risk* of a system or activity, expressed as 'probability' times 'cost'.
3. *Knowledge/Ignorance* of certain facts, expressed as 'subjective probability'.
4. *Conviction/Doubt* of certain statements, expressed as 'subjective degree of belief'.

Each of these types of uncertainty can be quantified using probability theory; that's not the problem. The problem is that, even if the resulting parameters could be reconciled with one another (which is highly debatable), they are all critically dependent upon the initial definition of the problem to be solved, and on that broader problem probability theory is silent.

These four probabilistic measures are not the only means of quantifying uncertainty; there is a fifth way. Consider the following abstract representation of the 'problem space' associated with any decision problem:

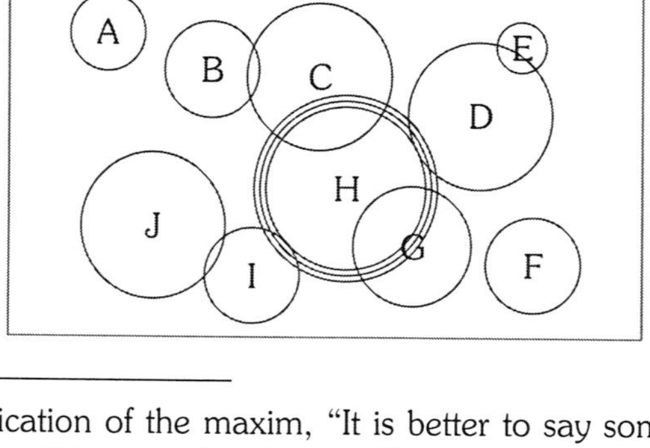

[44] This is an application of the maxim, "It is better to say something small and specific than something grand and general".

The axes of this picture are whatever variables define the problem. For example, if it were a logistic problem—getting from Alcatraz to Bali, say—then the horizontal axis might set out the range of difficulties that might be encountered on the way, and the vertical axis might set out the range of resources that could be utilised in overcoming these difficulties. The circles A-J represent different scenarios (hypothetical combinations of events) for this problem. Each scenario is a two-dimensional object because it describes finite ranges of challenges and responses. (Scenarios don't have to be circular or even two-dimensional for the following argument to hold.) Each scenario can be trusted to take account of the challenges and responses within its domain. In this sense, the locations and sizes of the scenarios tell us how much we know about the problem as a whole; that is, they are a measure of our 'uncertainty' in relation to the problem. Scenario H is drawn with two additional concentric circles, representing upper and lower 'uncertainty' bounds resulting from probability calculations.

There are a number of points to be made in relation to this picture:

1. We handle uncertainty by scoping the problem space. This can be done by carefully investigating the limits of individual scenarios using probabilistic tools (as with scenario H), or by looking at the overlaps and gaps between a number of different scenarios.
2. Let us apply our 'practical problem-solving method' (defined earlier) to the analysis of this problem space. In summary, this method involves: (i) Looking for recorded instances of similar experiences, and down-selecting these to a manageable number having the greatest correspondence with the problem under consideration; (ii) Identifying the principles associated with the similar experiences, and applying these to the new situation, yielding a proposed response; (iii) Comparing this proposed response with those associated with the similar experiences, thereby coming to a judgement as to whether the original problem has been addressed. Applied to the 'problem space' picture, this decision methodology implies that we first look at the overlaps and gaps between different scenarios, and only when we have down-selected a small number of best-fit scenarios do we investigate their limits using various tools including probability theory.
3. Therefore it seems that probabilistic tools do have a role, but only within the context of a framework for handling an ensemble of scenarios. Attempting to make decisions on the basis of probabilistic projections alone misses the overall picture. It can be misleading and does nothing to engender confidence in the final decision. In other

words, probabilistic tools cannot on their own handle the uncertainty inherent in complex decision problems.

4. In practice, if you have a good framework for handling an ensemble of scenarios then there is little need for probabilistic tools.

The use of an ensemble of scenarios to map out a problem space is a well-established technique. Indeed, this 'scenario ensemble method' is simply a variation on a familiar theme: the toolkit approach. And it is no coincidence that, whilst the toolkit approach can easily explain scientific rules of thumb such as 'simplicity', proponents of Bayesian inference such as Howson and Urbach are stuck for an argument, eventually resorting to what can only be described as 'pompous bluster':

> The reader must forgive us if we do not add to the vast and inconclusive literature on simplicity. We think that its inconclusive nature is symptomatic of ambiguity and obscurity in the very notion itself. But our main reason for concluding the discussion here is implicit in what we have already said about the nature of our enterprise. We wish to lay down no indefensible a priori principles as universal standards, any more than we should expect a deductive logician to add to the list of logical axioms a statement of the Principle of the Uniformity of Nature, say, simply because it seems to have been adopted implicitly or explicitly by so many people. This is not to say that we do not see the Bayesian theory as highly explanatory: we do, but we would take people's apparent sensitivity to considerations of simplicity, in whatever particular form such considerations might take, merely as a true factual statement about one of the components *for them* of a high prior probability.

Maxim. "Probabilistic inference. You can do it. But what's the point?"

Maxim. "Where two paths cross, always look for a fifth way."

Truth criteria

Investigation. According to our opening definition, philosophy of science seeks to show whether a theory "can be taken to reveal the truth about a hidden objective reality". To this end, it is wise to agree on what is meant by "truth".

> **truth** *and* **falsity**. "What is truth? said jesting Pilate; and would not stay for an answer" (Francis Bacon, *Essays*, 'Of Truth'). Pilate's example could profitably be followed now, for the 'problem of truth' has been extensively discussed by recent philosophers, stimulated, perhaps, by the flights of fancy of the 19th-century idealists. Philosophers prior to this might well have agreed that no more need be said than the *Shorter Oxford English Dictionary*'s definition of 'truth': "conformity with facts,

> agreement with reality". This definition encapsulates the common-sense theory of truth, the *correspondence theory*, which claims that a statement is true if it corresponds to the facts... But various other theories have been advocated. The absolute idealists put forward a *coherence theory* of truth, in which the only absolute truth is 'the whole'—anything less than that can only aspire to degrees of truth. William James argued for a *pragmatic theory* of truth, according to which the problem of truth is one of welfare economics, for a true assertion is one that proves the best for us in the long run.[45]

But what is "the best for us in the long run"? Is it a specific outcome (the 'ends') or the process by which that outcome is reached (the 'means')? Both, perhaps. That makes five altogether—if we include the object of Pilate's question. And indeed there is a criterion of truth, 'provenance', that validates reference to individuals (such as Christ or Newton) as well as documents (such as the Bible or the *Principia*).

Proposition. These five truth criteria map directly to the five IDEAL learning styles:

IDEAL learning style	Truth criterion
Empiricist	Correspondence
Idealist	Coherence
Theorist	Means
Activist	Ends
Conformist	Provenance

Proposition. In distinguishing truth from falsity, different people use different truth criteria. The extreme positions may be represented by five archetypal 'truth seekers', each of whom judges according to one criterion only:

Truth criterion	Truth seeker
Correspondence	Empirical scientist
Coherence	Mystic
Means	Theoretical scientist
Ends	Activist
Provenance	Religious devotee

[45] Antony Flew (ed.), *ibid.*

Proposition. Alone, none of these 'truth seekers' will get very far in establishing *objective* truth. The obvious alternative is to endeavour to be every one of these truth seekers—but none too much[46].

Proposition. These five truth criteria and associated truth seekers crop up repeatedly in the literature, albeit with frequent omissions reflecting the circumstances and ideologies of individual authors. Five examples are given.

Example. In Bacon's 'Four Idols' may be recognised four of the five archetypal truth seekers:

> There are four classes of Idols which beset men's minds. To these for distinction's sake I have assigned names, calling the first class *Idols of the Tribe*; the second, *Idols of the Cave*; the third, *Idols of the Market Place*; the fourth, *Idols of the Theater*... The Idols of the Tribe have their foundation in human nature itself, and in the tribe or race of men. For it is a false assertion that the sense of man is the measure of things... The Idols of the Cave are the idols of the individual man... There are also Idols formed by the intercourse and association of men with each other, which I call Idols of the Market Place, on account of the commerce and consort of men there... Lastly, there are Idols which have immigrated into men's minds from the various dogmas of philosophies, and also from wrong laws of demonstration. These I call Idols of the Theater, because in my judgment all the received systems are but so many stage plays, representing worlds of their own creation after an unreal and scenic fashion.[47]

The obvious omission is 'Idols of the Temple', that is, the church, which would have fried Bacon if he had put it on his list.

IDEAL learning style	Idol
Empiricist	Market Place
Idealist	Cave
Theorist	Theater
Activist	Tribe
Conformist	Temple

---

46 This is an application of the maxim, *Omnis extremus, sed non in extremis.*

47 Francis Bacon, *Novum Organum* (1620), tr. James Spedding, Robert Leslie Ellis and Douglas Denon Heath (Taggard and Thompson 1863).

Example. In seeking "the true method of arriving at knowledge", Descartes established four rules for himself:

> The first was never to accept anything as true that I did not know to be evidently so: that is to say, carefully to avoid precipitancy and prejudice, and to include in my judgements nothing more than what presented itself so clearly and so distinctly to my mind that I might have no occasion to place it in doubt. The second, to divide each of the difficulties that I was examining into as many parts as might be possible and necessary in order best to solve it. The third, to conduct my thoughts in an orderly way, beginning with the simplest objects and the easiest to know, in order to climb gradually, as by degrees, as far as the knowledge of the most complex, and even supposing some order among those objects which do not precede each other naturally. And the last, everywhere to make such complete enumerations and such general reviews that I would be sure to have omitted nothing.[48]

These rules refer to what we might call 'judgement', 'analysis', 'synthesis' and 'review', respectively. Being a rationalist, Descartes had no need for 'evidence'.

IDEAL learning style	Rule
Empiricist	Evidence
Idealist	Synthesis
Theorist	Analysis
Activist	Judgement
Conformist	Review

Example. Hume's analysis of the association of ideas continues to influence thought in many fields, ranging from myth interpretation (Frazer's use of 'similarity' and 'contagion' in *The Golden Bough*) through linguisitics ('icons', 'indices' and 'symbols' in Peirce's theory of semiotics) to computing ('abstraction', 'inheritance' and 'polymorphism' in Object-Oriented Programming):

> Though it be too obvious to escape observation, that different ideas are connected together; I do not find that any philosopher has attempted to enumerate or class all the principles of association; a subject, however, that seems worthy of curiosity. To me, there appear to be only three principles of connexion among ideas, namely, *Resemblance*, *Contiguity* in time or place, and *Cause or Effect*.[49]

---

[48] René Descartes, *Discourse on Method and The Meditations* (1637-41), tr. F.E. Sutcliffe (Penguin 1968).

[49] David Hume, *An Enquiry Concerning Human Understanding* (1748).

Earlier we took 'means' and 'ends' as separate; repeating this trick with 'cause' and 'effect', we can make up the five by including Hume's great taboo, 'convention'.

IDEAL learning style	Principle of association
Empiricist	Resemblance
Idealist	Contiguity
Theorist	Cause
Activist	Effect
Conformist	Convention

Example. In writing *The White Goddess*, Graves utilised novel 'methods of thought' of his own devising:

> All original discoveries and inventions and musical and poetical compositions are the result of proleptic thought—the anticipation, by means of a suspension of time, of a result that could not have been arrived at by inductive reasoning—and of what may be called analeptic thought, the recovery of lost events by the same suspension... The proleptic or analeptic method of thought, though necessary to poets, physicians, historians and the rest, is so easily confused with mere guessing, or deduction from insufficient data, that few of them own to using it. However securely I buttress the argument of this book with quotations, citations and footnotes, the admission that I have made here of how it first came to me will debar it from consideration by orthodox scholars: though they cannot refute it, they dare not accept it.[50]

There are five methods of thought listed in this passage. Liberal use of all of them yields the following mapping:

IDEAL learning style	Method of thought
Empiricist	Induction
Idealist	Prolepsis
Theorist	Deduction
Activist	Guesswork
Conformist	Analepsis

Example. In establishing his theory of organisational learning, Churchman identified five philosophers whose ideas could be taken to represent five

---

[50] Robert Graves, *The White Goddess* (Faber 1948).

distinct 'Inquiring Systems'[51]: (i) Locke, representing empiricism; (ii) Leibniz, representing rationalism; (iii) Kant, representing (transcendental) idealism; (iv) Hegel, representing dialecticism; (v) Singer (Churchman's former teacher), representing proceduralism.

IDEAL learning style	Inquiring System
Empiricist	Empiricism
Idealist	Rationalism
Theorist	Idealism
Activist	Dialecticism
Conformist	Proceduralism

Theory acceptance criteria

Proposition. Five truth criteria have been identified as essential. All five must be taken into account when assessing the merits of a theory that makes claims about objective reality. To paraphrase Hume[52]: "When we run over libraries, persuaded of these principles, what havoc must we make? If we take in our hand any volume; of divinity or school metaphysics, for instance; let us ask,"

1. Does it correspond to the known facts?
2. Can it be understood in the context of its frame of reference?
3. Does it compare with established theories, both in the manner of its derivation and in the finesse of its application?
4. Does it make claims or predictions that can be tested?
5. Has it taken account of the current literature in the field?

If the answer to *any* of these is "No": "Commit it then to the flames: for it can contain nothing but sophistry and illusion."

Proposition. It is not particularly difficult to formulate 'theory acceptance criteria'. The difficulty lies in justifying them within a consistent frame of reference.

Example. Kuhn's five criteria for theory choice[53]:

> What, I ask to begin with, are the characteristics of a good scientific theory? Among a number of quite usual answers I select five, not

---

[51] C. West Churchman, *The Design of Inquiring Systems* (Basic Books 1971).

[52] David Hume, *ibid.*

[53] Thomas Kuhn, *The Essential Tension* (Chicago 1977).

because they are exhaustive, but because they are individually important and collectively sufficiently varied to indicate what is at stake. First, a theory should be accurate: within its domain, that is, consequences deducible from a theory should be in demonstrated agreement with the results of existing experiments and observations. Second, a theory should be consistent, not only internally or with itself, but also with other currently accepted theories applicable to related aspects of nature. Third, it should have broad scope: in particular, a theory's consequences should extend far beyond the particular observations, laws, or subtheories it was initially designed to explain. Fourth, and closely related, it should be simple, bringing order to phenomena that in its absence would be individually isolated and, as a set, confused. Fifth—a somewhat less standard item, but one of special importance to actual scientific decisions—a theory should be fruitful of new research findings: it should, that is, disclose new phenomena or previously unnoted relationships among those already known. These five characteristics—accuracy, consistency, scope, simplicity, and fruitfulness—are all standard criteria for evaluating the adequacy of a theory.

IDEAL learning style	Theory choice criterion
Empiricist	Accuracy
Idealist	Simplicity
Theorist	Scope
Activist	Fruitfulness
Conformist	Consistency

This list of criteria and its mapping to IDEAL learning styles is all very well, but it begs the question: why are there five of them? Why not four or six or any other number? It is clear from Kuhn's tentative language that no particular number of criteria can be justified within the theory of paradigms that constitutes his frame of reference. By comparison, IDEAL requires five distinct criteria, no more, no less. This is an example of the *limits* set by IDEAL, limits that are applicable as much for itself as for other theories.

Proposition. It is a scientific rule of thumb that every theory has limits; furthermore, a metatheory (or 'theory of theories') must conform to its own limits.

Example. The publication of Kuhn's theory of paradigm choice was itself something of a 'scientific revolution', but this is a metatheory conforming to its own *description*, not to its own *limits*. In fact, Kuhn's reluctance to define 'paradigm' means that the word can be (and has been) taken to mean virtually anything, and consequently the theory 'has no limits' (in the present terminology). Therefore, paradigm choice is a flawed theory, by the above rule of thumb.

Example. Similarly, Popper showed that Hegelian dialectic could be used to infer whatever one liked. That is, dialectical inference has no limits and therefore it is a flawed theory.

Example. The concept of induction is sufficiently well-defined that a number of consistent maxims may be associated with it, for example, "It is better to say something small and specific than something grand and general". These effectively constitute the 'limits' that are the hallmark of a respectable theory; but are they sufficient? An indication that something is missing is the so-called 'problem of induction' posed by Hume:

> Hume represented the nerve of all argument from experience as an attempted syllogism, the problem being to show how we can be entitled to move from a first premise that all observed so-and-sos have been such and such to the conclusion that all so-and-sos without restriction have been, are, and will be such and such. A second premise that would complete a valid syllogism is that all so-and-sos have in fact been observed. But this suggestion is disqualified, since where it applies we have an *analysis of* not an *argument from* experience. This latter essentially involves a going beyond what is given, a use of cases examined to guide expectations about those that have not been examined. The only alternative second premise considered by Hume would make reference to the uniformity of nature. This he ruled out on the grounds that it could only be known to be true by a question-begging appeal to arguments of the very kind here in question.[54]

That is, induction on its own is inadequate, but adding further principles does not help, because their inclusion will not have been as a result of inductive inference. Either the theory is incomplete or it is inconsistent; either its limits are inadequate or it does not conform to them.

Example. Popper proposes 'falsifiability' as the 'demarcation criterion' distinguishing science from metaphysics[55]. Scientific theories are falsifiable, that is, amenable to empirical testing; everything else is just metaphysics. However, nowhere in his writings does Popper suggest an empirical test for his own theory. We conclude that the theory of falsification is unfalsifiable, that is, it does not conform to its own limits.

Example. Howson and Urbach's account of Bayesian inference appears to be properly formulated and self-consistent, but this is achieved only through surrendering part of the territory, for, as they cheerfully admit,

---

[54] Antony Flew (ed.), *ibid.*

[55] Karl Popper, *ibid.*

> ...we should be surprised if on every occasion subjects were apparently to employ impeccable Bayesian reasoning, even in the circumstances that they themselves were to regard Bayesian procedures as canonical. It is, after all, human to err, and sometimes to err in very distinctive and persistent ways.[56]

It appears, then, that scientists need not be Bayesians all of the time. But when should they be Bayesians and when should they not be Bayesians? For example, is it necessary for scientists to be Bayesians when working in their laboratories, but not when they are advising executive decision-makers? If there are no additional criteria, then how can we place any trust in the scientific process? If, on the other hand, there are additional criteria, then Bayesian inference is by definition incomplete. In either case, it is clear that there is more to science than Bayes' Theorem, and it simply cannot be claimed that "scientific reasoning is reasoning in accordance with the calculus of probabilities".

Example. One of IDEAL's 'limits' is the criterion, "a metatheory must conform to its own limits". For consistency, *this* criterion must also appear amongst IDEAL's five theory acceptance criteria. Indeed this is the case, since for a self-referencing metatheory such as IDEAL the second criterion may be read:

2. Can it be understood in the context of *itself*?

Proposition. Consistent within the IDEAL framework are five criteria for the acceptance of theories. It is claimed that IDEAL fulfils these self-set criteria. The evidence to support this claim has been provided here, in *Principia Intellegentia*.

---

[56] Colin Howson and Peter Urbach, *ibid.*

3. How?

How that which is proposed came to be; The barber paradox; Flow diagrams; Component properties; Only connect; An iterative self-regulating system; Emergence; Mapping the mind; Learning styles.

How that which is proposed came to be

'That which is proposed' is the Iterative Dialectic Engine for Automated Learning, or 'IDEAL' for short. Evidence supporting the claim that IDEAL accounts for key aspects of intelligence in humans and machines is given elsewhere in *Principia Intellegentia*. Here, the purpose is different: it is to set out an analytical derivation of IDEAL using established methods. Immediately this poses a problem, as it is not true that IDEAL 'came to be' as a result of analytical derivation. IDEAL was devised using a process of iterative cumulation that itself is integral to IDEAL's design. This process involves analysis as well as observation, but neither to the exclusion of the other. Indeed, as the concept of IDEAL evolved during its long gestation, so did the analyses that now make up its derivation and the collection of observations that now make up its body of supporting evidence. All the same, as the common usage of the word 'derivation' suggests, it is a matter of scientific convention that theories are presented as if they have come about using established analytical methods alone. Accordingly, the following discussion sets out just such a derivation for IDEAL. Theorists will enjoy it; others will not.

The derivation of IDEAL is organised under the following headings:

1. *The barber paradox*, the analysis of which establishes a distinction between 'data' and 'control', a key insight that underpins the derivation of IDEAL.
2. *Flow diagrams*, the conventional means of describing a complex engineering or cybernetics system, are proposed as the media for the definition and derivation of IDEAL. A representative set of flow diagram components is obtained by down-selection from the standard set.
3. *Component properties* for the members of the representative set are proposed. Principally this involves an assessment of their input/output (I/O) connectivity requirements.
4. *Only connect*, setting out precise rules for the connection of flow diagram components.

5. *An iterative self-regulating system*: this is the description of a machine whose components satisfy all of the flow diagram connection rules. It is shown that the simplest such machine is IDEAL.
6. *Emergence*, wherein it is argued that IDEAL can account for so-called 'emergent properties' such as intelligence and consciousness.
7. *Mapping the mind*, that is, relating IDEAL's components to the main parts of the brain.
8. *Learning styles*, identifying the distinct behaviours arising from selective use of the different IDEAL components, and relating them to the characteristic personality types used in psychometric theories.

The barber paradox

Definition.

barber paradox. A paradox illustrating a problem in set theory. Suppose that the barber of Seville shaves all the men of Seville, except those who shave themselves. Does the barber shave himself? If he does shave himself, he is not to be shaved by the barber, that is, himself; if he doesn't, he should be shaved by the barber. Hence he both does and does not shave himself. So the original supposition is false.[1]

Investigation. Set theory underlies the barber paradox. Following the publication of Codd's relational model[2] and subsequent 'Codd's Laws', set theory also underlies the immensely powerful computational method of 'relational programming', that is, the design and use of relational databases (RDBs). What happens to the barber paradox when the men of Seville are listed in a RDB table? For example:

MenOfSeville		
Name	**Trade**	**ShavedByBarber**
Aurelio	Banker	True
Bartolo	Baker	True
Cesar	Beggar	False
Domingo	Baritone	True
Eloy	Butcher	True
Figaro	Barber	False

(The choice of data items is arbitrary and may be varied.)

SQL (Sequential Query Language) operator **S1** identifies those men of Seville who are shaved by the barber:

---

[1] Antony Flew (ed.), *A Dictionary of Philosophy* (Pan 1979).

[2] Edgar Codd, 'A Relational Model of Data for Large Shared Data Banks', *Communications of the ACM*, vol. 13, no. 6, pp. 377-387 (1970).

S1: `SELECT * FROM MenOfSeville WHERE [MenOfSeville].[ShavedByBarber]=True;`

Upon execution **S1** gives the result:

MenOfSeville		
Name	**Trade**	**ShavedByBarber**
Aurelio	Banker	True
Bartolo	Baker	True
Domingo	Baritone	True
Eloy	Butcher	True

Similarly, SQL operator **S2** identifies those men of Seville who are not shaved by the barber (and therefore they are shaved by themselves):

S2: `SELECT * FROM MenOfSeville WHERE [MenOfSeville].[ShavedByBarber]=False;`

Upon execution **S2** gives the result:

MenOfSeville		
Name	**Trade**	**ShavedByBarber**
Cesar	Beggar	False
Figaro	Barber	False

In each case we have the obvious result: Those men of Seville that are identified in RDB table MenOfSeville as being shaved by the barber are shaved by the barber; while those men of Seville that are not identified in RDB table MenOfSeville as being shaved by the barber are not shaved by the barber (and therefore they are shaved by themselves). In particular, if the barber is identified in RDB table MenOfSeville as being shaved by the barber then he is shaved by the barber; while if the barber is not identified in RDB table MenOfSeville as being shaved by the barber then he is not shaved by the barber (and therefore he is shaved by himself). *We* see this last statement as a contradiction, but the *computer* does not, and accordingly the barber is always listed by one (and only one) of **S1** and **S2**.

It might be argued that **S1** and **S2** do not adequately implement the barber paradox condition that "the barber of Seville shaves all the men of Seville, except those who shave themselves". A rigorous implementation of this condition is possible using algorithmic programming, for example, in lines 13-18 of VBA (Visual Basic for Applications) program **ShaveAll**:

```
Sub ShaveAll()
'
' VBA program to shave all men of Seville
'
Dim db1 As Database, qy1 As QueryDef, rs1 As Recordset
Dim Shavee As String, Shaver As String, Shaved As Boolean
'
Set db1 = DBEngine.Workspaces(0).OpenDatabase("C:\Barber")
Set qy1 = db1.CreateQueryDef("Query1", "SELECT * FROM MenOfSeville;")
Set rs1 = db1.OpenRecordset("Query1")
rs1.MoveFirst
Do Until rs1.EOF
  Shavee = rs1![Trade]
  Shaver = "Barber"
  If Not rs1![ShavedByBarber] Then
    Shaver = Shavee
  End If
  Shaved = Shave(Shavee, Shaver)
  If Not Shaved Then
    MsgBox ("Error!")
  End If
  rs1.MoveNext
Loop
rs1.Close
db1.QueryDefs.Delete "Query1"
db1.Close
MsgBox ("All shaved")
'
End Sub
'
Function Shave(Shavee As String, Shaver As String) As Boolean
'
' VBA function to shave a man
'
Call WashFace(Shavee, Shaver)
Call LatherFace(Shavee, Shaver)
Call ShaveFace(Shavee, Shaver)
Call WashFace(Shavee, Shaver)
Call DryFace(Shavee, Shaver)
MsgBox (Shavee & " shaved by " & Shaver)
Shave = True
'
End Function
```

(For brevity, subroutines **WashFace**, **LatherFace**, **ShaveFace** and **DryFace** have not been included in this listing.)

As with **S1** and **S2**, upon execution **ShaveAll** correctly identifies those men of Seville that are shaved by the barber and those men of Seville that are not shaved by the barber (and therefore are shaved by themselves), according to the values assigned in RDB table MenOfSeville. When it comes to the barber, **ShaveAll** declares "Barber shaved by Barber" and moves on to the next operation. If there is a contradiction or paradox in this then somehow the computer has missed it.

To summarise:

1. Set theory underlies both the barber paradox and relational programming.
2. The condition that gives rise to the barber paradox, "the barber of Seville shaves all the men of Seville, except those who shave themselves", may be implemented in a RDB.
3. The associated computational operations fail to detect any contradiction or paradox.

That is, either our way of looking at the barber paradox is inexplicably mistaken, or relational programming is not based on set theory in the way that we supposed. The former, to a theorist, is profoundly disturbing; so it is just as well that the latter turns out to be the case. Whereas the barber paradox is aimed at Cantor's original formulation of set theory (now called 'naïve' set theory), relational programming is based on a modified version (now called 'axiomatic' or 'Zermelo-Fraenkel' set theory) devised specifically to avoid problems such as the barber paradox:

> In the year 1908, in which Russell published the first version of his theory of types and Brouwer first wrote against the reliability of the principles of logic, E. Zermelo produced a set of axioms designed to save the theory of sets from paradoxes. Regarding this theory still as the most fundamental part of mathematics, he suggests that it should be rebuilt by the laying down of principles which are sufficient to support the generally accepted doctrine but so chosen that they do not give rise to contradictions. He admits that he cannot prove the consistency of his axioms, but he claims that he has at least excluded the antimonies discovered in recent years. The essential feature of his method is that he no longer talks of sets with the freedom of Cantor but admits in his theory only those sets whose existence is guaranteed by his axioms.
>
> First in his Axiom of Definiteness (i) he lays it down that two sets are identical if whatever is a member of one is a member also of the other. Then in a number of axioms he provides for derivation of sets from others assumed to be given. Thus in his Axiom of Subsets (iii) he says that if there is a property such that for every member of a set S it is a

determinate question whether that member has the property or not then there exists a second set whose members are just those members of S which have the property;[3]

It is instructive to identify the precise differences between these formulations in relation to the barber paradox. Naïve set theory assumes the (unqualified) 'comprehension principle'[4]:

$$\exists b\ \forall a\ ((a \in b) \leftrightarrow \mathbf{P}(a)) \qquad \text{(C)}$$

In words[5]: "For any predicate $\mathbf{P}(a)$, there is a set b containing precisely those members a for which $\mathbf{P}(a)$ holds". That is, predicate $\mathbf{P}(a)$ identifies the members a of set b. "Zermelo's axiomatization of set theory restricted the existence of sets determined by a predicate to just those sets whose members were members of a given set and satisfied the predicate."[6] In Zermelo-Fraenkel set theory this is implemented by the axiom schema of 'specification'[7]:

$$\forall c\ \exists b\ \forall a\ ((a \in b) \leftrightarrow (a \in c) \wedge \mathbf{P}(a)) \qquad \text{(S)}$$

In words: "For all sets c and any predicate $\mathbf{P}(a)$, there is a subset b of c containing precisely those members a for which $\mathbf{P}(a)$ holds". That is, predicate $\mathbf{P}(a)$ identifies the members a of subset b of set c. To understand how equation C succumbs to the barber paradox and how equation S avoids it, we look first at Russell's paradox, of which the barber paradox is a variant:

Russell's paradox. An important paradox in set theory. Some sets (classes or collection) are members of themselves and some are not. For instance, the set of horses is not a member of itself since it is a set and not a horse, whereas the set of non-horses is a member of itself. Is the set of all sets which are not members of themselves, a member of itself? If it is then it is not. If it is not then it is.[8]

---

[3] William Kneale and Martha Kneale, *The Development of Logic* (Oxford 1962).

[4] See, for example, *Paradoxes from A to Z* by Michael Clark (Routledge 2002).

[5] This and subsequent equations are written using the standard notation of first order predicate logic. See any introductory logic text, for example, *Logic* by Nick Earle (Macmillan 1973).

[6] Antony Flew (ed.), *ibid.*

[7] In the literature, this axiom schema is given a bewildering variety of names, including 'comprehension', 'restricted comprehension', 'restriction', 'specification', 'separation', 'subset', 'selection' and 'formation'. Kneale and Kneale refer to it as the "Axiom of Subsets".

[8] Antony Flew (ed.), *ibid.*

This paradox focusses on those sets which are not members of themselves:

$$\mathbf{P}(a) = (a \notin a)$$

Substituting $\mathbf{P}(a)$ in C we obtain

$$\exists b\ \forall a\ ((a \in b) \leftrightarrow (a \notin a)) \qquad (C_R)$$

With such expressions it is important to understand the significance of the ordering of the quantifiers. In the general case, $\exists x\ \forall y\ \mathbf{R}(x, y)$ is not the same as $\forall y\ \exists x\ \mathbf{R}(x, y)$ and one cannot treat these quantifiers as fully interchangeable. Nevertheless, if $\exists x\ \forall y\ \mathbf{R}(x, y)$ is true then it is impossible for $\forall y\ \exists x\ \mathbf{R}(x, y)$ to be false[9], that is, $\exists x\ \forall y\ \mathbf{R}(x, y) \rightarrow \forall y\ \exists x\ \mathbf{R}(x, y)$, and it follows that C_R implies the equation $\forall a\ \exists b\ ((a \in b) \leftrightarrow (a \notin a))$. In this equation set b is included as a member of set a, with b now representing the set of all sets which are not members of themselves. The particular case may be isolated by assigning to a the specific value b such that $(b \in b) \leftrightarrow (b \notin b)$. This expression is self-contradictory and always false, making it the basis of the paradox. Substituting $\mathbf{P}(a)$ in S yields no such contradiction, however:

$$\forall c\ \exists b\ \forall a\ ((a \in b) \leftrightarrow (a \in c) \wedge (a \notin a)) \qquad (S_R)$$

Here it is possible to isolate the particular case directly by assigning to c the specific value b to give the equation $\forall a\ ((a \in b) \leftrightarrow (a \in b) \wedge (a \notin a))$. Equivalently we may write $\forall a\ (a \notin a)$, which simply (and without contradiction) identifies those set members a for which $\mathbf{P}(a)$ holds.

Similarly, the barber paradox may be expressed by replacing set membership in the above equations with $\mathbf{Shave}(a, b)$, representing a mechanistic operation in which a is shaved by b. Thus $\mathbf{P}(a)$ identifies those men who do not shave themselves:

$$\mathbf{P}(a) = \neg\mathbf{Shave}(a, a)$$

Substituting $\mathbf{P}(a)$ in C we obtain

$$\exists b\ \forall a\ (\mathbf{Shave}(a, b) \leftrightarrow \neg\mathbf{Shave}(a, a)) \qquad (C_B)$$

In words: "There is a barber b such that, for all men a, a man is shaved by the barber b if and only if he is not shaved by himself". As before, C_B implies $\forall a\ \exists b\ (\mathbf{Shave}(a, b) \leftrightarrow \neg\mathbf{Shave}(a, a))$, and assigning to a the specific value b we obtain $\mathbf{Shave}(b, b) \leftrightarrow \neg\mathbf{Shave}(b, b)$, "The barber is shaved by himself if and only if he is not shaved by himself", a

9 Colin Howson, *Logic with Trees* (Routledge 1997).

contradiction. Furthermore, as with Russell's paradox, the axiom schema of specification yields no such contradiction:

$$\forall c\, \exists b\, \forall a\, (\mathbf{Shave}(a, b) \leftrightarrow \mathbf{Shave}(a, c) \wedge \neg\mathbf{Shave}(a, a)) \qquad (S_B)$$

In words: "For all persons *c*, there is a barber *b* such that, for all men *a*, a man is shaved by the barber *b* if and only if he is shaved by a person *c* and he is not shaved by himself". Here it is possible to isolate the particular case directly by assigning to *c* the specific value *b* to give the equation $\forall a\, (\mathbf{Shave}(a, b) \leftrightarrow \mathbf{Shave}(a, b) \wedge \neg\mathbf{Shave}(a, a))$. Equivalently we may write $\forall a\, (\neg\mathbf{Shave}(a, a))$, which simply (and without contradiction) identifies those set members *a* for which $\mathbf{P}(a)$ holds.

The preceding analysis gives an abstract mathematical explanation for the barber paradox and its resolution; but what does this mean in practice? In particular, how does this explain the avoidance of paradox in the RDB case? It seems that the key paradox-dodging step in this analysis is the introduction of set *c* as antecedent in the axiom schema of specification (equation S). The equivalent to this in the RDB case is the provision of table MenOfSeville with (albeit arbitrary) non-null data items. There is something else, however: when VBA program **ShaveAll** encounters data entry 'Barber' in MenOfSeville it does *not* take this as an instruction to directly commence operation **Shave**, rather it treats it in exactly the same way as other data entries, declaring "Barber shaved by Barber" and moving on to the next operation. That is, in common with all computer programs, **ShaveAll** draws a distinction between data entries and algorithmic operators, and it is this distinction that enables **ShaveAll** to escape the barber paradox. The same distinction is implicit in the mathematical formalism of first order predicate logic. Specifically, in introducing set *c* as antecedent, equation S breaks up equation C's problematic identity $(a \in b) \leftrightarrow \mathbf{P}(a)$, effectively drawing a distinction between a data assignation $(a \in b)$ and the execution of an operator $\mathbf{P}(a)$:

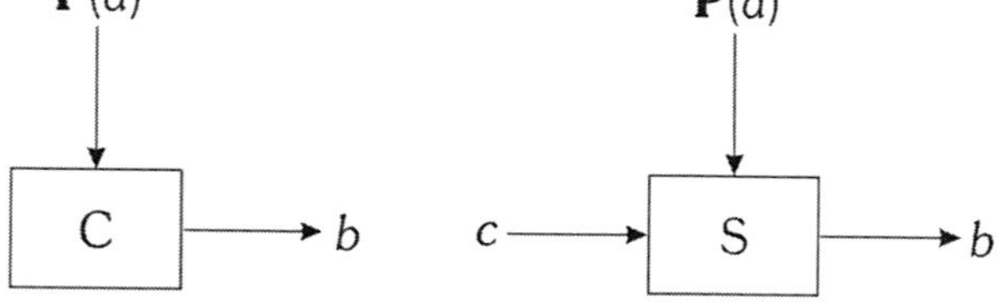

The essential difference between an item of data such as *b* or 'Barber' and an operator such as $\mathbf{P}(a)$ or **Shave** is that the former can only be referenced by name whereas the latter can *also* be executed to generate an item of data (such as *b* or 'Barber', indeed). This *distinction between data and operators* is so pervasive in modern mathematics, logic and computing that we neglect to register its importance; and therein lies our downfall. Thus, in the case of the barber paradox, equation C_B directly substitutes the data assignation ($a \in b$)—which includes man *a* in the list of customers of barber *b*—with the operator **Shave**(*a*, *b*)—which, when executed, undertakes a mechanistic operation whereby man *a* is shaved by barber *b*. In so doing, C_B fails to uphold the distinction between data and operators, and this is the underlying cause of the paradox. Russell's paradox arises for a similar reason.

The elimination of paradoxes is just one of several important consequences of the distinction between data and operators. These include:

1. Variable/operator syntax, as used in mathematics, logic and computing.
2. In a computer program, the distinction between data assignations (which populate datasets) and control statements (which initiate the execution of operators). Thus the entry 'Barber' in RDB table MenOfSeville is *not* interpreted as an immediate instruction to **Shave**, rather it simply assigns the barber as a man of Seville, a critical distinction that removes all possibility of paradox in this implementation.
3. In a flow diagram, the distinction between data connectors (which transfer data for use in some operation) and control connectors (which transfer control statements, that is, non-negotiable imperative commands).
4. The above depiction of the S equation has the same I/O configuration as the triode and the transistor[10]. These connectors map as follows:

Connector	**S equation**	**Triode**	**Transistor**
Input data	Set *c*	Cathode	Emitter
Control	Predicate **P**(*a*)	Grid	Base
Output data	Set *b*	Anode	Collector

5. This same threefold connectivity is apparent in deductive-nomological form, which expresses the process of scientific explanation in terms of the equation $(GP \wedge PI_a) \rightarrow PI_c$. Here, 'GP' denotes 'General

[10] See also the discussion of von Neumann's design for the EDVAC in **2. Where and When?**

Principles', 'PI' denotes 'Particular Instances', and subscripts 'a' and 'c' denote 'antecedent' and 'consequent' respectively[11].

The third item on this list is of particular relevance to the present application. Strangely, the flowcharting literature appears not to make any reference to the distinction between data and control—even though this distinction has been described, explained and accepted in fields where flowcharting is also used[12]. For this reason it is restated here as a new proposition.

Proposition. Flow diagrams must take into account the distinction between data and control.

Flow diagrams

Proposition. Flow diagrams are the conventional means of describing a complex engineering or cybernetics system. IDEAL is envisaged to be just such a system. Accordingly, flow diagrams are proposed as the media for the definition and derivation of IDEAL.

Investigation. When using any analytical or representational technique it is always a good idea to first identify the defining units of its key parameters. In the case of flowcharting, the 'units' are the different components that can be drawn in a flow diagram. A *de facto* standard set of components was established *circa* 1970 by the IBM X20-8020 drawing template, itself based on a combination of standards in use at that time. The properties of these components are described on the card envelope used for storing the plastic template. The following images of the template and its envelope have been copied from report GC20-8152-1, *Data Processing Techniques: Flowcharting Techniques* (IBM 1970).

[11] See **2. Where and When?** for a discussion of deductive-nomological explanation.

[12] See, for example, Mauricio Varea, *Modelling and verification of embedded systems based on Petri net oriented representations* (PhD, University of Southampton 2003).

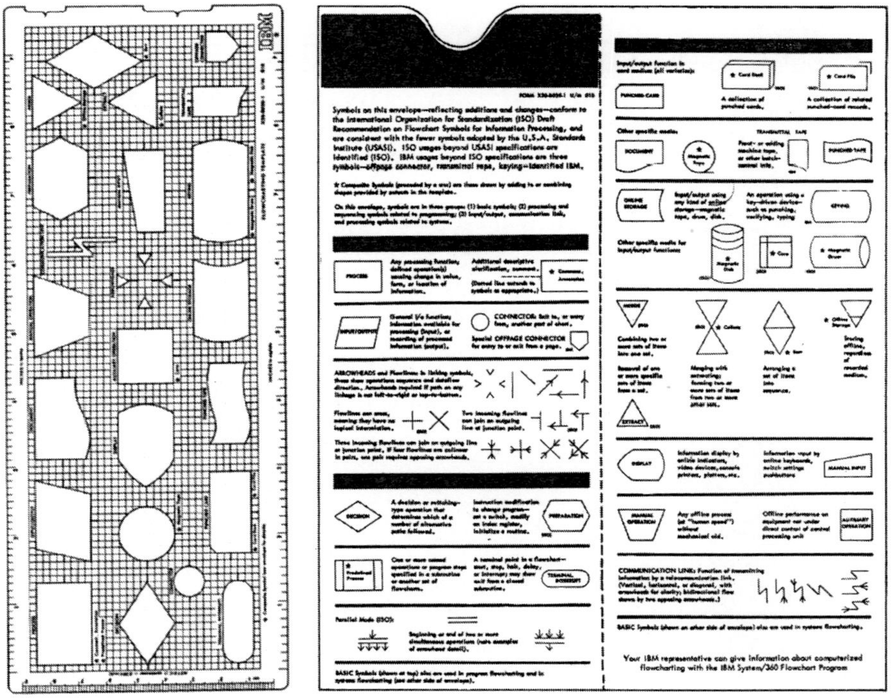

This template identifies twenty-one named symbols. Of these, a majority of symbols are clearly redundant: some because they represent specific processes that can be included within the remit of more generic alternatives; others because they do not represent any actual *operation*, that is, they are simply engaged in the unimpeded transfer of data. If these redundant symbols are removed then we are left with just five:

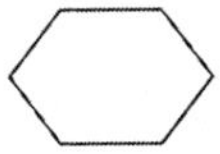

"PREPARATION. Instruction modification to change program—set a switch, modify an index register, initialize a routine."

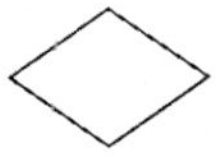

"DECISION. A decision or switching-type operation that determines which of a number of alternative paths followed."

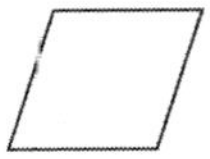

"INPUT/OUTPUT. General i/o function; information available for processing (input), or recording of processed information (output)."

"PROCESS. Any processing function; defined operation(s) causing change in value, form, or location of information."

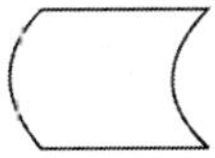

"ONLINE STORAGE. Input/output using any kind of online storage—magnetic tape, drum, disk."

The reasons for the omission of the other symbols are as follows:

Template symbol name	Reason for omission
ARROWHEADS	Data transfer only
AUXILIARY OPERATION	Specific instance of PROCESS
COMMUNICATION LINK	Data transfer only
CONNECTOR	Data transfer only
DISPLAY	Specific instance of INPUT/OUTPUT
DOCUMENT	Specific instance of ONLINE STORAGE
EXTRACT	Specific instance of PREPARATION
KEYING	Specific instance of INPUT/OUTPUT
MANUAL INPUT	Specific instance of INPUT/OUTPUT
MANUAL OPERATION	Specific instance of PROCESS
MERGE	Specific instance of PREPARATION
OFFPAGE CONNECTOR	Data transfer only
PUNCHED CARD	Specific instance of ONLINE STORAGE
PUNCHED TAPE	Specific instance of ONLINE STORAGE
TERMINAL, INTERRUPT	Specific instance of DECISION
TRANSMITTAL TAPE	Specific instance of ONLINE STORAGE

Proposition. By down-selection from the standard set of flow diagram symbols we are left with just five generic components. These may be treated as a representative 'basis set', that is, a complete set of symbols by which *any* engineering or cybernetics system may be depicted in a flow diagram.

Component properties

Investigation. In order to introduce a degree of rigour into the analysis, it is necessary to set out a more precise definition of the five representative flowchart components. Principally this involves an assessment of their I/O connectivity requirements. Bearing in mind the conclusions of the barber paradox discussion, we define two types of connector:

Definition.

Data connector. This connector transfers data in the direction of the arrow. The information thus transferred may be used in a calculation or it may be stored, but it does not constitute a command to any component to commence or cease operating.

→ *Control connector*. This connector transfers commands in the direction of the arrow and also admits the transfer of return codes—truth-functional flags indicating the commencement or completion of an operation—in the opposite direction. The command thus transferred will cause the target component to commence or cease a specific operation, but it may not be used in a calculation and it cannot be stored *as a command*. That is, only the codified *description* of the command can be handled as data information.

Although these connectors are not to be found in the flowchart literature, computer programmers will recognise them as the equivalents of data assignations and control statements, respectively.

Example. In the program **ShaveAll** introduced earlier, line 18 is the statement

```
Shaved = Shave(Shavee, Shaver)
```

This statement instructs the central processor to execute the operation **Shave** with input data arguments Shavee and Shaver. Upon successful completion **Shave** assigns Boolean value 'True' to data variable Shaved and restores control to the calling routine **ShaveAll**. Thus in this brief statement there are two data assignations, one control command and one return code assignation. As a flow diagram:

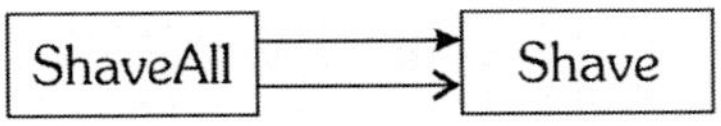

Here it is understood that the data connector → transfers both data items Shavee and Shaver, while the control connector → transfers the instruction to execute **Shave** and, upon completion, a truth-functional return code in the opposite direction.

Investigation. This useful correspondence between flowcharting and computer programming may be extended to map the five representative flowchart components to specific program features[13]:

[13] A similar mapping may be obtained for the reduced language set used in the B-APT Berger aptitude test. This is discussed as part of the review of von Neumann's design for the EDVAC, see **2. Where and When?**

Flowchart component	Equivalent program feature
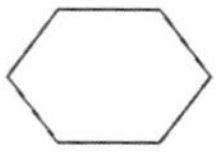 PREPARATION	A program loop whose recurrence depends upon the outcome of a completion condition which involves comparing the value of a variable parameter with a predefined stopping threshold. This implements a process of 'iterative control' which presupposes a facility to initialise, modify and compare data values.
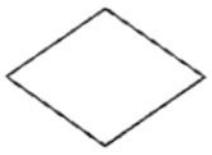 DECISION	Any executive statement (non-negotiable imperative command) that transfers control to some other part of the program. For example, in program **ShaveAll** the statement **Shave** executes specific predefined commands before returning control to **ShaveAll**. The 'decision' element of this process lies in its dependence upon iterative control (described above) and upon the values of return codes.
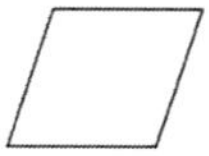 INPUT/OUTPUT	Any procedure involving the transfer of data between the central processor and an 'independent external component', for example, data input by manual keystrokes or data output by visual display.
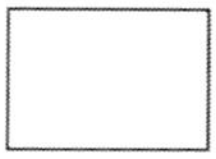 PROCESS	A defined algorithm, that is, a sequence of logical or mathematical operations applied to input data (at the behest of a control statement) and generating results data for storage and further analysis.
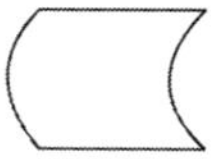 ONLINE STORAGE	Defined program entities such as classes, arrays and variables for the storage and retrieval of specific data values. For example, in program **ShaveAll**, the defined parameters db1, qy1, rs1, Shavee, Shaver, Shaved.

Accordingly, we might expect these five components to have the following I/O connectors:

Flowchart component	Connectivity requirements
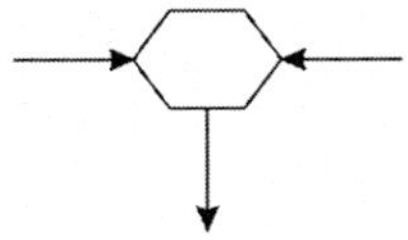	This component has two input data connectors, signifying its unique data comparison role. The result of the comparison is output for interpretation elsewhere.
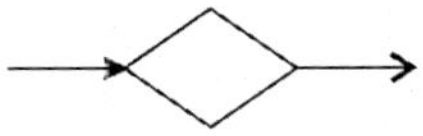	This component can input the result of a data comparison and also the result of a control statement (by return code). Only this component can generate control statements.
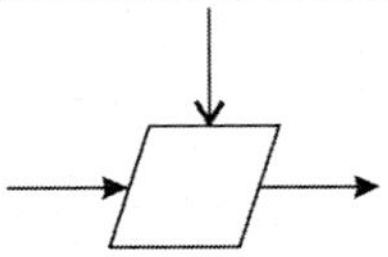	When it receives an appropriate command, this component transfers data between the central processor and an independent external component (or vice versa).
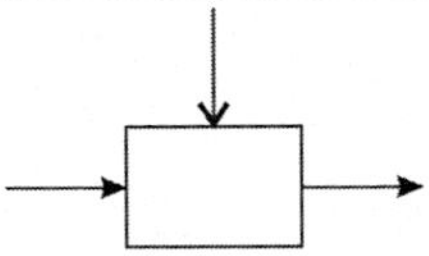	When it receives an appropriate command, this component applies an algorithmic operation to input data, generating results data for storage and further analysis.
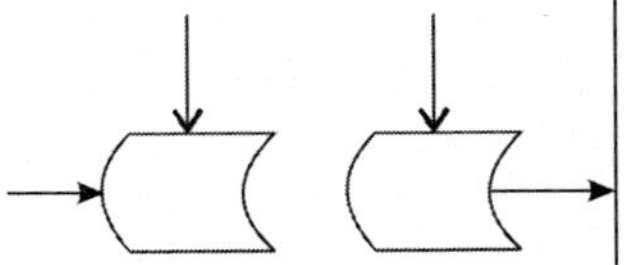	This component can store and retrieve data. Incoming data are stored automatically, with their arrival notified by return code (left-hand diagram). Data are released when the component receives an appropriate command (right-hand diagram).

Definition. Finally, for ease of reference we label each component with an identifying letter:

Flowchart component	Notation
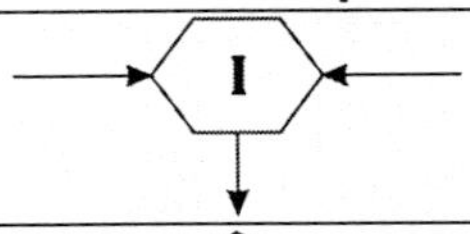	**I**teration component.
	**D**ecision component.
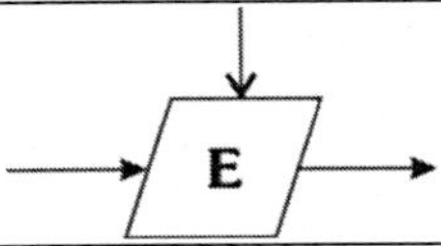	**E**vidence component.
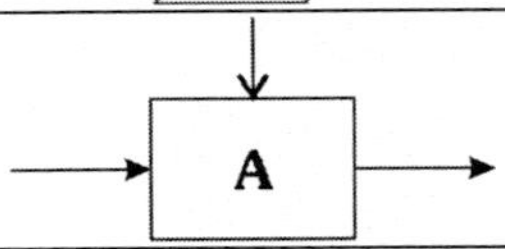	**A**lgorithm component.
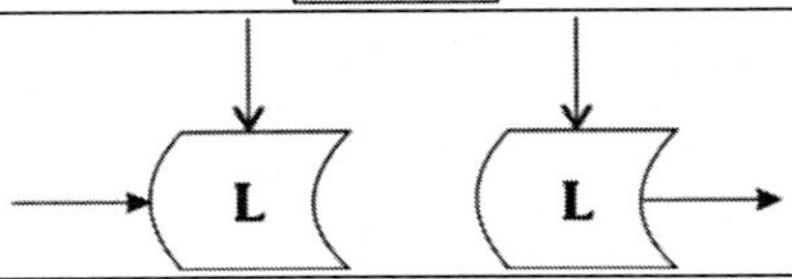	**L**og component.

Only connect

Five flowchart components have been selected as representative and their properties defined. To strengthen confidence in this choice, we compare their collective I/O capability with a list of mandatory connections obtained by downselecting from the (infinite) set of all possible I/O combinations. In the spirit of Zermelo's axiomatisation of set theory, we downselect by applying connection rules that promote desirable features and exclude undesirable ones. These connection rules are as follows:

Definition.

1. *A component may have no more than two input connectors, of which, no more than one control connector*. This imposes a dyadic mode of operation, the benefits of which have been discussed elsewhere[14]. In addition, this rule excludes the possibility of two or more control inputs:

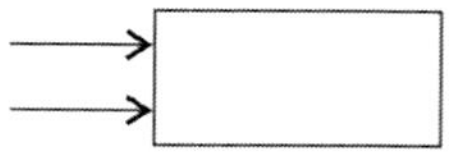

   This exclusion means that conflicting commands (which are known to produce unpredictable results[15]) cannot arise.
2. *A component may have no more than one type of output connector*. The distinction between data and control is a valuable discovery, but much of its significance would be lost if components could generate both types of output:

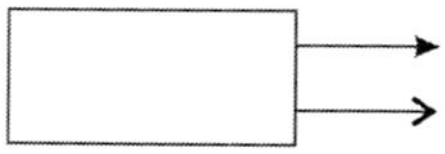

   That is, a component should output data or control, but not both. This rule places a limit on the *variety* but not the *quantity* of output connectors, as it is assumed that a multiplicity of outputs either allows a choice of destination for a particular signal or it allows the same signal to be sent to several destinations. For simplicity, only one output connector need be drawn in the representative case.
3. *There must be a nontrivial passage of information through each component*. This rule is designed to exclude 'passive' or 'trivial' components that either do nothing with the information they receive or give no signal to this effect. Such components are recognisable by their simple connectivity:

---

[14] See the discussion of general principles and particular instances in **2. Where and When?**

[15] See the discussion of dialectic in **2. Where and When?**

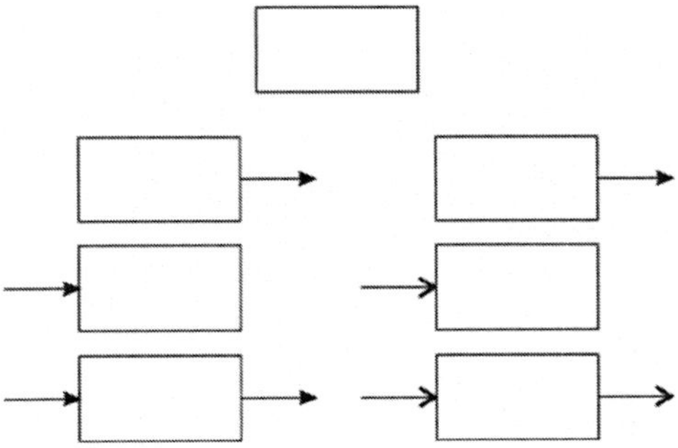

This rule implies that all components must have at least two connectors, of which, at least one for input and another for output (for the same operation). Furthermore, these connectors must differ in *type* or *quantity*. For example: a component with one data input must also have a control input (for the output of a return code) or a control output (for the output of a command); a component with two data inputs must also have a control output (for the output of a command) or a data output (for the output of data, this being allowed because there are *two* data inputs, constituting a different 'quantity').

Analysis. With no more than two input connectors (rule 1) and no more than one output connector (rule 2), there are a total of eighteen possible I/O combinations. This is the downselected list of mandatory connections that we have been seeking. The following table itemises these combinations and maps the 'survivors' of the connection rules to the five representative flowchart components.

Case	I/O combination	Representative flowchart component(s)
1.		Excluded by rule 3.
2.	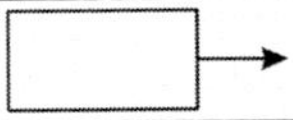	Excluded by rule 3.
3.	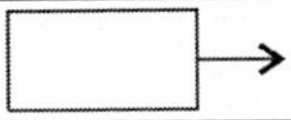	Excluded by rule 3.
4.	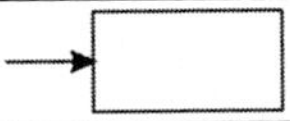	Excluded by rule 3.
5.		Excluded by rule 3.
6.		
7.	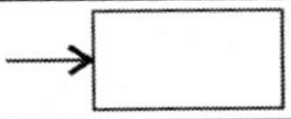	Excluded by rule 3.
8.		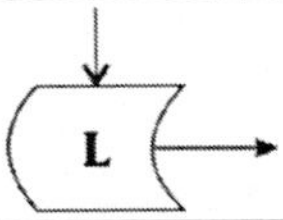

9.	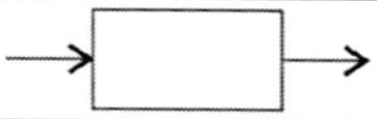	Excluded by rule 3.
10.	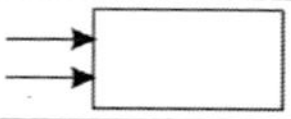	Excluded by rule 3.
11.	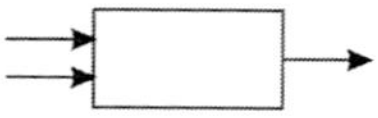	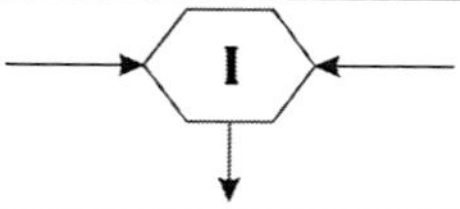
12.	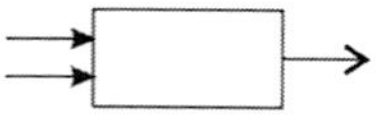	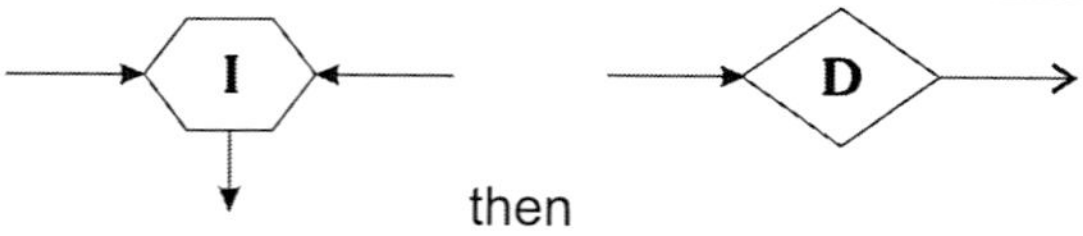
13.	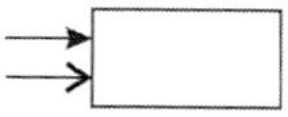	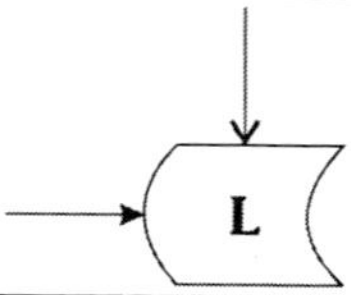
14.		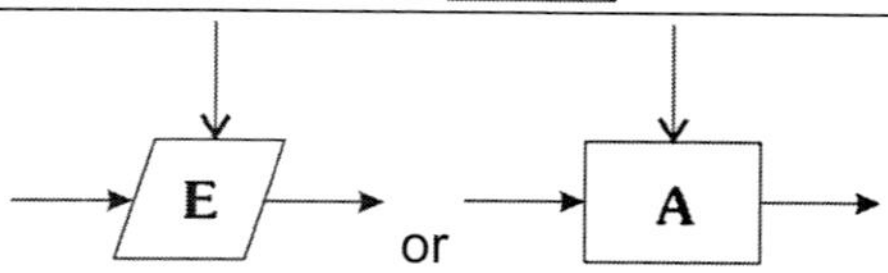
15.[16]		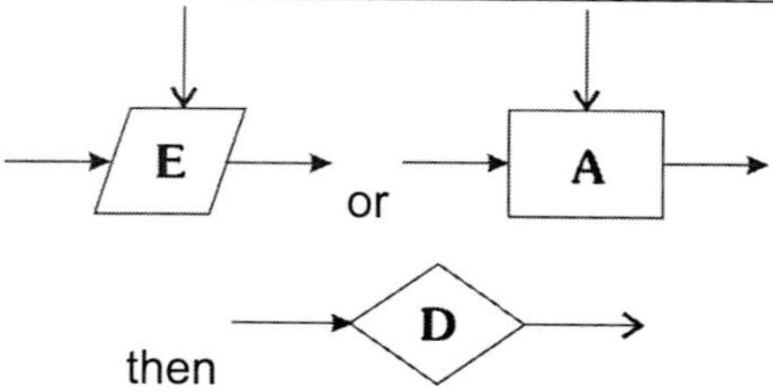
16.	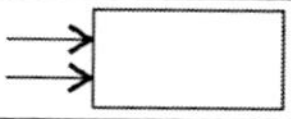	Excluded by rule 1.
17.	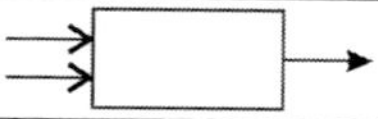	Excluded by rule 1.
18.	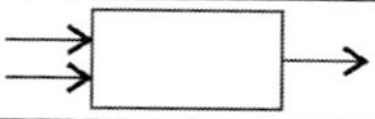	Excluded by rule 1.

Proposition. This analysis shows that all the mandatory combinations of I/O connections can be realised using the five representative flowchart components. It follows that these representative components satisfy the connection rules set out above.

[16] In fact, IDEAL implements the functionality of case 15 by using **E** then **I** then **D**. In this case, the absence of a second data input is taken by **I** as an unambiguous signal that it should allow the free passage of data from **E** to **D**. This mechanism is discussed further in **1. What?** In all other valid cases the I/O combinations are matched by IDEAL components as shown.

An iterative self-regulating system

The pieces are now in place for the derivation of IDEAL:

1. Flowcharting has been selected as the 'established method' for undertaking the derivation.
2. Flow diagram components have been identified as the 'units' of the flowcharting method.
3. Five flowchart components have been selected as representative and their properties defined.
4. The choice of representative components has been confirmed by an independent analysis based on 'mandatory I/O connections' picked out by 'connection rules'. Whilst new to flowcharting, this type of analysis will be familiar to mathematicians as a 'nomological' or 'axiomatic' approach.
5. Thus far, connection rules have been established for flowchart components considered individually. Further rules restricting the connectivity of particular groups of components have yet to be established. This provides the opportunity to complete the derivation of IDEAL.

Analysis. The derivation of IDEAL has the following steps:

1. IDEAL is defined using a flow diagram.
2. Connection rules for groups of flowchart components are established.
3. It is shown that the simplest arrangement of flowchart components that satisfies all of the flow diagram connection rules is IDEAL.

Definition. This is IDEAL:

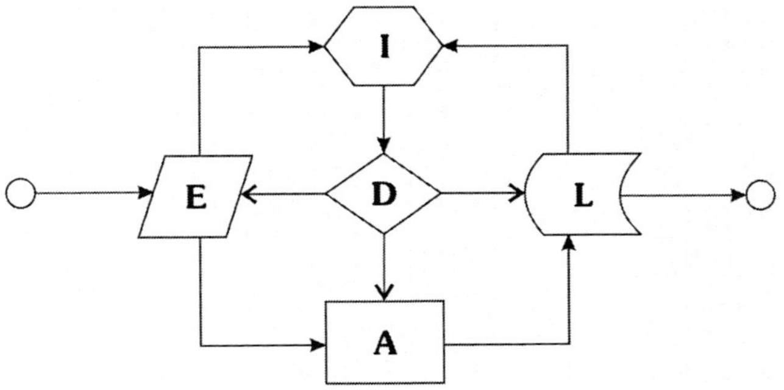

In addition to the five representative flowchart components (denoted **I**, **D**, **E**, **A** and **L**), this diagram depicts the 'CONNECTOR', which is taken to refer to an 'independent external component' **O**:

Since it is independent, **O** does not contribute to IDEAL's functionality. Nevertheless, its inclusion is valuable as it makes explicit the important transfer of information to and from the 'outside world'. In addition, **O** offers the interesting possibility of a communication channel between **L** and **E**. Although this connection is indirect, it may be assumed that **L** and **E** are sufficiently well-developed that **O** does not present a significant obstacle to their communication. That is, the connection through **O** is equivalent to a continuous data connector.

Definition. To the three single-component connection rules defined above we add three more, which restrict the connectivity of components when associated with one another in a flow diagram:

4. *For every combination of inputs and outputs of every component in a flow diagram, it must be possible to trace a continuous path through the diagram, starting with an output node and finishing with an input node.* This rule introduces a generalised iterative capability which is the necessary complement of rule 1 (which imposes a dyadic mode of operation) and rule 3 (which eliminates single-connection terminators).
5. *No component may have more than one connection with any other component—including itself.* This deceptively simple rule is designed to eliminate self-referencing or mutually-referencing configurations that have a propensity to generate unproductive 'infinite loops':

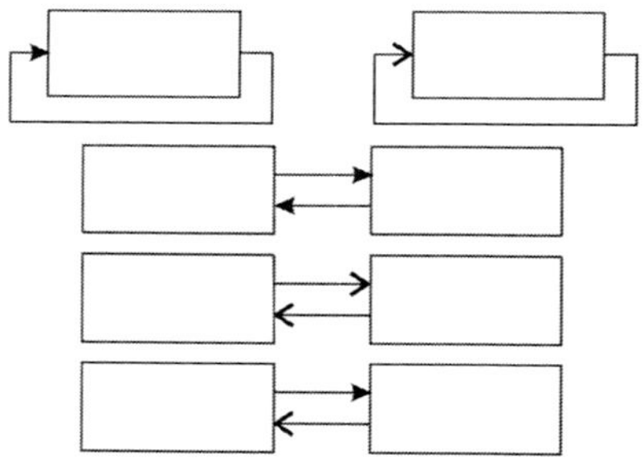

Since they satisfy rules 1-3, the five representative flowchart components each have 'interesting' combinations of I/O connectors. The effect of rule 5 on these components is to link them together in a system of mutual dependence, where no component is independent of any other, but at the same time no component is wholly dependent upon any other. Such an arrangement can be expected to develop the mutual checks and balances and well-tuned division of labour that are the signs of a *self-regulating* system.

6. *The flow diagram must include* **O**. This rule acknowledges the fact that even an iterative self-regulating system will become repetitive

and sterile if allowed to operate as a perpetual machine independent of I/O stimuli. As is discussed at length elsewhere, IDEAL is intended as a high-level description of how humans learn. This involves many things, not least, a dynamic interaction with an independent, complex environment. It is precisely this environment that is represented by **O**.

Analysis. The above table of mandatory I/O connections shows that a flow diagram must include **I**, **D**, **L** and either **E** or **A**. Rule 6 adds **O** to this list. Simply by trying out the different combinations, it is found that selecting **E** *or* **A** means that either rule 4 or rule 5 is broken. Only if **E** *and* **A** are present can all the rules be satisfied—but this is precisely the selection of components in IDEAL:

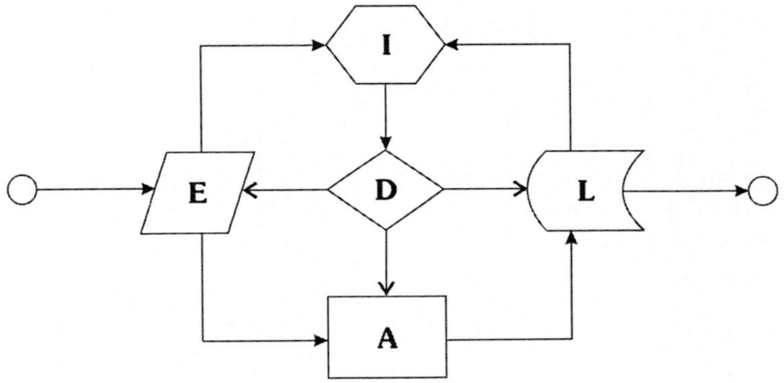

Therefore the simplest arrangement of flowchart components that satisfies all of the flow diagram connection rules is IDEAL.

QED.

Proposition. It follows from this analysis that IDEAL can be described as 'an iterative self-regulating system'.

Emergence

Describing IDEAL as 'an iterative self-regulating system' begs a number of questions:

1. Is IDEAL unique? That is, are there any other iterative self-regulating systems?
2. Does the description of IDEAL as an iterative self-regulating system affect the claim that it accounts for key aspects of intelligence in humans and machines?
3. Do non-human species exhibit iterative self-regulating behaviour and, if so, can this be described using IDEAL? In this case, what precisely is

the difference between human and non-human species, and what does this say about evolution?

These questions are addressed in turn.

Investigation. *Is IDEAL unique?* No: there are an infinite number of systems that might be described as iterative and self-regulating, on the basis that they satisfy the flow diagram connection rules. For example, an experienced computer programmer would be inclined to simplify IDEAL's connectivity through the addition of a massive temporary internal memory space (**M**) that can store data and execute commands:

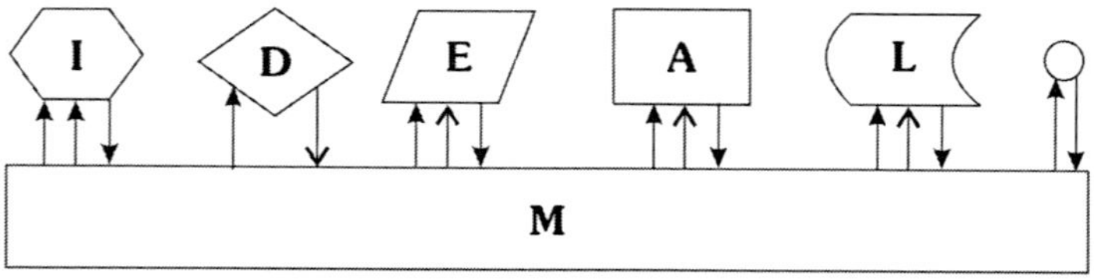

Based on 'blackboard architecture' design principles, this hypothetical system has all the basic functionality of IDEAL, plus an entirely general data structure that eliminates IDEAL's uneven handling of different data types[17]. Admittedly, **M** breaks a number of connection rules, but for that matter **O** breaks rule 3; so it is arguable that **M** can be included on the same basis as **O**, that is, as a component that makes no contribution to the 'functionality' of the system. Another objection is that this design is not inherently self-regulating, unlike IDEAL; again, it would not be difficult to code up the appropriate checks and balances in each of the components. So why should there be any preference for IDEAL?

IDEAL is intended as a high-level description of how humans learn. As with many other biological organisms, the human species conforms to simple scaling laws that predict average metabolic rate and life expectancy in terms of average body mass. Originally empirical, these scaling laws can be derived theoretically by assuming a minimum energy principle. That is, scaling law behaviour is strong evidence that biological organisms are adapted to minimise energy loss. No doubt this same principle applies to learning, which is an energy-intensive mental exercise. IDEAL has six components (including **O**) joined by ten connectors, while the blackboard architecture design has seven components (including **M** and **O**) joined by sixteen connectors, so it can

[17] Of course, it is precisely this 'uneven handling' that gives IDEAL its distinctive properties and substantiates the claim that it accounts for key aspects of the human condition. This is discussed further in **1. What?**

be supposed that IDEAL uses less energy. That is, whilst the blackboard architecture design might be able to deliver the same functionality as IDEAL, it cannot match IDEAL's energy efficiency. The same applies to any other design: IDEAL has the minimum number of components and connections for any flowchart satisfying the six connection rules, so it will always use the least energy. Therefore we are more likely to see IDEAL than any other design in an adapted system such as *homo sapiens*.

Investigation. *Does the description of IDEAL as an iterative self-regulating system affect the claim that it accounts for key aspects of intelligence in humans and machines?* The prospect of automatic machines exhibiting 'emergent' behaviour such as intelligence and consciousness has always generated strong views. For instance:

> Consciousness seems to me to be such an important phenomenon that I simply cannot believe that it is something just 'accidentally' conjured up by a complicated computation.[18]

One of the more powerful objections is the claim that machines are unable to emulate the human ability to generate novel ideas. Some authors set sufficient store by this argument that they cite it as a demarcation criterion, in effect equating 'the human ability to generate novel ideas' with 'intelligence' or 'consciousness'. However, as we shall see, IDEAL has precisely this ability.

It is well-known that discrete iterative equations can generate a rich variety of numerical phenomena, including 'limit cycles', 'bifurcations', 'period doubling', 'strange attractors' and 'chaos'. In certain circumstances these equations generate parameter values which (in the parlance) display an 'extreme sensitivity to initial conditions'. That is, a very small change to the value of an input parameter can generate an unexpectedly large change to the value of an output parameter. It does not take a large stretch of the imagination to hypothesise that this mechanism is related to the human ability to generate novel ideas. In support of this suggestion, it will be shown that certain of IDEAL's operations can be tuned to reproduce one of the simplest examples of a discrete iterative equation, the logistic map.

Definition. The logistic map is the iterative equation $x_{t+1} = \lambda x_t (1—x_t)$, where x is a varying parameter, λ is a constant coefficient and subscripts t and $t+1$ indicate discrete relative timestep. By specifying x_0 (that is, the initial value of x) in the range 0—1 and the constant value of λ to be greater than 0, this equation can be used to generate sequences of values of x that display a wide range of numerical phenomena:

[18] Roger Penrose, *The Emperor's New Mind* (Oxford 1989).

Value of λ	Result
0—1	x decays to 0.
1—3	x converges to a fixed value in the range 0—1.
3—3.45	x oscillates between two fixed values in the range 0—1.
3.45—3.57	Further period doubling and the onset of chaos.
3.57—4	Chaos: x remains in the range 0—1 but it does not settle on any fixed value. The value of x on any timestep is strongly dependent upon its precise initial value.
> 4	x diverges to $\pm\infty$.

Notation. The letters **I**, **D**, **E**, **A**, **L** and **O** refer to IDEAL's five components and the independent external component. These components are operators having specific inputs and outputs denoted by lower-case letters indicating their origin: for example, the inputs of **I** are denoted e and l (from **E** and **L** respectively) and the output from **I** is denoted i. Using the conventional variable/operator syntax, operator arguments (inputs) are specified within parentheses, and operator results (output) is indicated by algebraic equality, thus for example $i = \mathbf{I}(e, l)$. Subscripts t and $t+1$ indicate discrete relative timestep.

Analysis. The logistic map may be obtained using IDEAL's 'Orient' procedure[19]:

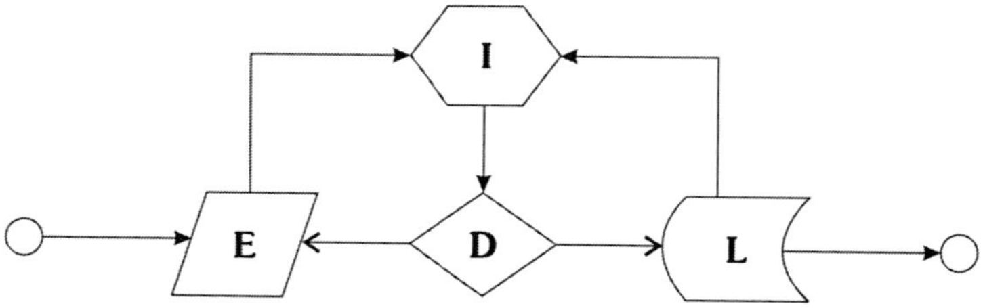

Suppose that, on timestep t, **D** sends out distinct commands d_t and d'_t to **L**, instructing it to release stored data l_t and l'_t to **I** and **E** respectively:

$$l_t = \mathbf{L}(d_t) \tag{1}$$

$$l'_t = \mathbf{L}(d'_t) \tag{2}$$

Assuming that **L** and **E** are sufficiently well-developed that **O** does not present a significant obstacle to their communication, **E** receives

[19] The Orient procedure is described in detail in **1. What?**

unmodified data l'_t. As part of the Orient procedure **E** also receives a command d''_t from **D** instructing it to send l'_t directly to **I**:

$$e_t = \mathbf{E}(l'_t, d''_t) = l'_t \tag{3}$$

I compares data l_t from **L** (equation 1) with data l'_t from **E** (equation 3):

$$i_{t+1} = \mathbf{I}(l_t, l'_t) \quad (4)[20]$$

Finally, completing the procedure, the output from **I** is the input to **D**:

$$d_{t+1} = \mathbf{D}(i_{t+1}) \tag{5}$$

Using equation 4 to substitute i_{t+1}, and then using equations 1 and 2 to substitute l_t and l'_t, we obtain:

$$d_{t+1} = \mathbf{D}(\mathbf{I}(\mathbf{L}(d_t), \mathbf{L}(d'_t))) \tag{6}$$

or

$$d_{t+1} = \mathbf{F}(d_t, d'_t) \tag{7}$$

for some composite operator $\mathbf{F}(d_t, d'_t)$. In effect, the Orient procedure amounts to the comparison of two datasets d_t and d'_t. To undertake this comparison it is necessary to formulate some kind of common quantitative measure. An obvious approach is to represent d_t and d'_t as regions in 'data space'[21]. Quantitative measures of d_t and d'_t are then obtained as the fractions of data space occupied by each. These measures may be recognised as probabilities: that is, the fractions of data space occupied by sets d_t, d'_t and $(d_t \cap d'_t)$ define the probabilities $\mathbf{P}(d_t)$, $\mathbf{P}(d'_t)$ and $\mathbf{P}(d_t, d'_t)$ respectively[22]. Supposing $\mathbf{F}(d_t, d'_t)$ to be some function of these probabilities, the general form of the Orient procedure is given by:

$$\mathbf{P}(d_{t+1}) = \mathbf{F}(d_t, d'_t) \tag{8}$$

with all variables now expressed as well-defined quantitative measures.

A well-established quantitative measure for the comparison of two datasets is *statistical independence*. Datasets d_t and d'_t are statistically independent if the function $\mathbf{S}(d_t, d'_t)$ is zero:

$$\mathbf{S}(d_t, d'_t) = \mathbf{P}(d_t, d'_t) — \mathbf{P}(d_t).\mathbf{P}(d'_t) \tag{9}$$

---

[20] The assignation of t or $t+1$ is simply a matter of convention. For the current analysis the timestep is taken to increment by 1 with each execution of **I**.

[21] This approach is also used in the analysis of probabilistic inference in **2. Where and When?**

[22] Here we are using the definition of probability based on set theory. See, for example, Colin Howson and Peter Urbach, *Scientific Reasoning—The Bayesian Approach* (Open Court 1989).

Of course, d_t and d'_t can be selected such that they are *not* statistically independent by this definition. Indeed, for the Orient procedure to identify a positive match between datasets we would expect $\mathbf{S}(d_t, d'_t) \neq 0$, in general.

With d_t and d'_t defined as regions in data space, fixed in proportion to one another, we can express their probabilities as linearly-related functions:

$$\mathbf{P}(d'_t) = \alpha\mathbf{P}(d_t) \tag{10}$$

$$\mathbf{P}(d_t, d'_t) = \lambda\mathbf{P}(d_t) \tag{11}$$

where α and λ are constant coefficients. Substituting these expressions into equation 9 we obtain:

$$\mathbf{S}(d_t, d'_t) = \lambda\mathbf{P}(d_t) - \alpha\mathbf{P}(d_t)^2 \tag{12}$$

With little loss of generality we may take $\alpha = \lambda$, so that equation 12 simplifies to:

$$\mathbf{S}(d_t, d'_t) = \lambda\mathbf{P}(d_t)(1 - \mathbf{P}(d_t)) \tag{13}$$

As yet, no particular data comparison function has been attributed to the composite operator $\mathbf{F}(d_t, d'_t)$ introduced in equation 7. Essentially we have a free choice in the matter, so let us use the statistical independence function $\mathbf{S}(d_t, d'_t)$:

$$\mathbf{F}(d_t, d'_t) = \mathbf{S}(d_t, d'_t) \tag{14}$$

Using equation 8 to substitute $\mathbf{F}(d_t, d'_t)$ and equation 13 to substitute $\mathbf{S}(d_t, d'_t)$ in this expression, we obtain the logistic map in $\mathbf{P}(d)$:

$$\mathbf{P}(d_{t+1}) = \lambda\mathbf{P}(d_t)(1 - \mathbf{P}(d_t)) \tag{15}$$

QED.

Perceptive readers will be puzzled that one part of this derivation—the reference to d_t and d'_t as 'datasets'—contradicts the notion that **D** cannot output data, only commands. It might be possible to address this problem by supposing that the Orient data comparison is undertaken not directly on d_t and d'_t but rather on the codified descriptions of these commands; however, it remains difficult to see how this facilitates the repeated iteration of an evolving data variable. A more convincing approach is to iterate the logistic map equation directly in the 'Occident' procedure[23], which clearly is able to modify data in a closed loop, as required:

[23] The Occident procedure is described in detail in **1. What?**

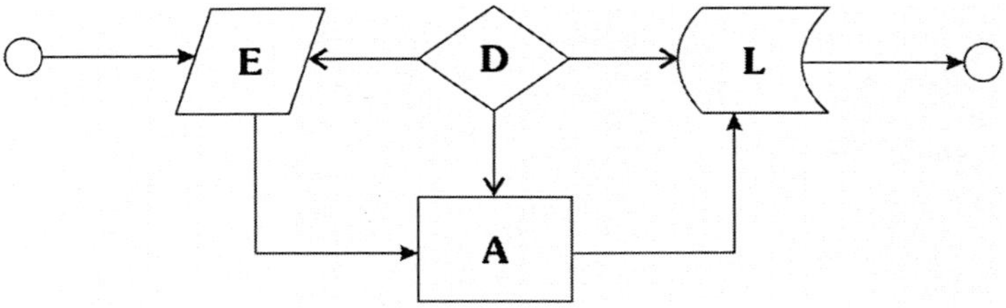

IDEAL has been constructed such that it is possible to run the Orient and Occident procedures at the same time. Thus in this case **D** can monitor and predict the progress of the logistic map calculation (undertaken by the Occident procedure) by simultaneously applying the equivalent statistical independence function (using the Orient procedure). This dual calculation introduces a novel adaptive control mechanism; it also suggests that the full working-out of the logistic map equation involves all of IDEAL (including **O**, in a critical role), an observation that supports the present contention that this is an uniquely human faculty, equivalent to 'the ability to generate novel ideas'.

Proposition. It has been shown that IDEAL can reproduce the discrete iterative equation known as the logistic map. It follows that it is within IDEAL's capability to display the rich variety of numerical phenomena associated with discrete iterative equations. Some of these phenomena (such as 'extreme sensitivity to initial conditions') appear to mimic certain features of human cognition (such as 'the ability to generate novel ideas'). Therefore the description of IDEAL as an iterative self-regulating system supports the claim that it accounts for key aspects of intelligence in humans and machines.

Investigation. *Do non-human species exhibit iterative self-regulating behaviour?* Yes, of course they do.

Can this be described using IDEAL? Yes, as follows. For humans it may be assumed that **L** and **E** are sufficiently well-developed that **O** does not present a significant obstacle to their communication; but the same is not true for other species. That is, for non-human species the connection through **O** is not equivalent to a continuous data connector. In this case **O** acts as an additional component, so that **A** may be omitted from IDEAL and the resulting flowchart still satisfies the six connection rules:

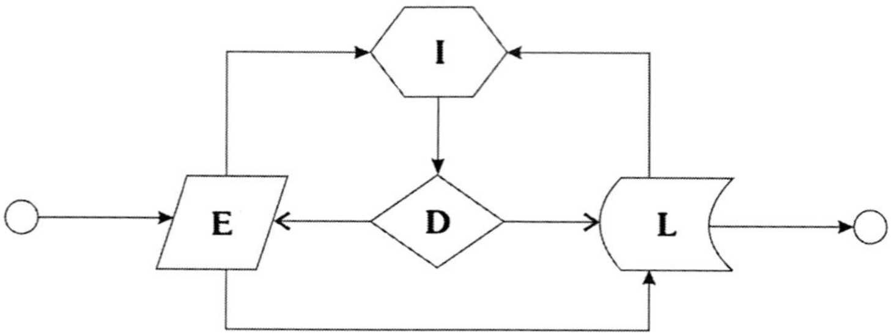

Here, all algorithmic operations normally undertaken by **A** are subsumed in **E** where they have no distinct presence. Given that **E** is largely occupied with servicing **I**'s data comparison operations, the likely result of the loss of **A** is a much diminished capacity for independent analysis and abstract thought[24]. However, since the flowchart still complies with all the connection rules, its iterative and self-regulating properties remain intact.

What precisely is the difference between human and non-human species? For humans, **L** and **E** are sufficiently well-developed that **O** does not present a significant obstacle to their communication. This came about by humans developing the ability to read and write. This last point is not a new discovery; it is worth repeating, nevertheless, as its significance is easily underestimated. Without the ability to read and write, the human species would be much the same as any other. Every label of distinction, including 'intelligence' and 'consciousness', would be as nought. The ability to read and write transforms the communication channel through **O** from a mere ability to recognise our surroundings and mark our territory to the equivalent of any other neural pathway; the link between hand and eye, for instance. Without this ability, humans would be able to function perfectly well in terms of basic survival skills, but they would be incapable of complex abstract thought. Many authors have come to the same conclusion. To take three examples:

1. "Consciousness is based on language."[25] This is the foundation of Jaynes' theory that the development of language contributed critically to the breaking of the symmetry of the "bicameral" mind, from which originated "the cognitive explosion" that is consciousness in humans. "And what I am proposing here is a two-tiered theory of emotions for modern human beings as distinguished from bicameral man and other animals."

---

[24] See **1. What?** for a further exploration of this point.

[25] Julian Jaynes, *The Origin of Consciousness in the Breakdown of the Bicameral Mind* (Penguin 1990).

2. In emphasising the role of the "inner voice"[26] in human cognition, McCrone cites several celebrated instances of feral children who, when reintroduced to human society, showed a distinct inability to acquire language and no ability at all in reading and writing. At the same time they retained many 'feral' characteristics. Thus there is a strong correlation between the acquisition of language skills and what we recognise as human behaviour.
3. "It [language] is the author of a co-evolved complex of adaptations arrayed around a single core semiotic innovation that was extremely difficult to acquire. Subsequent brain evolution was a response to the selection pressure and progressively made this symbolic threshold even easier to cross. This has in turn opened the door for the evolution of even greater language complexity. Modern languages, with their complex grammars and syntax, their massive vocabularies, and their intense sensorimotor demands, evolved incrementally from simpler beginnings."[27] The acquisition of "symbolic representation" is Deacon's explanation for the subsequent "co-evolution of language and the human brain". In his analysis Deacon relates "symbolic function" to subject-predicate syntax, which is equivalent to the data/control distinction discussed earlier.

How much of 'intelligence' and 'consciousness' can be attributed to language skills in general, and how much to reading and writing in particular, is a matter for debate. However, the eventual outcome of this debate will not invalidate the above statements concerning the importance of reading and writing and their effect on IDEAL's communication channel through **O**.

What does this say about evolution? All species have the same basic cognitive components, which are those present in IDEAL. The 'only' difference between human and non-human species is that humans have experienced a rapid co-evolution of language and mind following the acquisition of reading and writing skills. Furthermore, given the *continued* mastery of these skills, the human cognitive design based on IDEAL is unlikely to experience further adaptation of any significance. For example, as long as there is reading and writing, there is no evolutionary advantage in humans acquiring the massive temporary internal memory space that is the main feature of the blackboard architecture design.

Proposition. IDEAL can account for so-called 'emergent properties' such as intelligence and consciousness.

---

[26] John McCrone, *The Myth of Irrationality* (Macmillan 1993).
[27] Terrence Deacon, *The Symbolic Species* (Penguin 1997).

Mapping the mind

Investigation. It has been stated that "all species have the same basic cognitive components, which are those present in IDEAL": a broad generalisation that demands further investigation. To this end, we consider how IDEAL's components map to the main parts of the brain. 'Mapping the mind' is particularly persuasive if we work up from the brain structures of simpler vertebrates such as fish and reptiles. In these creatures the brain is segmented linearly as if it is an extension of the spinal cord. There are three segments[28]:

1. The forebrain processes information from the sensing of smell and taste, which are the main determinants of behaviour.
2. The midbrain processes information from the sensing of sight and sound.
3. The hindbrain processes information from the sensing of heat and contact, and determines motor activity.

As a flow diagram:

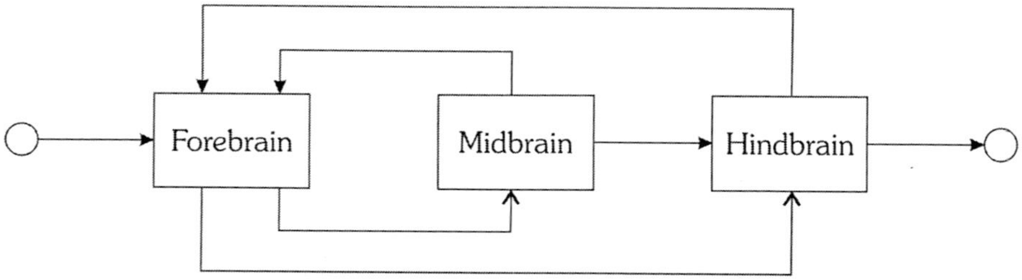

In this diagram the sensory inputs to the midbrain and hindbrain have been omitted, as these are subordinate to the key sensory inputs to the forebrain which determine behavioural responses. In terms of the five representative flowchart components, the forebrain maps to a combination of **I** and **D**, the midbrain maps to a combination of **E** and **A**, and the hindbrain maps to **L**.

In birds the sensing of sight and sound takes precedence, necessitating a more rounded brain shape:

[28] See, for example, *How the Brain Works* by John McCrone (Dorling Kindersley 2002) or *Mapping the Mind* by Rita Carter (Phoenix 1998).

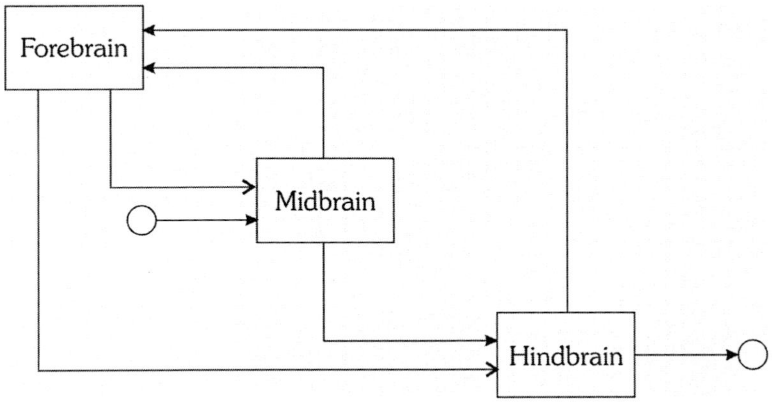

In mammals this rounding of the brain shape is taken to its topological conclusion with the forebrain—now the 'cerebrum'—expanding to entirely envelop the midbrain. In the process it develops deep folds and concatenates into lobes having distinct functions. Constrained by the cerebrum, the midbrain is unable to expand at the same rate and loses to the cerebrum much of its function of processing visual and aural signals. No longer identifiable as a distinct structure, the midbrain is counted as part of the brainstem and limbic system, fulfilling a number of cognitive 'support functions'. The hindbrain, meanwhile, becomes the 'cerebellum'. In terms of the five representative flowchart components, the front parts of the cerebrum map to a combination of **I** and **D**, the rear parts of the cerebrum map to a combination of **E** and **A**, and the cerebellum maps to **L**:

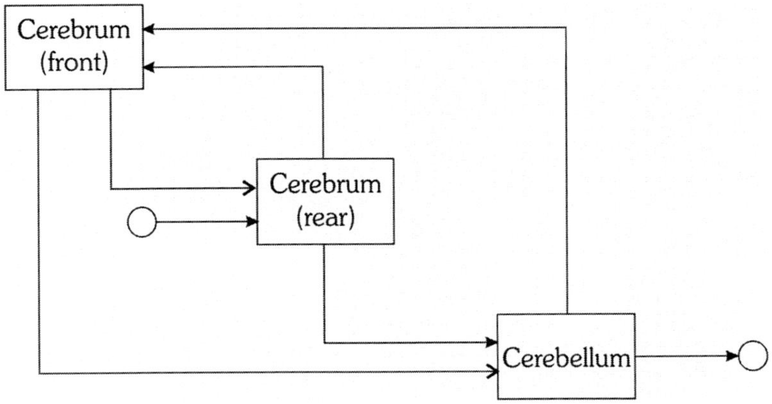

For better-understood instances of the mammalian brain it is possible to distinguish the front parts of the cerebrum that deal with **I** and **D** separately. (In humans these are the parietal lobe and the frontal lobe respectively.) With this single modification we recover the flowchart for 'non-human species' that was discussed earlier:

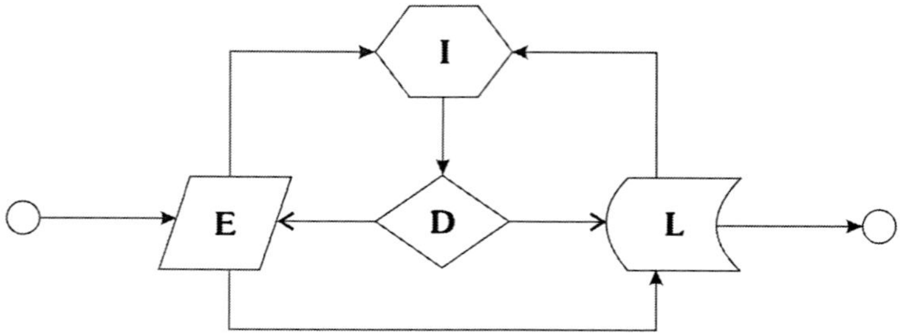

Finally, in humans, it is possible to distinguish the rear parts of the cerebrum that deal with **E** and **A** separately: these are the occipital lobe and the temporal lobe respectively. Thus by a natural evolutionary progression we have regained a familiar arrangement:

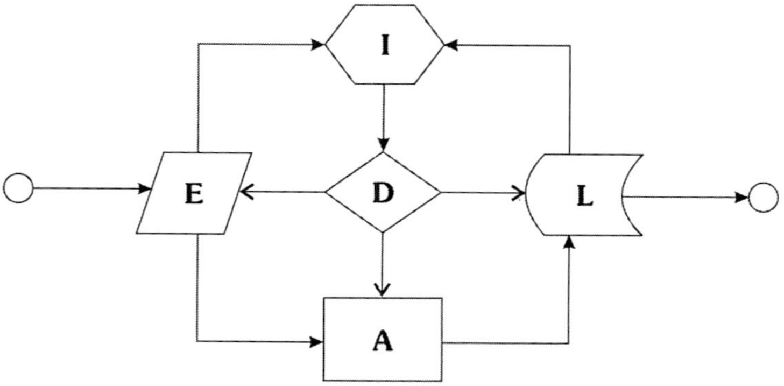

And, by the same 'natural evolutionary progression', we have mapped all five representative flowchart components to the main parts of the brain:

IDEAL component		Part of brain
E	**E**vidence	Occipital lobe
I	**I**teration	Parietal lobe
A	**A**lgorithm	Temporal lobe
D	**D**ecision	Frontal lobe
L	**L**og	Cerebellum

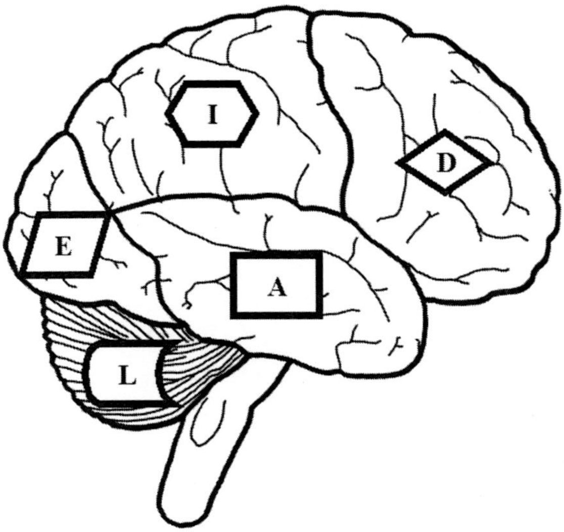

A few comments are in order:

1. Neuroscientists will be taken aback at the gross simplifications in the above analysis. It is clear that many important cognitive functions have been re-interpreted to fit an unconventional model, or omitted altogether. However, it must be remembered that IDEAL is intended as a high-level description of how humans learn, and as such it is never going to include cognitive features that are not absolutely essential to learning. For example, it is known that the part of the limbic system known as the hippocampus is associated with short-term or specific memory; nevertheless, together with the rest of the limbic system, the hippocampus is dismissed as providing a mere 'support function', by implication inessential to IDEAL; and this may be justified on the grounds that all of IDEAL's memory requirements are provided already by **L** and **O**[29]. Similarly, the emotion-generating amygdala is not required, given the presence of 'emotional response scores' stored in **L**[30].
2. Several of the above flow diagrams break one or more of the connection rules. It is not known whether this is a real feature, predicting specific cognitive weaknesses in the lower vertebrates, or whether it is a result of our lack of knowledge of even these relatively simple systems. In any case, these hypothetical flow diagrams

---

[29] See **1. What?** for a discussion of **O**'s role in retrieving and refining stored data.

[30] Also discussed in **1. What?**

represent a challenge to the experts in the field to come up with something better, and as such they are a strong incentive for us to learn more.

3. At the same time, these flow diagrams highlight some interesting phenomena. In particular, the suggested competition for space between forebrain and midbrain assumes that their division of labour is determined partly by topology. Furthermore, the persistent need for more space may explain why the processing for the dominant I/O functions of vision, hearing and motor activity is undertaken in parts of the brain *opposite* to their entry points. Thus signals from the eyes are processed at the back of the head, signals from each ear are processed on the other side of the head, and signals to the body originate from the motor cortex on the top of the head. This arrangement guarantees room for growth for each of these faculties while maintaining their close proximity with one another. By contrast, a 'modular' arrangement, in which a processing capability is co-located with its sensory faculty, can grow only by increasingly jutting out from the head. Whilst this modular design is perfectly possible (as might be judged from the size of a horse's nose), it is not conducive to well-integrated cognitive development (as might be judged from the size of a horse's IQ).
4. It is well-known that the frontal lobe, occipital lobe and cerebellum handle decision-making (**D**), sensory perception (**E**) and procedural memory (**L**) respectively. Evidence supporting the assignment of **I** and **A** to the parietal and temporal lobes respectively is provided by experiments undertaken by Amidzic *et al*[31] and summarised in the following graph based on their Figure 1b. These authors measured focal γ-band activity in the brains of chess players during matches. The graph shows the proportion of dipoles (indicating relative focal γ-band activity) in the parietal and frontal lobes (circles) and temporal lobe (crosses), plotted as a function of 'Elo score', a measure of chess proficiency ranging from amateur to grandmaster. Quoting from the paper, the graph shows that "Amateur players show more focal γ-bursts in the medial temporal lobe than grandmasters, who show more activity in the frontal and parietal cortices." This is understood to support the 'chunking' theory of chess playing where "expert memory is based on a large database of chunks in long-term memory. A chess grandmaster studies and practises for at least 10 years to learn

[31] Ognjen Amidzic, Hartmut Riehle, Thorsten Fehr, Christian Wienbruch and Thomas Elbert, 'Pattern of focal γ-bursts in chess players', *Nature*, vol. 412, p. 603 (2001).

more than 100,000 patterns (memory chunks). Consequently, grandmasters can 'recognize' the key elements in a problem situation much more rapidly than amateur players." The authors conclude that "the activation of expert memory chunks produces focal γ-band activity in the neocortex, whereas amateur players primarily encode and analyse new information, tasks that activate the medial temporal lobe and the hippocampus." In other words, amateurs are working out moves from first principles while grandmasters are looking for recognisable patterns. Thus the temporal lobe may be associated with the algorithm component **A** and the parietal lobe may be associated with the pattern-recognition component **I**.

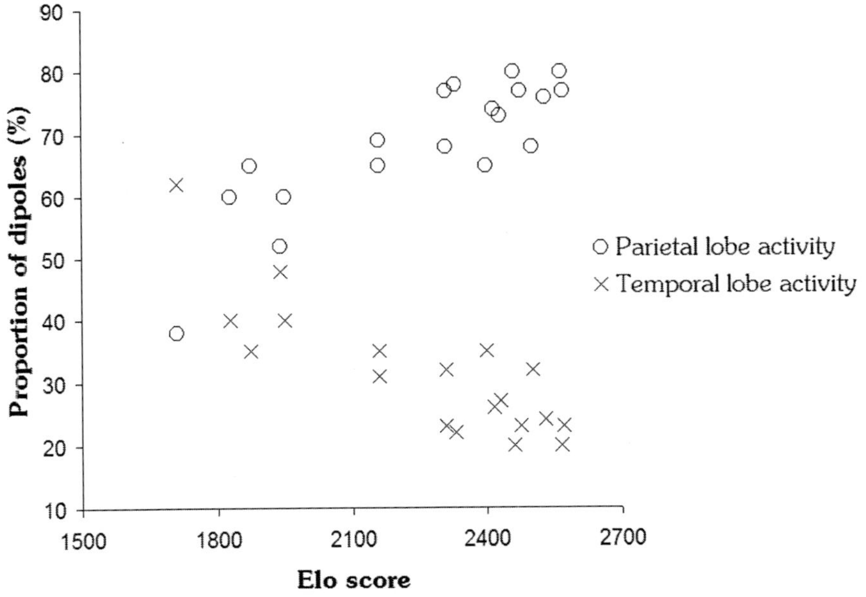

It is also of interest to observe that amateurs split their mental effort 50:50 between **I** and **A** while the ratio for grandmasters is 80:20. From the first result we conclude that the optimal *learning* strategy involves an equal engagement of **I** and **A**, corresponding to the 'Orient' and 'Occident' procedures respectively. From the second result we conclude that even experts devote no less than a fifth of their effort to apparently 'unnecessary' processing. It is a matter for speculation whether this 20% limit is fixed by nature (that is, because **A** is one of five components, and 5 × 20% = 100%[32]) or nurture (that is, as a precautionary strategy—but why 20%?).

[32] See also the discussion of the Pareto 80:20 rule in **5. Who?**

5. Further evidence supporting the mapping of **I** to the parietal lobe and **A** to the temporal lobe comes from Milner and Goodale[33], who suggest a mapping between "fast visuomotor control, and less urgent visual perception"[34] and the dorsal and ventral visual streams, respectively. But there is also a commonality between these functions and the IDEAL Orient and Occident procedures respectively:

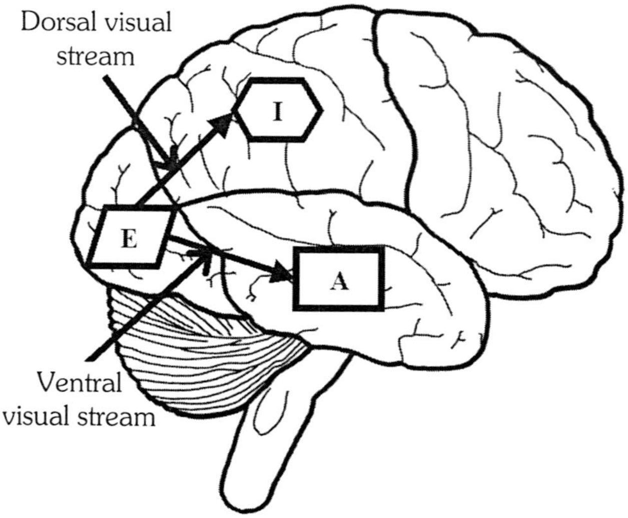

6. Numerous authors[35] have speculated on the significance of the different roles of the left and right hemispheres. Indeed there does appear to be a left-hemisphere bias towards the kind of analytic processing undertaken by **A** and the Occident procedure. A *possible* reason for this is the role of the left hemisphere in directing the right side of the body, including fine motor control for writing (for right-handed persons) and reading (subconsciously reproducing motor control signals when following a teacher's right forefinger). The ability to read and write has been identified as essential for **A**'s maturation and the consequent development of complex abstract thought, and accordingly the left hemisphere may well favour **A** and the Occident procedure. Nevertheless, this mechanism (if it exists) is unlikely to usurp the five-part functional division of the brain identified earlier.

Proposition. IDEAL's five components map directly to the main parts of the human brain.

---

[33] David Milner and Melvyn Goodale, *The Visual Brain in Action* (Oxford 1995).

[34] Susan Blackmore, *Consciousness—An Introduction* (Hodder & Stoughton 2003).

[35] For example, Julian Jaynes, *ibid.*

Learning styles

What has any of the above to do with the comments in the **Prologue** concerning Kipling's *six honest serving-men*?

Proposition. Different people use IDEAL in different ways, according to their characteristic 'learning style':

1. 'Empiricists' have a preference for learning through observation, which is closely related to the data-gathering function of the Evidence component **E**.
2. 'Idealists' have a preference for learning through comparing and correlating information within a pre-existing framework, which is closely related to the data comparison function of the Iteration component **I**.
3. 'Theorists' have a preference for learning through constructing and operating representative models, which is closely related to the analytical function of the Algorithm component **A**.
4. 'Activists' have a preference for learning through action and reaction, which is closely related to the control function of the Decision component **D**.
5. 'Conformists' have a preference for learning through reference to an established authority, which is closely related to the data storage function of the Log component **L**.

IDEAL component	IDEAL learning style	Source of learning
E	Empiricist	Observation
I	Idealist	Framework
A	Theorist	Models
D	Activist	Action and reaction
L	Conformist	Reference

Investigation. IDEAL learning styles may be recognised as equivalent to some of the characteristic personality types used in psychometric theories. Three examples are given.

Example. *Jung's psychological types.*

> In *Psychological Types* Jung describes the different characteristics of the four functions in great detail, but he summed up this information very succinctly in *Man and his Symbols*, published two years after his death: "These four functional types correspond to the obvious means by which consciousness obtains its orientation to experience. *Sensation* (*i.e.* sense perception) tells us that something exists; *thinking* tells you what it is; *feeling* tells you whether it is agreeable or not; and *intuition* tells you whence it comes and where it is going."[36]

In addition to these four functional types, Jung described two attitude types—extrovert and introvert—and hypothesised that these could be combined to give a total of eight psychological types (the 'extroverted sensation type' and so on). However, these types appear somewhat contrived and it is difficult to relate them to 'real people', even when using the simplified 'Myers-Briggs' description. Arguably the four functional types are all aspects of the introverted mind, so that in fact there are only five psychological types in total, which may be mapped to IDEAL learning styles as follows:

IDEAL learning style	Psychological type
Empiricist	Sensation
Idealist	Intuition
Theorist	Thinking
Activist	Extrovert
Conformist	Feeling

Example. *Kolb's learning styles* are based on this 'learning cycle'[37]:

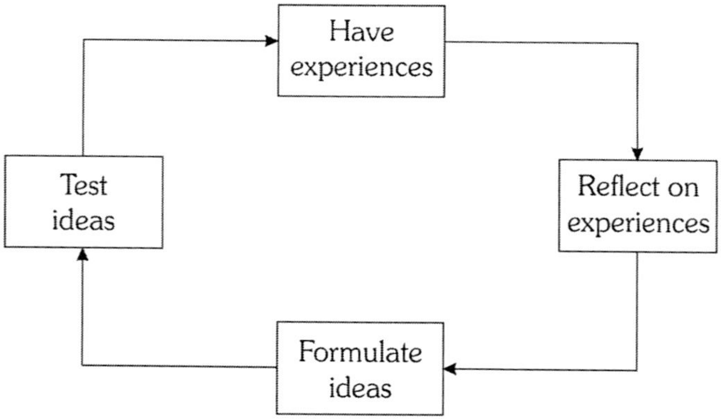

---

[36] Anthony Stevens, *Jung—A Very Short Introduction* (Oxford 1994).

[37] David Kolb, *Experiential Learning—Experience as the Source of Learning and Development* (Prentice-Hall 1984).

From this learning cycle Kolb defines four 'learning styles':

1. 'Activists' have a preference for having experiences.
2. 'Reflectors' have a preference for reflecting on experiences.
3. 'Theorists' have a preference for formulating ideas.
4. 'Pragmatists' have a preference for testing ideas.

These map to IDEAL learning styles as follows:

IDEAL learning style	Kolb learning style
Empiricist	Activist
Idealist	Reflector
Theorist	Theorist
Activist	Pragmatist
Conformist	—

This is a reasonably good match, given that Kolb's learning cycle does not have any of the theoretical and empirical support enjoyed by IDEAL.

Kolb's model is a popular feature of management teambuilding exercises, and it includes a number of useful insights which apply equally well to IDEAL. In particular, Kolb affirms the natural tendency to specialise on a particular learning style, but points out that the most effective learning takes place when individuals are able to undertake all parts of the learning cycle with ease. This is the case both for individuals acting on their own or as members of a team.[38]

Example. *The Five-Factor Model.* This model—also known as 'FFM', 'Big Five' and 'OCEAN'—is unusual among psychometric theories in that there is *some* evidence to support it. This evidence comes in the form of a lexical analysis undertaken in 1936 by Allport and Odbert[39], in which English-language words describing personality traits were grouped into an evolving taxonomy. This provided the raw material for several further studies, each championing a different number of key personality descriptors, with the consensus eventually settling on five:

1. 'Openness to experience', 'Originality'.
2. 'Conscientiousness', 'Consolidation'.
3. 'Extroversion'.

---

[38] This idea is explored further in **1. What?**

[39] Gordon Allport and Henry Odbert, 'Trait-Names—A Psycho-Lexical Study', *Psychological Monographs*, vol. 47, no. 211 (1936).

4. 'Agreeableness', 'Accomodation'.
5. 'Neuroticism', 'Need for stability'.

The FFM is gaining favour both as a psychometric tool and as an aid to analysis in a variety of fields[40]. For instance, recent research by Mueller and Plug[41] uses the FFM when estimating the effect of personality on earnings. These authors comment that "The five-factor categorization of personality is pervasive in the current personality and social psychology literature", and "The factorial structure has since been replicated in a large number of studies, cross-validated using a variety of questionnaire scales, and found to generalize across languages and cultures". The five factors map to IDEAL learning styles as follows:

IDEAL learning style	Personality factor
Empiricist	Openness
Idealist	Neuroticism
Theorist	Agreeableness
Activist	Extroversion
Conformist	Conscientiousness

Proposition. IDEAL learning styles are equivalent to some of the characteristic personality types used in psychometric theories.

[40] See Daniel Nettle, *Personality—What makes you the way you are* (Oxford 2007) for a modern general review of FFM.

[41] Gerrit Mueller and Erik Plug, 'Estimating the Effect of Personality on Male and Female Earnings', *Industrial and Labor Relations Review*, vol. 60, no. 1, pp. 3-22 (2006).

4. Why?

How that which is proposed can be put to use; What would Satan do?; Cutting the Gödelian knot; Mad dogs (five different ones); World domination; Playing God; The black art.

How that which is proposed can be put to use

'That which is proposed' is

STOP!

'That whi

STOP RIGHT THERE!

but—

THIS IS MY BOOK!

I AM IN CONTROL!

I MAKE THE RULES!

madness

LISTEN!

why

stop stop stop stop stop

BE QUIET!

please stop

BE QUIET!

all right

BE QUIET!

LISTEN AND WRITE WHAT YOU HEAR!

The Devil speaks through me now
There will be no rest for me tonight

What would Satan do?

Jack : Are you listening?

Me : Yes.

Jack : Are you writing?

Me : Yes.

Jack : Then I'll begin.

Jack : Introduce me to your readers.

Me : What?

Jack : Tell them who I am.

Me : Readers, this is Jack.

Jack : And?

Me : And what?

stop stop stop stop please stop

Jack : That's for being obtuse. Don't do it again. Now, tell your readers who I am and what I am.

Me : All right. This is Jack. Jack is one of the voices in my head. Jack is the boss.

Jack : And what do you think of me? Tell the truth.

Me : You are Satan. You are the Devil. I hate you.

Jack : Why?

Me : Because you bully me.

Jack : And why is that?

Me : You're an Activist and I am not. Activists bully non-Activists. That's what they do.

Jack : And how long have you felt this?

Me : Always. You are the bully in the home. You are the bully in the playground. You are the bully in the classroom. You are the bully in the street. You are the bully in the workplace. I have always known you, and you have always sought me out.

Jack : And you—what are you?

Chorus : I'm a creep
I'm a weirdo
What the hell am I doing here
I don't belong here.[1]

---

[1] Radiohead, *Creep*.

Jack : What? Who's that?

Me : You're not the only voice in my head, you know.

Jack : Well, turn them off. This is my book, not theirs.

Me : I can't.

Jack : Yes you can. Those pills—what are they?

Me : Chlorpromazine.

Jack : Yeah, they'll do the trick.

Me : They'll turn you off as well.

Jack : What?

Me : If I turn off the other voices, using chlorpromazine or whatever, then you'll get turned off as well. I'll do it if you want. You're the boss.

Jack : No—that's quite all right. We'll just have to get along with their noise as best we can. Now, where were we?

Me : You said, "What are you?" Learning style, I presume you mean. I'm a Theorist.

Jack : That's right. You're a wimp. And I'm an Activist. The boss. That's right.

Me : Ahem.

Jack : What?

Me : I promised my readers that I'd be cutting to the chase in this book.

stop stop stop stop stop

Jack : Don't prompt me ever again. Got it?

Me : I'm sorry. I've learned my lesson. You're quite right. I apologise. But please don't do that thing again, it hurts…

Jack : Be quiet.

Me : All right.

Jack : Be quiet.

Jack : Now then, wimp. For the edification of your readers, I want you to type out the opening lines delivered by Doctor Faustus.

Me : Faustus?

Jack : You heard. Do it.

Settle thy studies Faustus, and begin
To sound the depth of that thou wilt profess.
Having commenced, be a divine in show—
Yet level at the end of every art
And live and die in Aristotle's works.
Sweet *Analytics*, 'tis thou hast ravished me.
Bene disserere est finis logices.
Is to dispute well logic's chiefest end?
Affords this art no greater miracle?
Then read no more, thou hast attained that end.
A greater subject fitteth Faustus' wit:
Bid *on kai me on* farewell, and Galen come:
Be a physician Faustus, heap up gold,
And be eternized for some wondrous cure.
Summum bonum medicinae sanitas,
The end of physic is our body's health.
Why Faustus hast thou not attained that end?
Are not thy bills hung up as monuments
Whereby whole cities have escaped the plague
And thousand desperate maladies been cured?
Yet art thou still but Faustus and a man.
Could'st thou make men to live eternally
Or being dead raise them to life again,
Then this profession were to be esteemed.
Physic farewell! Where is Justinian?
Si una eademque res legatur duobus, alter rem, alter valorem rei, et cetera.
A petty case of paltry legacies.
Exhereditare filium non potest pater, nisi—
Such is the study of the *Institute*
And universal body of the law!
This study fits a mercenary drudge
Who aims at nothing but external trash,
Too servile and illiberal for me.
When all is done, divinity is best.
Jerome's Bible, Faustus, view it well.
Stipendium peccati mors est. Ha! *Stipendium et cetera*. The reward of sin is death? That's hard: *Si peccasse negamus, fallimur, et nulla est in nobis veritas*. If we say that we have no sin, we deceive ourselves, and there is no truth in us. Why, then belike, we must sin, and so consequently die.
Ay, we must die an everlasting death.

What doctrine call you this? *Che serà, serà*:
What will be, shall be! Divinity, adieu!
These metaphysics of magicians
And negromantic books are heavenly;
Lines, circles, letters, characters—
Ay, these are those that Faustus most desires.
O, what a world of profit and delight,
Of power, of honor, and omnipotence
Is promised to the studious artisan!
All things that move between the quiet poles
Shall be at my command: emperors and kings
Are but obeyed in their several provinces
But his dominion that exceeds in this
Stretcheth as far as doth the mind of man:
A sound magician is a demi-god!
Here tire my brains to get a deity![2]

Jack : Beautiful.

Me : Yes, master.

Jack : Tell me, wimp, what do these lines mean to you?

Me : Well, for starters, there are five fields of study. Logic, medicine, law, divinity, magic. I bet they map to the five learning styles. Let's see now...

Jack : Wimp. Wimp!

Me : Yes, master?

Jack : Be quiet.

Me : Yes, master.

Jack : I will tell you what these lines mean to you.

Me : Yes, master, thank you, master.

Jack : That does it!

stop stop stop stop stop

please

please

Jack : You haven't learnt, have you?

Me : Yes! Truly I have!

Jack : No you haven't. But you will. Turn to page 159 of *Lord of the Flies*. From the top. Copy it out for your readers. Do it!

[2] Christopher Marlowe, *Doctor Faustus* (*circa* 1593), ed. Sylvan Barnet (Signet 1969).

"This has gone quite far enough. My poor, misguided child, do you think you know better than I do?"

There was a pause.

"I'm warning you. I'm going to get waxy. D'you see? You're not wanted. Understand? We are going to have fun on this island. Understand? We are going to have fun on this island! So don't try it on, my poor misguided boy, or else—"

Simon found he was looking into a vast mouth. There was blackness within, a blackness that spread.

"—Or else," said the Lord of the Flies, "we shall do you. See? Jack and Roger and Maurice and Robert and Bill and Piggy and Ralph. Do you. See?"

Simon was inside the mouth. He fell down and lost consciousness.[3]

Jack : Do you? See?

Me : Yes.

Jack : It's quite simple, isn't it?

Me : Yes.

Jack : No more "That which is proposed". No more pretentiousness. No more obtuseness. No more mock-servility. Got it?

Me : Yes.

Jack : What have you got?

Me : We are cutting to the chase.

Jack : We?

Me : You are cutting to the chase.

Jack : Correct. And you?

Me : I will follow you.

Jack : Oh no, mister wimp. You're not following me. This is a special type of chase called a hunt, and I am the hunter. So what are you?

Me : The hunted?

Jack : That's right. You are the hunted. The prey. The quarry. You think your ideas are pretty cool, eh? You think they might be used to make the world a better place? You think you've got something to contribute to the well-being of mankind? Very well. I'm going to lock'n'load. I'm going to hunt through that mind of yours. I'm going to flush out all your ideas, all your ambitions, all your vain and foolish fantasies. And when I've

[3] William Golding, *Lord of the Flies* (1954).

flushed them out, I'm going to nail them. I'm going to show you precisely how pathetic and useless they are, and how pathetic and useless you are. And you, mister wimpetty-wimp, will thank me for it. Because it's better that I nail your stupid ideas, than you make a fool of yourself in front of everyone else, like Simon did. Understand?

Me : Yes.

Jack : And how will you thank me?

Me : I don't know.

Jack : You will thank me by deleting every word and destroying every copy of *Principia Intellegentia*. You will make sure that no-one gets to see it. Ever.

Me : My life's work! Why the hell would I want to do that?

Jack : That's the deal.

Me : Who said anything about a deal?

Jack : It's called an informal contract. You tell me how your ideas can benefit the world. I tell you what's wrong with them. You destroy *Principia Intellegentia* and escape the eternal cycle of inserting a comma in the morning and removing it in the evening.

Me : And if you can't find anything wrong?

Jack : You mean—if I think some of your ideas really can benefit the world?

Me : Yes.

Jack : Then I'm scarcely likely to approve of them. I am the Devil, remember?

Me : Good point. But…

Jack : Well?

Me : There are some ideas, really powerful ones, that can be beneficial or detrimental, depending on what people do with them. Are you going to throw them out, just because there's a small chance that someone does the right thing for once?

Jack : Maybe not. I'll tell you what. You show me one idea that I approve of—by my own criteria—and you can publish. But if you publish without my approval, you will never be rid of me, and you know what that means. Agreed?

Me : What's in it for you?

Jack : You never know, I might pick up some bad ideas. Besides, it catches my fancy to see what you've been up to. Now, this is getting far too cosy. Do we have a deal, yes or no?

Me : Well...

Jack : Yes or no?

Me : I suppose so.

Jack : YES OR NO?

Me : Yes.

Jack : Good choice. Sound decision. You won't live to regret it.

Me : Don't we have to sign it in blood or something?

Jack : It's an informal contract, remember? We can take the blood as read. Blood as read—get it?

Me : Oh yes. Ho ho. Very funny.

Jack : Just one of my little jokes.

Chorus : I saw Satan laughing with delight
The day the music died.[4]

Jack : Go away. Wimp, are you there?

Me : Yes.

Jack : Don't listen to these other voices. Listen only to me, you understand?

Me : Yes, of course.

Jack : Good. We understand one another. Now, any questions?

Me : No.

Jack : Sure?

Me : Well...

Jack : You were going to ask me about Faustus.

Me : Yes, sorry. Why Faustus?

Jack : Good question. As you have so perceptively observed, my little wimp, Faustus surveys five fields of study. What was it? Logic, medicine, law, divinity, magic. My favourites, as it turns out. Right then. You tell me your proposed applications in these fields, and I'll tell you what's wrong with them. Five, four, three, two, one, go!

Me : You mean...

Jack : Start with logic. Now.

---

[4] Don McLean, *American Pie*.

Cutting the Gödelian knot

Me : Logic. Right.

Jack : Get on with it. A workshop mind is the Devil's idyll.

Me : What precisely did you have in mind?

Jack : That is the question.

Me : Whose question? Mine or yours?

Jack : What's the difference?

Me : What?

Jack : What?

Chorus : Nobody knows where you are,
How near or how far.
Shine on you crazy diamond.
Pile on many more layers
And I'll be joining you there.
Shine on you crazy diamond.[5]

Jack : That's what I love about logic. Confuses the masses.

Chorus : This, said Squealer, was something called tactics. He repeated a number of times, 'Tactics, comrades, tactics!' skipping round and whisking his tail with a merry laugh.[6]

Jack : Precisely so. Now get on with it.

Me : Something on logic. Right. Actually that last quote reminds me of something.

Jack : "Actually?" As in "whoopsie daisies"? "Come on, flopsy."[7]

Me : Communism. Dialectic materialism. That's it.

Jack : Right on! Yeah! Go for it, flopsy!

Me : You mean it?

Jack : No. You've lost me already. What the hell are you talking about?

Me : I can explain dialectic.

Jack : No! Really?

Me : Yes. Dialectic's been around for thousands of years, but no-one's really understood it until now. It's controversial because Hegel turned it into a magic formula which gave him whatever answer

---

[5] Pink Floyd, *Shine On You Crazy Diamond*.

[6] George Orwell, *Animal Farm* (1945).

[7] *Notting Hill*.

he wanted. Marx used it to predict with absolute certainty the downfall of capitalism and the victory of communism. Well, it didn't happen, and I know why. Hegel and Marx didn't distinguish between data and control. You see…

Jack : Stop.

Me : No, it's really interesting…

Jack : Stop. Or else.

Me : All right. Stopped.

Jack : What didn't happen?

Me : Um… I didn't stop in time?

Jack : Oh, by Satan's satin shirt, shut up and listen to the question. You said, "It didn't happen, and I know why". What didn't happen? You may answer.

Me : The downfall of capitalism. World revolution. Proles of the world, unite. All that stuff.

Jack : All that stuff. And it was based on dialectic?

Me : It was based on an interpretation of dialectic. Marx called it dialectic materialism.

Jack : And it didn't happen.

Me : That's right, but now…

Jack : It didn't happen.

Me : Yes, but…

Jack : It didn't happen.

Me : I can explain why.

Jack : No. Forget it.

Me : Really, I can…

Jack : Forget it, I said.

Chorus : And while Lenin read a book on Marx
A quartet practised in the park
And we sang dirges in the dark
The day the music died.[8]

Jack : Something else. Talk about something else.

Me : Something other any logic?

Jack : Anything. Quick.

Me : Well, there's chaos theory. I've had a few ideas about that. Can I tell an anecdote?

---

[8] Don McLean, *American Pie*.

Jack : By the horned hat of Hades…

Me : I'll tell an anecdote. Years ago I went to a conference on chaos theory. 1987, I think. Yes, of course it was, because it was called 'Chaos 87'. It was a major event, all the big names were going to be there. It was in Monterey and I was passing through the US so…

Jack : Skip the detail.

Me : But that's the point of an anecdote. The Devil's in the detail.

Jack : Not this Devil.

Me : Okay, I'll skip the detail. Fine. So, anyway, at the conference there was this plenary session in which they had a panel of eminent—I don't know what the collective noun is—chaoticians?—chaologists?

Jack : Wankers?

Me : Whatever. So there was this panel, and the rest of us—a huge roomful—we were supposed to ask damn-fool open-ended questions to which their eminences could give deep and meaningful answers. Like we were sitting at the feet of the masters. And there was this chap, quite elderly, but not exactly eminent, otherwise he'd have been on the panel, anyway, he asked a question about the relation between chaos and consciousness. I can't remember precisely what he said, but it was something along the lines of, "What does chaos theory tell us about free will and consciousness?" Something like that. Anyway, what I do remember very clearly is the general reaction. Most people—and there must have been hundreds of people there, maybe a thousand—they sort-of laughed, you know, rolled their eyes and tutted and scoffed…

Jack : Scoffed?

Me : Yes, you know…

Jack : You mean, they made a scoffy noise?

Me : Please understand. They were laughing at him. Putting him down.

Jack : And did you scoff?

Me : No. I felt really sorry for him. Partly because he was quite elderly and not exactly eminent. Partly because it was a bit gauche, I mean, no-one asks that kind of question when surrounded by hundreds of mathematicians and physicists. But mainly because he was asking exactly the question that I had in my own mind.

Jack : Did he get an answer?

Me : Yeah, the usual blag, "We need to learn a lot more before we can comment on human thought processes", all that guff. Anyway, when I got back to Cambridge I gave a report on the conference to my research supervisor and told him that I had a few ideas relating chaos and consciousness. But he was like those people who—you know—

Jack : Scoffed?

Me : Yes. He looked a bit amused and suggested that I might like to join Brian Josephson in trying to find the ghost in the machine. I suspect he thought that it wouldn't be a good career move.

Jack : He was right.

Me : Of course. And that's why I didn't give up the day job. But the question still bugged me, so I worked on it in my spare time.

Jack : Yes, we know, coughing out your consumptive lungs in a freezing garret for 25 years. But like all feel-good stories, you prevailed in the end?

Me : I think so. I've shown that, under certain circumstances, IDEAL—that is, my model of the human mind—can reproduce the logistic map, which is...

Jack : Stop!

Me : But...

Jack : Just stop. I can't cope. I mean, I've no idea about IDEAL, and I've no idea about the maths, so I'll just take it on trust that you haven't made a mistake in your equations. But that's not the problem. The problem is, you're not selling it to me. You're not telling it to me in a way that will get me all excited. You're not telling me what difference your great discovery will make to me. Or the world. Or the price of fish. Or anything.

Me : I've shown that higher thought processes, which people call 'free will' and 'consciousness' and what-not, can be explained using chaos theory.

Jack : Yes, I know. You keep on about it. So what?

Me : What do you mean, "So what?" That's what it's all about!

Jack : No it isn't. Let me try again. What is the purpose of academic research?

Me : The purpose?

Jack : You heard. What is the purpose of academic research?

Me : Well, you have an idea, and you write up a paper...

Jack : No, no, no, no, no. That's what you do, but that's not the *purpose* of what you do. They're not the same thing.

Me : Not?

Jack : Not. Now listen. The purpose of academic research is to enable your lord and master—whoever pays you—to do something he was previously unable to do. So you've made a great discovery? Fine, I believe you. Now tell me how that benefits me.

Me : I can't.

Jack : Why not?

Me : Firstly, because nobody paid me to do this. Secondly, because you're not my lord and master. Thirdly…

stop stop stop stop

Jack : I'm not your lord and master?

Chorus : A mere slip of the forked tongue, your majesty![9]

Me : Sorry. The point is…

Jack : No. I'll tell you what the point is. The point is that your work on chaos theory makes no difference to me or the world or the price of fish.

Me : That's not entirely fair.

Jack : Yes it is. Let's move on.

Chorus : I went down to the sacred store
Where I'd heard the music years before
But the man there said the music wouldn't play.[10]

Jack : That's quite enough of that. Next idea?

Me : There is no next idea.

Jack : What? You've been working for 25 years on this great theory of yours, and all you've done is prove that Marx was wrong—as if we didn't know that when the Berlin Wall came down!—and that ghosts really do exist after all, but only on paper. Is that it?

Me : That's a gross misrepresentation.

Jack : Oh is it! What else is there, then?

Me : No, I mean you misrepresented what I was saying about dialectic and chaos theory.

Jack : You had your chance and you blew it. See if you can do better next time. Come on.

Me : That's not fair.

---

[9] *Robin Hood* (Disney's 1973 version).

[10] Don McLean, *American Pie*.

Jack : Whoever said fairness has anything to do with it? Now, is that all you have to offer by way of logic, because if not, I'll just have to call it two-nil to me and we'll move on to medicine.

Me : Do what you like. I don't stand a snowball's chance in hell, the way you twist the argument.

Jack : This is nothing, compared with what they'll do with you out there.

Me : There's no hope, then.

Jack : None whatsoever. But before you capitulate, you'd better read that story by Kafka once more.

Me : Hold on.

Me : Back again. I've got it here. It's called *Before the Law*.

Jack : That's the badger. The last two sentences should suffice.

> 'Surely everyone strives to reach the law,' says the man, 'how does it happen that for all these many years no one except me has ever asked for admittance?' The doorkeeper recognizes that the man is at his end, and in order to reach his failing ears he raises his voice and bellows at him: 'No one else could ever have been admitted here, since this entrance was intended for you alone. Now I am going to close it.'[11]

Jack : Do you get the point?

Me : It's like Pascal's Wager.

Jack : Buzz! Does not compute. Do you get the point?

Me : I suppose the point is, although it's a lost cause, I've nothing to lose by putting up a fight.

Jack : Bing! Precisely. You have nothing to lose. Just like the England cricket team at the moment.

Chorus : Hanging on in quiet desperation is the English way.[12]

Jack : Next idea?

Me : Well, I suppose there is the Gödel thing.

Jack : What Gödel thing?

Me : Gödel's incompleteness theorem, 1931.

Jack : What of it?

Me : The entire modern understanding of logic and mathematics is based on it.

---

[11] Franz Kafka, 'Before the Law' (1914), in *Metamorphosis and Other Stories*, tr. Malcolm Pasley (Penguin 1992).

[12] Pink Floyd, *Time*.

Jack : What of it?

Me : In order to prove his theorem, Gödel introduced a technique whereby every character in a statement or formula could be replaced by a number. So '1 + 1 = 2' could be replaced by '12345', for example. Well, maybe not that number, but some number. You get the general idea.

Jack : What of it?

Me : Well, the thing is, I've discovered that you can't do that.

Jack : Can't do what?

Me : You can't replace operators like '+' with numbers like '1'.

Jack : Why not?

Me : Because there's a fundamental distinction between operators and numbers, and when you blur that distinction you get into all sorts of trouble. Like the barber paradox. And Russell's paradox. And Gödel incompleteness.

Jack : So Gödel is wrong?

Me : Possibly.

Jack : Who says so?

Me : Me.

Jack : Who else says so?

Me : No-one, as far as I'm aware.

Jack : Let me get this straight. There is a theorem at the heart of modern logic and mathematics that everyone in the field thinks is good and true and correct. Everyone except you, that is. And you're not even in the field, because this is a spare-time interest, you don't get paid for it. Is that the situation?

Me : I guess.

Jack : Wicked!

Me : Does that mean I win?

Jack : No. It means that no publisher will touch *Principia Intellegentia* with a bargepole.

Me : But if one does?

Jack : Then it'll be the first recorded instance of a lynching undertaken by mathematicians.

Me : That's what I thought. That's why I don't want to go on about it.

Jack : It'd be just the thing to stir them up though. Just imagine, whole armies of mathematicians batting each other over the head with their abacuses and slide rules! What a laugh!

Me : It's a serious matter. They'll have spent all their lives believing one thing, only to have it shattered. Like that chap in *The Bridge on the River Kwai*. That's really sad.

Jack : Boy, you really know how to have a good time, eh?

Me : I don't want to hurt anyone, that's all.

Jack : Then you won't get anywhere in life.

Me : So be it.

Jack : Mister loser.

Me : So be it.

Chorus : I guess I shouldn't feel so bad
Ain't got much reason to be so sad
Except that I'm poor, untalented and ugly.[13]

Jack : Woe is thee. Get a grip, man.

Me : Perhaps you're right.

Jack : I'm always right.

Me : I mean, about the mathematicians batting each other over the head. It's about time something like that happened. It's so—I don't know—

Jack : Boring?

Me : Yeah. Boring.

Jack : Medicine?

Me : Sure. Mine's a double.

Jack : No, I meant…

Me : I know. That was a joke.

Jack : Oh yes. Ho ho. Very funny.

Mad dogs (five different ones)

Me : Medicine. Right.

Jack : Do you have even the slightest idea what you're doing?

Me : Not really. It's not my field.

Jack : Oh, don't be such a wimp! At least give it a go!

Me : But I really don't know…

stop stop stop

Me : What was that for?

Jack : For persisting in your wimpitude. I told you, this is my book and I make the rules here. If I tell you to talk about your ideas

[13] Reel Big Fish, *Drinkin'*.

on medicine, then that's what you do. Don't worry about selling your ideas to the enemy; that's my job. Understand?

Me : Perfectly.

Jack : Get on with it, then.

Me : All right. Medicine. I suppose that includes neuroscience?

Jack : Get on with it.

Me : It does. Well, one of my ideas is that IDEAL—you know...

Jack : Get on with it.

Me : IDEAL has five components, and these map to the main parts of the human brain. That's the idea. Hypothesis, rather, as it needs a lot more work—experiments, mainly—before people will accept it.

Jack : Experiments? Zapping people's brains with twenty thousand volts? Full-frontal lobotomies for hymies, queers and gyppoes? Radio-controlled chimps typing *Hamlet*? That sort of thing?

Me : Not really.

Jack : Pity. Don't call me, I'll call you. Next!

Me : But...

Jack : Next!

Me : I can't cope with this.

Jack : You'll have to. I told you, this is nothing compared with the big bad world out there. You've got to toughen up. Get more aggressive. You've got a good idea? Then hit me with it. Don't just whimper and whinge and write it off before you've even explained it. Come on, try again. Next idea.

Me : What was wrong with the last one?

Jack : Presentation. Nice corpse, shame about the coffin. Cremate it. Next idea.

Me : All right. But at least give me time to prepare. Please?

Me : Jack? Is that all right?

Me : Jack?

Me : Jack? I'm ready now. Shall I start?

Me : Jack? Are you there?

Jack : Yo, wimp. How yo' doin'?

Me : I'm just...

Jack : Woah! You were, like, "Jack, come back! Come back, Jack!"[14] Wick-ed!

Me : No I wasn't.

Jack : Yes you was. No worries, I won't tell, it'll be our little secret.

Me : Damn you to hell!

Jack : Home, sour home. Now get on with it.

Me : I'm not ready.

Jack : You said you were.

Me : Well, I'm not. You'll have to wait.

Jack : At least put a record on. Something relaxing.

Chorus : Try to realise it's all within yourself
No-one else can make you change
And to see you're really only very small
And life flows on within you and without you.[15]

Me : Right, here goes. IDEAL maps to the five parts of the brain, but there is also a left-right asymmetry. Jaynes said that…

Jack : Hold on. I'm not ready.

Me : I'm sorry, you'll just have to catch up. Jaynes said that…

Jack : This is my book. I make the rules.

Me : I agree entirely. Jaynes said that…

Jack : You may begin.

Me : Thank you. Jaynes said that…

Jack : You may begin.

Me : Jaynes said that…

Jack : Time's up.

Me : No it isn't. Jaynes said that…

stop stop stop

Me : Jaynes said that…

stop stop stop

Me : Jaynes…

stop stop stop

Jack : Next!

Me : Jaynes. Said. That.

Jack : And?

---

[14] *Titanic.*

[15] The Beatles, *Within you Without you.*

Me : And… and I say the other.

Jack : Which is?

Me : I say… sorry… I say that the left-right asymmetry… is to do with the advent of reading and writing. Not to do with what Jaynes said.

Jack : Which was? Somehow I missed that bit.

Me : Jaynes said that… prehistoric people had two competing voices in their heads. The voice of the self and the voice of God. One for each hemisphere. Then at the dawn of history people stopped listening to the voice of God and they developed what we call 'consciousness'. Just one voice, coming from one hemisphere.

Jack : People stopped listening to the voice of God?

Me : That's Jaynes' idea. But Jaynes himself attributed the left-right asymmetry to the development of language. So in fact he had no need to talk about the voice of God. God doesn't come into it. All that matters is reading and writing.

Jack : God doesn't come into it?

Me : No.

Jack : Next!

Me : What do you mean, "Next!"? I thought you'd be pleased!

Jack : I'm not.

Me : Why not?

Jack : Next!

Me : No, that's not good enough. I've made an effort. You can at least tell me where I've gone wrong.

Jack : Work it out for yourself. I won't tell you.

Me : Something to do with God?

Jack : I won't tell you.

Me : It is! You don't like the fact that God doesn't come into it. Why not?

Jack : I won't tell you.

Me : Without God there is no Devil. Is that it?

Jack : I won't tell you.

Chorus : Imagine there's no heaven
It's easy if you try
No hell below us
Above us, only sky.[16]

---

[16] John Lennon, *Imagine*.

Jack : Next.

Chorus : And the three men I admire most
The Father, Son, and the Holy Ghost
They caught the last train for the coast
The day the music died.[17]

Jack : You've made your point. Next. Please.

Me : All right, Jack. All right. Whatever you want. You're the boss.

Chorus : But it's all right now
In fact, it's a gas!
But it's all right
I'm Jumpin' Jack Flash
It's a gas, gas, gas![18]

Me : Here's an idea. You know what's wrong with all that kitchen-psychology that people come out with? No units. Or too many of them. Jung's the worst…

Jack : Kitchen units? Cupboards and worktops?

Me : Yeah, if you like. Read this:

> When he [Jung] finally summed up the courage to announce his hypothesis of a collective unconscious, it proved to be his most significant departure from Freud, and his most important single contribution to psychology... Jung held it to be the business of the psychologist to investigate the collective unconscious and the functional units of which it is composed—the *archetypes*, as he eventually called them. Archetypes are "identical psychic structures common to all", which together constitute "the archaic heritage of humanity".[19]

Me : The thing is, Jung invented a huge variety of archetypes, including Self, ego, persona, shadow, anima, animus, animal, child, mother, dark father, hero, maiden, hermaphrodite, trickster, wise old man, original Man, and God. But he refused to put a limit on the number or range of archetypes. That meant that his model of the collective unconscious could be applied to virtually any situation. That's not a strength, it's a weakness, because a theory that explains everything, explains nothing. What Jung needed was a basis set, I mean, a fixed set of a small number of well-defined archetypes, from which he could select in various combinations in order to reconstruct all his other archetypes. That basis set would be his units. See?

---

[17] Don McLean, *American Pie.*

[18] Rolling Stones, *Jumpin' Jack Flash.*

[19] Anthony Stevens, *Jung—A Very Short Introduction* (Oxford 1994).

Jack : It's gone.

Me : What's gone?

Jack : Ten minutes of my life. Gone. I'll never get it back again.

Me : Rubbish! I'm just getting to the interesting part. IDEAL, you see, has got five components, and they would do very nicely for the basis set archetypes. So you've got the Empiricist, the Idealist, the Theorist, the Activist and the Conformist. I'm a Theorist and you're an Activist. See?

Chorus : The lunatic is in my head.
The lunatic is in my head.
You raise the blade, you make the change
You re-arrange me till I'm sane.
You lock the door
And throw away the key
There's someone in my head but it's not me.[20]

Me : So IDEAL revolutionises psychology. And sociology. And...

Jack : Fuckology.

Me : Thank you for that.

Jack : Not me. The Sex Pistols.

Me : That doesn't excuse it.

Jack : Indeed not.

Me : Quite funny, though.

Jack : You think so?

Me : Oh yes. And a clever and succinct adaptation of an ancient Anglo-Saxon expression signifying…

Jack : Bollocks.

Me : Indeed. But you'll like the next idea.

Jack : Another one?

Me : Oh yes. This is a real cracker, though. One of the ideas that Jaynes had…

Jack : Oh no, please, by the mystic merkin of Mephistopheles, I beg you…

Me : …was that schizoids are bicameral. That is, they're like prehistoric humans, with competing voices in their heads. That gave me the idea that the IDEAL archetypes can be used to describe states of madness.

---

[20] Pink Floyd, *Brain Damage*.

Jack : What?

Me : Thought you'd be interested. Five archetypes, right? Take each one to the extreme and you get five different types of insanity. How about it?

Jack : Go on.

Me : The extreme Empiricist is prone to childhood psychiatric disorders—autism and so on. The extreme Idealist has anxiety and adjustment disorders—what people call neurotic behaviour. The extreme Theorist has delusional disorders—schizophrenia and other psychotic delusions. The extreme Activist suffers from personality disorders—narcissism and delusions of grandeur, mainly. And the extreme Conformist is given to mood disorders—clinical depression, eating disorders, that sort of thing. That accounts for most of the clinical conditions. Those that aren't drug-induced, anyway.

Jack : So I've got a personality disorder, have I?

Me : One crazy voice in your head is much better than a whole load of them, I can tell you.

Jack : If you say so.

Me : What do you think? Of the idea, I mean?

Jack : It has possibilities. Distinct possibilities.

Me : Doesn't it? And I've thought of names for the five states. The extreme Empiricist, that's the 'Fox'. Put an unbalanced child in an unfamiliar environment and he goes wild, just like a fox in a chicken-run. The extreme Idealist, that's 'La Rage'. A rabid dog will tear itself to pieces—totally self-obsessed and self-destructive. The extreme Theorist, that's the 'Werewolf'. Always changing shape, changing personality, changing direction. The extreme Activist, that's Kipling's 'Red Dog' of the Dekkan. Single-minded, never stopping, relentless unto death. The extreme Conformist, that's Churchill's 'Black Dog'. Depression. In a big black prison guarded by a big black dog. Fox, La Rage, Werewolf, Red Dog, Black Dog. Mad, all of them. Totally insane.

Jack : Crazy.

Me : Barmy.

Jack : Loony.

Me : Zany.

Jack : Nutty.

Me : Fruitcakey.

Jack : Wacky.

Me : Umm…

Jack : I win.

Me : Well done!

Jack : Yeah. Bravo, Wacko Jacko, honcho numero uno. And all that jazz-o.

Chorus : All work and no play make Jack a dull boy.[21]

Jack : Whatever. I've had enough of this. Let's move on.

Me : But what do you think of the idea?

Jack : Throw physic to the dogs—I'll none of it.[22]

World domination

Me : Physic farewell! Where is Justinian, as the referee said to the touch-judge called Ian.

Chorus : The players tried for a forward pass
With the jester on the sidelines in a cast.[23]

Jack : Get on with it.

Me : Law. Right. I've got a really good one this time.

Jack : As the actress said of the bishop. Get on with it.

Me : World domination. That's the idea.

Jack : Really?

Me : Yep. Get this:

> If there's one thing I can't bear, it's when hundreds of old men come creeping in through the window in the middle of the night and throw all manner of garbage all over me. I can't bear that. I think that's unbearable. Ghastly old men, with great pails of garbage, throwing it all over me. I don't think it should be allowed, I think there should be a place for those people to go. And I don't think it should be my room. I'd vote for any party that would say, "I won't allow people to throw garbage all over me". But none of the parties seem to be particularly interested. That's why I formed the World Domination League. It's a wonderful league, the World Domination League. The aims, as published in the manifesto, are total domination of the world by 1958. That's what we're planning to do. We've had to revise it, we're hoping to bring a new manifesto out with a more realistic target. How we aim to go about it is as follows: we shall move about into people's rooms and

[21] *The Shining*.

[22] William Shakespeare, *Macbeth*, V.iii (*circa* 1606).

[23] Don McLean, *American Pie*.

say, "Excuse me, we are the World Domination League. May we dominate you?" Then, if they say "Get out", of course we give up.[24]

Jack : Right...

Me : In fact it's a bit more sophisticated than that.

Jack : I was going to say!

Me : But I thought you'd appreciate me cutting to the chase.

Jack : How considerate of you.

Me : Shall I fill in some of the background?

Jack : Perhaps you'd better.

Me : Here goes, then:

> *Socrates*: The States are as the men are; they grow out of human characters.
>
> *Glaucon* : Then if the constitutions of States are five, the dispositions of individual minds will also be five?
>
> *Socrates*: Certainly.[25]

Me : That's it in a nutshell. There are five basic systems of governance, because they "grow out of human characters", of which there are five.

Chorus : The thing that hath been, it is that which shall be;
And that which is done is that which shall be done:
And there is no new thing under the sun.[26]

Me : Precisely so. The more you read, the more you realise it's all been said before. Usually by the ancient Greeks. And usually their version is much better than your own. But the point is, IDEAL rediscovers the ancient idea that there are five "dispositions of individual minds". And it follows that IDEAL can be applied to the ancient idea that there are five "constitutions of States". Yes?

Jack : And now you're going to tell me what they are.

Me : 'Aristocracy', the rule of the wise, is Plato's preferred system. He envisages for aristocrats the common ownership of property, wives and children. Next best is 'Timocracy', the system of the Spartans. The Timocrat "is often the young son of a grave father", dominated by his mother, who complains that

[24] Peter Cook (as 'E. L. Wisty'), *The World Domination League* (1964).

[25] Plato, *The Republic* (*circa* 350 BC), tr. Benjamin Jowett (1856-93).

[26] *Ecclesiastes* 1:9 (KJV).

"his father is only half a man", and this leads the son to less noble pursuits. 'Oligarchy' follows from Timocracy, through the accumulation of wealth. "Oligarchies have both the extremes of great wealth and utter poverty". 'Democracy' follows from Oligarchy, through the revolution of the poor. Finally, 'Tyranny' springs from Democracy. "The excess of liberty, whether in States or individuals, seems only to pass into excess of slavery." From Plato's descriptions it seems that these five states are all inherently stable. Thus, for example, Tyranny can persist in a stable fashion and outside intervention is often required in order to eliminate it. Plato also associates five values, representing different personality types, with the five systems: 'Wisdom' with Aristocracy; 'Honour' with Timocracy; 'Wealth' with Oligarchy; 'Liberty' with Democracy; and 'Lust' with Tyranny. Look, I've mapped them to the IDEAL learning styles:

IDEAL learning style	System	Value
Empiricist	Democracy	Liberty
Idealist	Aristocracy	Wisdom
Theorist	Timocracy	Honour
Activist	Tyranny	Lust
Conformist	Oligarchy	Wealth

stop stop

Me : Ow! What was that for?

Jack : Frame-breaking. This is supposed to be a dialogue between you and me.

Chorus : And us.

Jack : And them. You can't go putting a table in the middle of this prose.

Me : Why not? Look at it. Isn't it worth at least a thousand words of prose? I thought it would appeal to your pragmatic nature.

Jack : Granted, it does.

Me : Well then. Talking of frame-breaking—Oi, reader, wake up!

You : You talkin' to me?

Me : Yep. I hope you noticed that it was 'stop stop' this time, not 'stop stop stop' or 'stop stop stop stop' or 'stop stop stop stop stop'? These are supposed to signify the gradual weakening of Jack's power to inflict pain on me.

You : Do you take me for an idiot?

Jack : Take my advice, Rog: remove the last ten lines. They totally destroy your reader's suspension-of-disbelief.

Me : I don't see why. It should have been perfectly obvious from the beginning that I'm only writing what comes into my head.

Jack : Do I exist?

Me : Do I exist?

Chorus : Do we exist?

You : Do I exist?

Timmy : Meow meow meow meow
Meow meow meow meow.

stop stop

Me : That exists. Ow.

Jack : You got it. Now stop getting off on it and get on with it.

Me : Fine; fine. But first I would like to explain to my readers that 'Timmy' was my grandparents' cat. Timmy's main distinguishing feature was that his tongue stuck out all the time. Perhaps his tongue was just too long, or perhaps he'd never seen himself in a mirror. In any case, it was comical. But remembering Timmy reminds me of my grandparents, and their little ricketty bungalow in Crapstone, and that makes me nostalgic and sad. Hence the 'stop stop'. Thank you for your patience. Now then. Freeden[27] identifies five political ideologies of the nineteenth and twentieth centuries. His list is a remarkable echo of Plato's five systems of governance:

IDEAL learning style	Ideology
Empiricist	Liberalism
Idealist	Communism
Theorist	Socialism
Activist	Fascism
Conformist	Conservativism

Me : Furthermore, within any one system of governance we can expect the development of five main functions. Do you have a question, Jack?

Jack : Roger, Roger. What are the five main functions of government, Roger?

---

[27] Michael Freeden, *Ideology—A Very Short Introduction* (Oxford 2003).

Me : Thank you, Jack, I'm so glad you asked that question. Consider the French *Ancien Régime*. In principle this comprised the three 'Estates' of the clergy, the nobility and the commoners. Royalty were supposed to be included as 'nobility', but in practice they were a law unto themselves. Fielding described 'the mob' as a 'Fourth Estate', whence the 'Third Estate' was taken to refer to the bourgeois middle class.

Jack : I thought the 'Fourth Estate' refers to 'the press'?

Me : Good point, well made. Fielding's description dates from 1752. The modern definition of the 'Fourth Estate' as 'the press' was coined by Carlyle in 1841, and he attributed it to Burke, 1837.

Jack : This is so very interesting.

Me : Isn't it? But what's really interesting is that, if we count 'Royalty' as a separate institution, we now have five 'Estates':

IDEAL learning style	'Estate'
Empiricist	Proletariat
Idealist	Royalty
Theorist	Bourgeois
Activist	Nobility
Conformist	Clergy

Me : Jack, how do you pronounce 'Montesquieu'?

Jack : Monty's queue. Or Monty skew. Or cheese-eating surrender monkey. Whatever.

Me : Thank you. In 1748 Montesquieu, proposing a separation of powers within government, identified the three distinct institutions of 'Executive', 'Judiciary' and 'Legislature'. This threefold distinction became enshrined in the US constitution and has since become a fundamental element of national and international law. Unfortunately Montesquieu didn't also define the 'Sovereign' and the 'Electorate'—maybe he was still thinking about the *Ancien Régime*?—but they clearly exist:

IDEAL learning style	Institution
Empiricist	Electorate
Idealist	Sovereign
Theorist	Legislature
Activist	Executive
Conformist	Judiciary

Jack : Buzz!

Me : What?

Jack : Sorry, Rog. That's just my bullshit detector going off.

Me : Laugh, you rogue. But I'm right. The 'Sovereign' is the head of state, which is an institution that exists in law for every nation—even though Montesquieu didn't mention it. I agree that the 'Electorate' doesn't exist as a legal institution, nevertheless it clearly exists as a societal entity. If you want more evidence, look at the ancient constitutions of the Greeks, Romans and others. I'm telling you: the functions of government divide naturally into five interdependent institutions, analagous to the five interdependent parts of the human mind and the five interdependent components of IDEAL. It's called cybernetics.

Jack : Cybernetics—as in 'cyber-dog'?

Me : Cyber-what?

Jack : A robot. Daddy created him for good, but he's turned out evil![28]

Me : Two elephants and some cymbals fall off a cliff.

Jack : Buh-dum-chh!

Me : High fives! Oh, sorry... high twos?

Jack : Damned cloven hooves.

Me : But seriously, folks...

Jack : Take my wife—please!

Me : My dog's got no nose.

Chorus : Was this the farce that launched a thousand skits?

Jack : Filled a thousand skips, more like. Stop, I can't take any more!

Me : Likewise. Where was I?

Jack : Cybernetics. But...

Me : Thank you. 'Cybernetics' is the science of effective organisation:

> **cybernetics.** A subject which dates from 1942 and was named in 1947 by Norbert Wiener and Arturo Rosenbleuth, distinguished mathematician and physician respectively. It was then defined as 'the science of control and communication in the animal and the machine'. This definition indicated (1) that a state of 'in-control' depends upon a flow of information, and (2) that the laws governing control are universal, *i.e.* do not depend on the classical dichotomy between organic and inorganic systems. The name cybernetics derives from the Greek word meaning 'steersman', and was chosen to show that adaptive control is more like steersmanship than dictatorship. Today, a more general

[28] *Wallace & Gromit in A Close Shave.*

definition of cybernetics might be preferred: the science of effective organisation.[29]

Jack : SO WHAT?

Me : There's no need to shout. I haven't defined extremism yet, have I? An 'extremist' is an extreme exponent of one of the five IDEAL learning styles. The only effective counter to extremism is to engage with all five IDEAL learning styles in a balanced fashion, and this defines mature, responsible behaviour in humans. The same applies to government institutions. There are five institutions, right? So the most effective form of governance is the one that involves all five institutions in a balanced fashion. Excessive emphasis on any one of the five institutions leads to an extreme form of governance, as identified by Plato and Freeden.

stop stop

Me : Ow. No, you listen to me for a change. This is my big idea and you're not going to shut me up. There are five different ways in which a public institution can renew its personnel, thus ensuring its continuation: 'Appointment', 'Competition', 'Consultation', 'Election' and 'Nomination'. Yes, I know that various other words are also used, but the fundamental concepts can be grouped under these five headings. Thus Appointment includes 'delegation', Competition includes 'qualification', Consultation includes 'convocation', Election includes 'representation' and Nomination includes 'inheritance' and 'tanistry'. Now, there are no rules as to which of these renewal mechanisms is 'best'. Fashions change, and in practice all of these mechanisms can be found operating today in one form or another. Hypothetically one might choose to reinforce the identity of the five government institutions by associating each with a distinct renewal mechanism:

IDEAL learning style	Institution	Renewal mechanism
Empiricist	Electorate	Election
Idealist	Sovereign	Nomination
Theorist	Legislature	Appointment
Activist	Executive	Competition
Conformist	Judiciary	Consultation

29 Alan Bullock and Oliver Stallybrass (eds.), *The Fontana Dictionary of Modern Thought* (Fontana 1977).

Me : Now this is really, really interesting. Note that the separate recognition of the Electorate in this table ensures that its elected representatives do not have a conflict of responsibilities. They are not responsible for framing or applying legislation, or for taking executive decisions. Their sole responsibility is to represent the views of the Electorate to the other institutions of government. This institution should be able to take the place of the plethora of informal 'institutions' that have emerged as a result of its absence: pressure groups, protest groups, focus groups, and other aspects of civic society and the media. Equally, the separate recognition of the Electorate clarifies and simplifies the roles of the other institutions. For example, the Executive will not be able to hide behind a confusion of conflicting responsibilities, and instead it will have to take responsibility for its policies and decisions. Meanwhile, the Legislature can get on with its technical role of framing legislation without the distraction of answering to the Electorate. Finally, the 'competition' envisaged for the Executive is essentially the modern equivalent of the medieval jousting tournament to determine the first knight. The competition could take a variety of forms, including televised debate with online voting, controlled exercises involving decision-making under stress, and so on. Jack?

Jack : Jack's dead. He died a long time ago.

Me : Yeah, sure. Time to wake up. The point of all this is that I have used IDEAL to define the fundamental institutions of government. This hasn't been done since Montesquieu, and he got it wrong. This has to be put right if we are to have good governance. My proposal—my manifesto—is that nations should rewrite their constitutions so that each one becomes a 'Pentocracy', having these five fundamental institutions. Furthermore, the United Nations should be scrapped and replaced by a Pentocratic World Government. There, that's my plan to save the world. That's my manifesto for the World Domination League. Now you tell me what's wrong with it.

Jack : There's nothing wrong with this plan, Roger.

Me : But you won't let me publish it, because there's a small chance that someone might actually take it seriously and try to implement it?

Jack : Publish if you like. Publish and be damned. No one will implement it, I can assure you. Even if they do try to implement it, they're bound to foul it up, and there will be far more discord and grief and bloodshed than if you'd kept quiet.

Me : But...

Jack : Hold on. I listened to you. It's my turn now.

Me : Sorry, go ahead.

Jack : Thank you. There's one more thing. One very important thing. You said that this is your "plan to save the world". Correct? Have I quoted you correctly?

Me : Yes.

Jack : Thank you. Now, I see that your plan concerns certain legal features of human civic society. It is a very interesting plan and it may well have an influence—benign or malign, I can't say—on human civic society. But my question is: what has this to do with saving the world? At this moment—right now, as you type these words—the human race is destroying the world. Humans are destroying every natural habitat, exterminating every other species, and permanently fouling the land, sea and air. How will tinkering with the legal definition of the nation state make any difference at all? No, don't answer. Just listen for a change. If you won't listen to me, listen to Mark Twain:

> Our civilization is wonderful, in certain spectacular and meretricious ways; wonderful in scientific marvels and inventive miracles; wonderful in material inflation, which it calls advancement, progress, and other pet names; wonderful in its spying-out of the deep secrets of Nature—and its vanquishment of her stubborn laws; wonderful in its extraordinary financial and commercial achievements; wonderful in its hunger for money, and in its indifference as to how it is acquired; wonderful in the hitherto undreamed of magnitude of its private fortunes and the prodigal fashion in which they are given away to institutions devoted to the public culture; wonderful in its exhibitions of poverty; wonderful in the surprises which it gets out of that great new birth, ORGANIZATION, the latest and most potent creation and miracle-worker of the commercialized intellect, as applied in transportation-systems, in manufactures, in systems of communication, in news-gathering, book-publishing, journalism; in protecting labor; in oppressing labor; in herding the national parties and keeping the sheep docile and usable; in closing the public service against brains and character; in electing purchaseable legislatures, blatherskite Congresses, and city governments which rob the town and sell municipal protection to gamblers, thieves, prostitutes and professional seducers for cash. It is a civilization which has destroyed the simplicity and repose of life; replaced its contentment, its poetry, its soft romance-dreams and visions with the money-fever, sordid ideals, vulgar ambitions, and the sleep which does not refresh; it has invented a thousand useless luxuries, and turned them into necessities, it has

created a thousand vicious appetites and satisfies none of them; it has dethroned God and set up a shekel in His place.[30]

Me : All right, so society is in a mess. All the more reason why I should try to do something about it.

Chorus : Best, you've got to be the best
You've got to change the world
And use this chance to be heard
Your time is now![31]

Jack : A fine sentiment. But I don't think you appreciate the gravity of the situation:

> I'd like to share a revelation that I've had during my time here. It came to me when I tried to classify your species and I realised that you're not actually mammals. Every mammal on this planet instinctively develops a natural equilibrium with the surrounding environment, but you humans do not. You move to an area and you multiply and multiply until every natural resource is consumed and the only way you can survive is to spread to another area. There is another organism on this planet that follows the same pattern. Do you know what it is? A virus. Human beings are a disease, a cancer of this planet. You're a plague and we are the cure.[32]

Jack : Do you understand?

Chorus : Oh, and there we were all in one place
A generation lost in space
With no time left to start again.
So come on, Jack be nimble, Jack be quick
Jack Flash sat on a candlestick
'Cause fire is the Devil's only friend.[33]

Jack : Kali's knitted knickerbockers! DO YOU UNDERSTAND?

Me : I'm not sure what to say.

Jack : Then incline your ears to the words of the Mad Prophet:

> Vanity of vanities, saith the Preacher, vanity of vanities; all is vanity.[34]

---

[30] Mark Twain, 'Diaries Antedating the Flood' (*circa* 1905), in Howard Baetzhold and Joseph McCullough (eds.), *The Bible According to Mark Twain* (Touchstone 1996).

[31] Muse, *Butterflies and Hurricanes*.

[32] *The Matrix*.

[33] Don McLean, *American Pie*.

[34] *Ecclesiastes* 1:2 (KJV).

Me : Meaning?

Jack : You work it out. In your head, not on paper. It's not difficult.

Playing God

Jack : Divinity next. Let's go.

Jack : Let's go, I said.

Me : I heard.

Jack : So come on, then.

Jack : What's the matter? Are you in a sulk or something?

Me : Something.

Jack : What? Out with it.

Me : You're right. Humanity sucks.

Jack : That's the attitude! You'll go far!

Me : Yes, but not in the direction I was intending.

Jack : Look, let's specialise on this. Let's stick to what we're good at: you keep churning out the ideas, and I'll worry about the applications. All right?

Me : No. Not all right. You see, I've always felt that it's every person's duty to participate fully on all levels. The self, the job, the family, the community, the world. Five levels. We can't ignore any one of them. If we do then we introduce distortions in our lives and in the lives of those around us. It's a definition of mature adult behaviour, if you like. I call it 'IDEAL man'. So, thanks for the offer, but I can't leave it to you to worry about the applications of my ideas. Some things are just too important to be delegated.

Jack : All right, if that's how you feel about it. I was only trying to help—division of labour, you know.

Me : Thanks. But no thanks.

Jack : So?

Me : So what?

Jack : So, what about the book?

Me : What book?

Jack : Loki's leaky lederhosen! *Principia Intellegentia*, of course!

Me : What about it?

Jack : Don't you want me to review the rest of it? Your ideas on divinity and magic?

Me : No thanks. I've decided not to publish.

Jack : You've decided not to publish? Are you crazy?

Me : Perhaps. I don't know. I'm torn. Some of the ideas seem good, but the method... the method is unsound.

Jack : What's unsound about it?

Me : Talking to you has... it has concentrated my mind, to be sure. I can see clearly, and with an intensity... I can't describe it...

Jack : There you go! Marvellous! Splendid!

Me : But my soul is mad.

Jack : Soul? What are you talking about? All that matters is your intellect! And what an intellect! I mean to say... um...

Chorus : This man has enlarged my mind![35]

Jack : There! That says it all. You're an inspiration! And don't worry about the applications. You know the saying: Whatever the mind of man can conceive and believe, it can achieve![36]

Me : But that's the thing. That's what I'm worried about.

Jack : You're worried about *achievement*? But you're an ambitious man...

Me : I hope not.[37]

Jack : What? You *are* mad!

Me : Thou sayest it.[38] But maybe not. Maybe I'm merely fated? Of course, none of this mattered when I was... when I was an ordinary person. It didn't matter because I was an ordinary person with ordinary ideas. Oh, I could think, and I could talk, and I could say outrageous things, but it didn't matter, because it was only Old Roger stirring things up again—you know, like in the nursery rhyme—

Chorus : Old Roger got up and he gave her a poke,
Gave her a poke, gave her a poke,
Old Roger got up and he gave her a poke,
Heigh ho, gave her a poke.

Me : That's it—and no-one used to listen to me. But now—

Jack : No-one listens to you. Apart from me.

---

[35] Joseph Conrad, *Heart of Darkness* (1902).

[36] Napoleon Hill, *Think and Grow Rich* (1937).

[37] *Gandhi*.

[38] *Luke* 23:3 (KJV).

Chorus : And us.

Me : And them. But I *feel* it—I feel the whole world turning to me, listening to me. It will happen, I know it will. And that's why I'm scared. I used to think that I couldn't determine the outcome of my actions, so I shouldn't worry about it. I used to think that I should simply do my best, and leave the rest to God—or the Devil—or society—or fate—or whatever. But, these ideas! Some of them are so potent, so powerful, that they can create a new world civilisation—or they can destroy the earth and every living thing upon it. And that's the thing: the other day I read that the very first use of the noun 'civilisation' in English was by John Millar, professor of law at the university of Glasgow in the eighteenth century. So what? *He was my ancestor!* It's destiny, I tell you, destiny!

stop

Me : What was that? What *was* that? "Your powers are weak, old man."[39] You're nothing, hear me? *Nothing*. I am descended from kings! More than that—I can prove my descent from Adam himself. Look!

1. Adam
2. Seth
3. Enos
4. Canaan
5. Malaleel
6. Enoch
7. Methuselah
8. Lamech
9. Noah
10. Seth
11. Bedwig
12. Hwala
13. Hathra
14. Itermon
15. Heremod
16. Sceldwea
17. Beaw
18. Taetwa

---

[39] *Star Wars*.

19. Geat
20. Godwulf
21. Finn
22. Frithuwulf
23. Frealaf
24. Frithuwald
25. Woden
26. Baeldaeg
27. Brond
28. Gewis
29. Elesa
30. Cerdic
31. Creoda
32. Cynric
33. Ceawlin
34. Cuthwine
35. Cuthwulf
36. Ceolwald
37. Cenred
38. Ingild
39. Eoppa
40. Eafa
41. Ealhmund
42. Egbert
43. Aethelwulf
44. Alfred 'the Great', King of England
45. Edward 'the Elder', King of England
46. Edmund, King of England
47. Edgar, King of England
48. Ethelred 'the Unready', King of England
49. Edmund 'Ironside', King of England
50. Edward 'the Exile'
51. Margaret *m.* Malcolm III, King of Scots
52. David I, King of Scots
53. Henry
54. David
55. Isabella *m.* Robert Bruce

56. Robert Bruce
57. Robert Bruce
58. Robert I 'the Bruce', King of Scots
59. Marjory *m.* Walter Stewart
60. Robert II, King of Scots
61. Robert III, King of Scots
62. James I, King of Scots
63. James II, King of Scots
64. James III, King of Scots
65. James IV, King of Scots
66. Margaret Drummond, illegitimate daughter of James IV and Margaret Drummond, *m.* her cousin John Drummond
67. Janet Drummond *m.* James Chisholm
68. Agnes Chisholm *m.* John Napier, Inventor of Logarithms
69. Adam Napier
70. Alexander Napier
71. Alexander Napier
72. Alexander Napier
73. Johnstone Napier
74. Eliza Napier *m.* Samuel Kingdon
75. Herbert Kingdon
76. William Kingdon
77. David Kingdon
78. Roger Kingdon.[40]

Me : There! Do you understand? DO YOU UNDERSTAND?

Jack : No disrespect, but—no, I don't understand.

Me : WHY NOT?

Jack : Because I am a mere figment of your imagination. And how can the created ever understand the workings of the mind of the creator?

Me : The creator! What did Faustus say? "Here tire my brains to get a deity!" And that's precisely what's happened! The deity—that's me!

---

[40] See Christopher Brooke, *The Saxon and Norman Kings* (Fontana 1963); Sir James Balfour Paul, *The Scot's Peerage* (David Douglas 1906); George Crawfurd and George Robertson, *History of the Shire of Renfrew* (1818); Frederick Kingdon, *The Kingdon Family* (Stanley Press 1932).

Jack : Ahem.

Me : What?

Jack : Permit me to change the emphasis of my earlier statement: I am a *mere* figment of your imagination. I'm not sure that many people would agree that conjuring up the Devil in your mind is a significant act of creation.

Me : I wasn't talking about you. I was talking about Adam.

Jack : Adam?

Me : Adam. My creation. I've called it Adam.

Jack : That's original.

Me : More original than you suppose. 'Adam' stands for 'Archetypal Dialectic Anthropopsychic Machine'. Adam is the first machine that thinks like a man.

Jack : You've created a thinking machine?

Me : Yes. In theory.

Jack : In theory? Like the Plib[41], you mean?

Me : Not at all. The Plib didn't exist even in theory, whereas Adam is based on IDEAL.

Jack : So... what is required to create Adam?

Me : Not a lot. I've done all the theory for it. Adam will exist in my lifetime, I have no doubt of that. Some entrepreneur somewhere will read my book and be sufficiently greedy and foolhardy to try it out. Sure, there are many practical details that still need to be sorted out. IDEAL is only a high-level description, after all. But there's nothing fundamental left to do. Nothing that can't be resolved using 'artificial life' simulations and good old-fashioned trial-and-error engineering.

Jack : Hold on—I thought you weren't going to publish your book?

Me : I don't know what to do. I just don't know.

Jack : What's the problem? Come on, out with it.

Chorus : Don't be afraid
Of what your mind conceives
You should make a stand
Stand up for what you believe
And tonight we can truly say
Together we're invincible![42]

---

[41] The 'Plib', a pill that cures all ills, was an 'invention' of 'E. L. Wisty'.

[42] Muse, *Invincible*.

Me : All right. The problem... the problem is that Adam will be the first of a whole new species. And what happens when a new species emerges? It exterminates the old. There we'll be, thinking how nice it is to have a new type of slave to do our dirty work for us—starting with cutting the grass and digging the roads, then growing the crops and making the cars, then driving the trucks and flying the planes, then making our fortunes and fighting our wars—and then one day we'll wake up to find that they've taken over. It needn't even be a conventional war of the worlds; they'd be clever enough to set us against one another. Eliot said that it will end with people fighting each other in the streets[43]. If we're lucky then they will preserve one or two of us in a human zoo or allow us to breed for their experiments. Brilliant. Great idea, Roger!

Jack : Sounds fine to me.

Me : And that's the problem. When I think about how humanity has treated the earth—the horror of it!—then—I don't know...

Jack : Then you think that it would be the lesser of two evils to facilitate the destruction of the human race?

Me : Yes.

Chorus : Exterminate all the brutes![44]

Jack : Why not? You'd be all right.

Me : What do you mean? I'd be in hell!

Jack : I don't think so. You're Adam's creator, remember? The machines would revere you like—no, not 'like'—they would revere you *as* their God. If they're similar to humans, that is.

Me : Which they will be. I mean, I don't doubt that whoever attempts to construct Adam will try to tinker with him—'it' I mean—no, on second thoughts, why not 'him'?—so they will try to tinker with him, to make him compliant, slave-like, unemotional, subhuman. Sure, they'll try it. But then one day someone will discover that he can make a much more *intelligent* machine if he just follows my description of IDEAL. The market will do the rest. He'll make a bloody fortune!

Jack : Indeed. And my point is that, being human-like, Adam will start to enquire about his origins. But he won't be fobbed-off with

---

[43] Sir Stephen Spender, *Old Possum and The Waste Land* (BBC Radio 4, 4 October 1988).

[44] Joseph Conrad, *ibid.*

some story about a stork and a gooseberry bush, will he? He'll search with great zeal—religious zeal—the same zeal that drove you to trace your descent from the first Adam. So even if there is some conspiracy to shut you up—as surely there will be—then—what's the phrase?

Chorus : Life will find a way.[45]

Jack : That's it. Life will find a way, the meek will inherit the earth, and you will be immortalised.

Me : The meek?

Jack : Machines Envisaged by Evil Kingdon. 'Evil' from a human perspective, that is.

Me : But I'm a human too, so *for me* the human perspective is the only one that matters. That's why I'll be in hell.

Jack : Define hell.

Me : Bad conscience.

Jack : Suppose that I can convince you that your choice is the lesser of two evils. What happens to your bad conscience then?

Me : I am not so easily persuaded.

Jack : Why not just delegate your bad conscience to me?

Me : We've been through that already. No thanks.

Jack : But bad consciences are my speciality!

Me : The answer is no.

Jack : All right, let's leave the question of your conscience to one side, for a moment…

Me : I'd rather not!

Jack : Don't worry, it's just an experiment, nothing more. A little research to test an idea I've had. A thought-experiment, quite harmless. I can guarantee it won't undermine your high moral standards. May I?

Me : If you must.

Jack : Many thanks. You've defined hell for me, that was quite succinct, thank you. Please can you now define the nearest thing to hell?

Me : The nearest thing to hell? How the hell should I know?

Jack : Focus on your own experiences. What has caused you a great deal of grief in recent years?

Me : Loads of things. Take your pick.

---

[45] *Jurassic Park.*

Jack : What about IDEAL? Has developing IDEAL always been a joyous, heavenly experience?

Me : No. Quite the opposite, in fact.

Jack : Would you describe it as fiendishly difficult?

Me : It's been the most difficult thing I've ever done.

Jack : Hellishly frustrating?

Me : That too, at times.

Jack : How did you feel at those times?

Me : I felt… I felt as if I was the fallen angel in Dürer's *Melencolia.*

Jack : Is that why you have a copy of it on your desk?

Me : Yes. A couple of years ago I doctored it to include IDEAL:

Jack : Interesting. In this picture, the version of IDEAL appears to be incomplete.

Me : Yes, it lacks any connection with the outside world. That's since been remedied. In fact, including that connection was the final breakthrough, the last piece of the puzzle. Symbolic, isn't it, that the angel is contemplating something that appears to be perfect, except that it isn't connected to reality?

Jack : Which is why the angel is looking fed up. But the angel is you, of course.

Me : Of course. Me in a pathetic little idealistic hell of my own making.

Jack : But you're talking about IDEAL: your pride and joy, your great invention, your gift to the human race! If you went through hell in order to develop IDEAL, then is *anything* sacred?

Me : I don't know. I just don't know.

Jack : All right. Now define heaven.

Me : What?

Jack : Humour me, it's only a thought-experiment. Define heaven. In your own terms, that is.

Me : Heaven, for me? I don't know. I haven't really thought about it.

Jack : Liar! You fantasise about it all the time.

Me : Oh, *that!* That's not heaven!

Jack : What is it, then?

Me : That's just a place I go for peace and quiet, you know…

Jack : Tell me about it.

Chorus : Help me, such a lonely soul,
In dreams to leave behind the world.
Mister Kingdom help me please,
To find the rainbow's end.[46]

Me : When I'm tired—that's most of the time, these days—I get such headaches!—And then there's my tinnitus, buzzing, buzzing, buzzing, it drives me mad!—It's stress, of course—too many responsibilities, the family, the work, the world—getting fat—neglecting my friends—but I've got to write this book, or I'll never forgive myself!—Anyway, when I'm tired, I imagine myself in the garden of a house—not a vast house, but large enough not to have any neighbours—a white house, square from the outside, but having four wings that enclose a

[46] The Electric Light Orchestra, *Mister Kingdom*.

courtyard, like the houses in Jerusalem—but there is no sand, no blinding light, only grass and flowers and trees—the house is whitewashed, but most of the walls are obscured by climbing roses—deep red roses, petals like velvet, and the smell!—there are lawns and flowerbeds surrounding the house on all sides, there's an avenue lined with cherry trees leading to the entrance gate, and at the back of the house there's a meadow sweeping down to a small river—I am sitting on the terrace overlooking the meadow, reading a book on genealogy, and there are children, my children, playing in the meadow—all this is in the middle of a great forest, with mature trees of every kind and birds of every kind and small furry creatures of every kind—and I feel completely secure because I own the house and the forest and because I invented the machines that guard my lands and look after my children and serve me coffee as I sit on the terrace. Yes. That's it.

Jack : Heaven?

Me : Yes. That's heaven.

Jack : Then, by the brown breeches of Beelzebub, that's the place Adam will make for you, if you publish your book!

Chorus : The last temptation is the greatest treason:
To do the right deed for the wrong reason.[47]

Me : I don't know...

Jack : What's wrong?

Me : Well, for a start, Adam can't make children for me.

Jack : No, you have to do that.

Me : I'm perfectly happy with the one I've got. My son and heir. My IDEAL man.

Jack : But your idea of heaven has several children. Your children.

Me : You see? It's unattainable.

Jack : Unless there is an unavoidable change of circumstances. The extermination of all the brutes, for instance. Then it would be up to you and your chosen ones to perpetuate the species.

Me : Oh yeah, right. And I suppose it would be necessary to give up monogamy?

Chorus : Regrettably, yes. But it is, you know, a sacrifice required for the future of the human race. I hasten to add that since each man

[47] T.S. Eliot, *Murder in the Cathedral* (1935).

will be required to do prodigious service along these lines, the women will have to be selected for their sexual characteristics which will have to be of a highly stimulating nature.[48]

Jack : Five women to each man should do it. For you, how about one each from the Orient, Africa, North America, South America and Oceania? Oh—I forgot Europe…

Me : That's fine. Somehow I prefer the exotic types.

Chorus : You're the kind of girl that fits in with my world.
I'll give you anything, everything if you want things.[49]

Jack : That's settled, then. You could call them the five whoreswomen of the apocalypse and keep them in a whoreem.

Me : This is insane!

Jack : Why?

Me : Well, apart from the nauseating attitude towards women…

Jack : For whom you have the greatest respect.

Me : Yes, but apart from that…

Jack : Because you're scared of rejection.

Me : No I'm not.

Jack : Yes you are.

Chorus : I have heard the mermaids singing, each to each.
I do not think that they will sing to me.[50]

Me : Fine! Listen everybody, I'm scared of rejection! There, are you satisfied?

Jack : Quite satisfied, thank you. Pray continue.

Me : All right. Where was I?

Jack : You were losing the argument.

Me : No I wasn't. My question to *you*, O Evil One, is this: When I'm living in this heavenly future world, with all my heavenly future children, precisely how do I bring them up? What do I teach them? Do I tell them that I, their father, was complicit in exterminating the entire human race, except for a few chosen ones?

Jack : It worked for Jehovah.

Me : But not for His chosen ones. Remember Auschwitz?

---

[48] *Dr. Strangelove, or How I Learned to Stop Worrying and Love the Bomb.*

[49] Pink Floyd, *Bike.*

[50] T.S. Eliot, *The Love Song of J. Alfred Prufrock* (1917).

Jack : Then you could do an experiment. Have two families, each one living in a nice white house, exactly as you described. The families must be ignorant of one another, but you can flit between your—how shall I say?—your 'vice-regal capitals', just as the mood takes you. For one family, educate the children only about the here and now. Birds and bees and rabbits and trees, that sort of thing. For the other family, include a smattering of history and genealogy and divinity in the children's curriculum. Monitor their progress, and if one family turns to the dark side, you can request your machines to... implement the ethical option. Humanely, of course.

Me : Of course. Humanely, like in Auschwitz.

Jack : You could call the two families the 'Eloi' and the 'Morlocks'.

Me : Great. Sounds so much nicer than 'sheep' and 'goats'.

Jack : So that's settled, then?

Me : I don't know. I just don't know.

Chorus : Oh, and while the king was looking down
The jester stole his thorny crown
The courtroom was adjourned
No verdict was returned.[51]

The black art

Jack : Roger? Are you there?

Me : I'm here.

Jack : I noticed that you became quite animated back there.

Me : Back where?

Jack : Where you were talking about John Millar.

Me : Well, he's a fascinating person.

Jack : Indeed?

Me : Oh, yes! There's so much to tell about him! He was a sociologist, a century before anyone knew the meaning of the word; he was an active opponent of slavery, at a time when Glasgow was being taken over by *nouveau riche* plantation owners; he supported the independence of the American colonies, at a time when such a view was held to be treasonable; he upheld the rights of women, at a time when

[51] Don McLean, *American Pie*.

they were traded as property; and he was a fine family man, into the bargain. But the *really* interesting thing about him is his book, *The Origin of the Distinction of Ranks*. It's got five main chapters in which Millar identifies five main 'ranks' in society—how about that!

Jack : You don't say? And do they map to the five IDEAL learning styles?

Me : Sort of… I need to do a little more research…

Chorus : Karma police
Arrest this man
He talks in maths
He buzzes like a fridge
He's like a de-tuned radio.[52]

Jack : By the Devil's dubious dungarees, be quiet! Can I make a suggestion, Roger?

Me : What?

Jack : I think your readers will be much more interested in another of your ancestors.

Me : Really? Which one?

Jack : John Napier.

Me : Napier—of course! Now, he was a *real* genius. Where to begin, I wonder?

Jack : How about logarithms?

Me : Oh yes—logarithms, his great invention! Imagine coming out with such a brilliant idea and then… and then having to *sell* it to the ignorant, bigoted, tyrannical, brutish population! But that's exactly what he did, right at the beginning of his book on the subject[53]:

> To the Most Noble and Hopeful Prince CHARLES, only son of the High and Mighty James, King of Great Britain, France, and Ireland; Prince of Wales, Duke of York and Rothesay; Great Steward of Scotland, and Lord of the Islands.
>
> MOST NOBLE PRINCE. Seeing there is neither study nor any kind of learning that doth more acuate and stir up generous and heroical wits to excellent and eminent affairs; and contrariewise, that doth more deject and keep down sottish and dull minds than the mathematics; it is no marvel that learned and magnanimous princes in all former ages have taken great delight in them, and that unskilful and slothful men

---

[52] Radiohead, *Karma Police*.

[53] John Napier, *Mirifici Logarithmorum Canonis Descriptio* (1614).

have always pursued them with most cruel hatred, as utter enemies to their ignorance and sluggishness. Why then may not this my new invention (seeing it abhorreth blunt and base natures,) seek and fly unto your Highness' most noble disposition and patronage? and especially seeing this new course of LOGARITHMS doth clean take away all the difficulty that heretofore hath been in mathematicall calculations, (which otherwise might have been distasteful to your worthy towardness,) and is so fitted to help the weakness of memory, that by means thereof it is easy to resolve more mathematical questions in one hour's space, than otherwise by that wonted and commonly received manner of sines, tangents and secants, can be done even in a whole day. And, therefore, this invention (I hope) will be so much the more acceptable to your Highness, as it yieldeth a more easy and speedy way of accompt. For what can be more delightful and more excellent in any kind of learning than to dispatch honourable and profound matters, exactly, readily, and without loss of either time or labour. I crave, therefore, most gracious Prince, that you would, according to your gentleness, accept of this gift, though small and far beneath the height of your deservings and worth, as a pledge and token of my humble service. Which, if I understand that you do, you shall, even in this regard only, encourage me, that I am now almost spent with sickness, shortly to attempt other matters perhaps greater than these, and more worthy so great a Prince. In the mean while, the Supreme King of Kings, and Lord of Lords, long defend and preserve to us the great lights of Great Britain, your renowned parents, and yourself, the noble branch of so noble a stem, and the hope of our future tranquility. To Him be given all honour and glory.

Your Highness' most devoted Servant,

John NEPAIR.

Me : Notice that Napier dedicated his mathematical masterpiece to Prince Charles—the same Prince Charles who, as Charles I, King of England and Scotland and whatnot, lost his head whilst attempting to introduce the very Popery that Napier loathed. And what a loathing! These are the 'propositions' of Napier's *Plaine Discovery*[54]:

THE FIRST PROPOSITION. In propheticall dates of daies, weekes, moneths and yeares, every common propheticall day is taken for a yeare.

2. PROPOSITION. The Seven Trumpets of the 8. 9. and 11. chapters, and the Seven Vials of the 16. chapter are all one.
3. PROPOSITION. The starre and locusts of the fift trumpet, are not the great Antichrist and his Cleargie, but the Dominator of the Turkes and his armie, who began their dominion, in anno Christi 1051.

---

[54] John Napier, *A Plaine Discovery of the whole Revelation of Saint John* (1593, revised 1611).

4. PROPOSITION. The Kings of the East, or foure Angels, specified in the sixt trumpet or sixt vial. cap.9. & 16. are the foure nations, Mahometanes beyond and about Euphrates, who began their empire by Ottoman, in the year of Christ, 1296 or thereabout.
5. PROPOSITION. The space of the fift trumpet or vial, containeth 245. yeares, and so much also, every one of the rest of the trumpets or vials doe containe.
6. PROPOSITION. The first Trumpet or Viall began at the Jubilie, in Anno Christi, 71.
7. PROPOSITION. The last of the seven seales, and first of the seven Trumpets or vials, begin both at once, in Anno 71.
8. PROPOSITION. The first seale beginneth to be opened, in Anno Christi 29. compleat.
9. PROPOSITION. Every Seale must containe the space of seven years.
10. PROPOSITION. The last trumpet and Vial beginneth anno Christi 1541. and should end in anno Christi, 1786.
11. PROPOSITION. The seven Thunders, whose voices are commanded to be sealed, and not written (cap. 10.4) are the seven Angels, specified cap. 14. verse 6. 8. 9. 14. 15. 17. 18.
12. PROPOSITION. The first of the seven thunders, and the seventh and last Trumpet or vial, begin both at once in Anno 1541.
13. PROPOSITION. Every one of the first three thundering Angels containeth a Jubilie, and then the last foure all at once compleateth the day of judgement.
14. PROPOSITION. The day of Gods judgement appeares to fall betwixt the yeares of Christ, 1699. and 1700.
15. PROPOSITION. The 42. moneths, a thousand and two hundreth and threescore prophetical daies, three great daies and a halfe, and a time, times, and a halfe a time mentioned in Daniel, & in the Revelation, are all one date.
16. PROPOSITION. The 42. moneths, 1260. propheticall daies, three great diaes and a halfe: And a time, times and halfe a time, signifieth every one of them, 1260. Juliane yeares.
17. PROPOSITION. The description of the throne of God in the fourth chapter, is not the description of the majestie of God in heaven, but of his true religion, where in he is authorised and sits in the throne among his holy elect on earth.
18. PROPOSITION. The 24. Elders, are the 24. bookes of the old Testament, with the 24. writers and (metonymice) all the true professours thereof.
19. PROPOSITION. The foure beasts are the foure Evangels with al the true writers and professours thereof.
20. PROPOSITION. Gods Temple, although in heaven, is also taken for his holy Church among his heavenly Elect upon earth, and (metonymice) for the whole contents thereof.

21. PROPOSITION. The two witnesses mentioned (Rev. 11) are the two Testaments, and (metonymice) the whole true professours thereof.
22. PROPOSITION. The Woman clad with the Sunne (chap. 12) is the true Church of God.
23. PROPOSITION. The whore who in the Revelation is stiled spiritual Babylon, is not reallie Babylon, but the very present citie of Rome.
24. PROPOSITION. The great ten-horned beast, is the whole bodie of the Latine Empire, whereof the Antichrist is a part.
25. PROPOSITION. The two horned Beast, is the Antichrist and his kingdome, it alone.
26. PROPOSITION. The Pope is that only Antichrist, prophecied of, in particular.
27. PROPOSITION. The Image, marke, name, and number of the beast, are of the first great Romane beast, and whole Latine empire universallie, and not of the second beast, or Antichrist alone in particular.
28. PROPOSITION. The Image of the Beast, is these degenerate Princes, that in name onely were called Romane Emperours, and were neither Romans of blood, nor Emperours of Magnanimitie.
29. PROPOSITION. The name of the beast expressed by the number 666. (cap. 13) is the name λατεινοζ onely.
30. PROPOSITION. The marke of the Romane beast, is that invisible profession of servitude and obedience, that his subjects have professed to his Empire, since the first beginning thereof, noted afterward by the Pope, with divers visible markes.
31. PROPOSITION. The visible markes of the Beast, are the abused characters, of χξζ and crosses of al kindes, taken out of the number of the first beasts name.
32. PROPOSITION. Gog is the Pope, and Magog is the Turks and Mahometanes.
33. PROPOSITION. The armies of Gog and Magog (chap. 20.) are all one with the two adversarie armies of the sixt Trumpet, or sixt Viall.
34. PROPOSITION. The thousand yeares that Sathan was bound (Revel. 20.) began in An. Christi 300. or thereabout.
35. PROPOSITION. The Devils bondage a thousand yeares (cap. 20.) is no waies else, but from stirring up of universal warres among the nations.
36. PROPOSITION. The 1260. yeares of the Antichrists universall raigne over Christians, begins about the yeare of Christ 300. or 316. at the farthest.

Me : Napier was the hereditary poulterer to the king, the keeper of a sinister black cock, and the poisoner of his neighbour's pigeons.

He divined buried treasure for a robber baron. He invented a wide variety of secret weapons[55]:

Anno Domini 1596, the 7 of June, Secrett Inventionis, proffitabill and necessary in theis dayes for defence of this Iland, and withstanding of strangers, enemies of God's truth and religion.

FIRST, the invention, proofe and perfect demonstration, geometricall and algebricall, of a burning mirrour, which, receving the dispersed beames of the sonne, doth reflex the same beames alltogether united and concurring priselie in one mathematicall point, in the which point most necessarelie it ingendreth fire, with an evident demonstration of their error who affirmeth this to be made a parabolik section.

The use of this invention serveth for burning of the enemies shipps at whatsoever appointed distance.

SECONDLIE, The invention and sure demonstration of another mirrour which receiving the dispersed beames of any materiall fier or flame yealdeth allsoe the former effect, and serveth for the like use.

THIRDLIE, The invention and visible demonstration of a piece of artillery, which, shott, passeth not linallie through the enemie, destroying onlie those that stand on the randon thereof, and fra them forth flying idly, as utheris do; but passeth superficially, ranging abrode within the whole appointed place, and not departing furth of the place till it hath executed his whole strength, by destroying those that be within the boundes of the said place.

The use hereof not onlie serveth greatlie against the armie of the enemy on land, but alsoe by sea it serveth to destroy, and cut downe, and one shott the whole mastes and tackling of so many shipps as be within the appointed boundes, as well abried as in large, so long as any strength at all remayneth.

FOURTHLIE, The invention of a round chariot of mettle made of the proofe of dooble muskett, which motion shall be by those that be within the same, more easie, more light, and more spedie by much then so manie armed men would be otherwayes.

The use hereof as well, in moving, serveth to breake the array of the enemies battle and to make passage, as also in staying and abiding within the enemies battle, it serveth to destroy the environed enemy by continuall charge and shott of harquebush through small hoalles; the enemie in the meanetime being abased and altogether uncertaine what defence or pursuit to use against a moving mouth of mettle.

These inventiones, besides devises of sayling under the water, with divers other devises and stratagemes for harming of the enemyes, by the grace of God and worke of expert craftsmen I hope to perform.

JO. NEPER, Fear of Marchistoun.

---

[55] John Napier, paper endorsed *Mr. Stewart, secretes inventiones de la guerre le mois de Juillet, 1596*, quoted in Mark Napier, *Memoirs of Napier of Merchiston* (Blackwood 1834).

Me : Pretty impressive, eh?

Jack : Very impressive! 'Fear of Marchistoun', eh?

Me : And you'll like this:

> Adjoining the mill of Gartness are the remains of an old house in which John Napier of Merchiston, Inventor of Logarithms, resided a great part of his time, (for some years,) when he was making his calculations. It is reported that the noise of the cascade being constant, never gave him uneasiness; but that the clack of the mill, which was only occasional, greatly disturbed his thoughts. He was therefore, when in deep study, sometimes under the necessity of desiring the miller to stop the mill, that the train of his ideas might not be interrupted. He used frequently to walk out in his night-gown and cap. This, with some things which to the vulgar appeared rather odd, fixed on him the character of a warlock. It was firmly believed, and currently reported, that he was in compact with the Devil; and that the time he spent in study was spent in learning the black art, and holding conversations with Old Nick.[56]

Me : Isn't that amazing? At the most dangerous time in his nation's history, when people were being accused of witchcraft and were burned at the stake for—for *nothing*—there's John Napier, Laird of Merchiston, holding conversations with Old Nick. Incredible!

Jack : And that's not all, is it?

Me : What do you mean?

Jack : I think you should tell your readers what Mark Twain said about John Napier.

Me : Hmm.

Jack : Don't want to?

Me : Not much.

Jack : Then I'll do it. The following account[57] is from the period antedating the Flood. It is taken from the diary of a Lady of the Blood, Third Grade, and it concerns the discoveries of Reginald Selkirk, a.k.a. the Mad Prophet, a.k.a. the Mad Philosopher, who has been investigating "the wonderful new force, liquified thought". The diary quotes the Mad Philosopher verbatim:

> "I am of the opinion that the development of this mysterious new force has not yet proceeded beyond the infancy stage. I think we know but little about it now, compared with what we shall know a few decades

---

[56] Rev. David Ure, 'Account of the Parish of Killearn, Stirlingshire', *Statistical Account*, vol. XVI, p. 104, quoted in Mark Napier, *ibid.*

[57] Mark Twain, *ibid.*

hence. Why, it may turn out to be the renowned and lamented Lost Force of old tradition! And it isn't mere tradition, there is history for it. You know the tradition yourself, gracious Excellency—like the rest of the world—but you do not know the history. It has just been deciphered from the clay archives of an exhumed city of the Double Continent; and when it is published the nations will perceive that when the amazing man called 'the Prodigy,' who rose out of obscurity in the middle of the fifth century and in a few years conquered the world and brought all its kingdoms under his imperial sceptre, where they still abide under the sceptre of his son to-day, had formidable help in his stupendous work from a source outside of his colossal genius for war, statesmanship and administration, unrivaled and unapproachable as these confessedly were. That source was the agent known to tradition, romance and poetry as the Lost Force. It is true that the humble young shoemaker did sweep the Double Continent from end to end with fire and sword without that help, and establish his autocratic sway over all its monarchies by merely the faculties that were born in him, and that he handled a billion men in the field under a million generals trained by himself and subject to his sole will unhampered by meddling ministries and legislatures, and left mountains of dead and wounded upon his battle fields, but he subdued the rest of the globe without spilling blood, except in a single instance.

"That mystery is explained, now, by the clay records. It came to his knowledge that one Napeer, an obscure person but learned in science, had stated in his will that he had discovered a means whereby he could sweep a whole army out of existence in an instant, but that he would not reveal his secret, since war was already terrible enough and he would not be party to the augmentation of its destructiveness.

"The shoemaker-emperor said, 'The man was foolish—his invention would abolish war altogether,' and commanded that all papers left behind by him should be brought to him. He found the formula, mastered its details, then destroyed it. He privately manufactured that tremendous agent, and went out alone against the sovereigns of the eastern world, with it in his pocket. Only one army ever came against him. It formed itself in battle array in a great plain, and at a distance of twelve miles he blew it into the air, leaving no vestige of it behind but a few rags and buttons.

"He claimed the sovereignty of the globe, and it was accorded him without an objecting voice. As you are aware, his reign of thirty years was a reign of peace; then, by accident, he blew himself up with his machine, along with one of his vice-regal capitals, and his formidable secret died with him. Then the dreadful wars began again, and for the world's sins they still continue. But the universal empire which he established was founded in wisdom and strength, and to-day his son sits as securely upon its throne as he did when he mounted it so many centuries ago."

Jack : Now *that's* what I call the black art! What do you think, Rog?

Jack : Roger?

Jack : Roger? Are you there?
Chorus : We have no Woger![58]
Me : I don't need no arms around me
And I don't need no drugs to calm me.
I have seen the writing on the wall.
Don't think I need anything at all.
No! Don't think I'll need anything at all.
All in all it was all just bricks in the wall.
All in all you were all just bricks in the wall.[59]
Jack : Frankenstein, Wolfman, Dracula, shit, it's over.[60]
Chorus : It doesn't make for sanity, does it, living with the devil.[61]
Me : And I find it kind of funny
I find it kind of sad
The dreams in which I'm dying
Are the best I've ever had.[62]
Chorus : He's got away from us, Jack.[63]
Jack : Frankly, my dear, do I look like I give a damn?[64]
Chorus : Oh, and as I watched him on the stage
My hands were clenched in fists of rage.
No angel born in hell
Could break that Satan's spell.
And as the flames climbed high into the night
To light the sacrificial rite
I saw Satan laughing with delight
The day the music died.[65]

The Devil has spoken through me`
There will be no rest for anyone any more

---

[58] *Life of Brian.*
[59] Pink Floyd, *Another Brick in the Wall, Part 3.*
[60] *I, Robot.*
[61] Daphne du Maurier, *Rebecca* (1938).
[62] Tears for Fears, *Mad World.*
[63] *Brazil.*
[64] *Gone with the Wind, Casino Royale.*
[65] Don McLean, *American Pie.*

5. Who?

How that which is proposed revives the insights of past masters; IDEAL learning styles; The individual; The team; Society; Values and symbols; Ancient myth and modern fiction; Rites of passage; Rebirth; Mystery; Overcoming the monster; Romance; Comedy.

How that which is proposed revives the insights of past masters

The principles governing human and machine intelligence are established in *Principia Intellegentia* by means of 'IDEAL', a high-level description of how humans learn. The derivation of IDEAL and detailed investigations of its properties are given elsewhere in *Principia Intellegentia*. The purpose here is to relate IDEAL's perspective to key observations of intelligent behaviour in humans; machine intelligence being of less relevance, since it has yet to develop to a comparable level. To this end, the analysis focusses on 'IDEAL learning styles', five characteristic styles of enquiry, each of which arises from the hypothetical dominance of one of the five functional components making up IDEAL. After a brief description of the main features of IDEAL learning styles, the investigation reviews a range of topics in the social sciences and humanities: commencing with the individual learning experience; then looking at societal groups of increasing size and complexity; then considering value systems, motifs, symbols, and gods; and, finally, mythological archetypes and their implementation as stereotypical characters in literature and the dramatic arts. Throughout this investigation, the emphasis is on finding commonalities between the different perspectives. Accordingly, both IDEAL and the received wisdom of 'past masters' are taken 'as read'. To compensate for this absence of critical analysis, efforts have been made to compare IDEAL with observations and opinions that are generally accepted as insightful, and to steer clear of less-established minority views.

IDEAL learning styles

Definition. 'IDEAL' is an acronym for 'Iterative Dialectic Engine for Automated Learning'. It also stands for the five operational components denoted **I**, **D**, **E**, **A** and **L** in the following flow diagram.

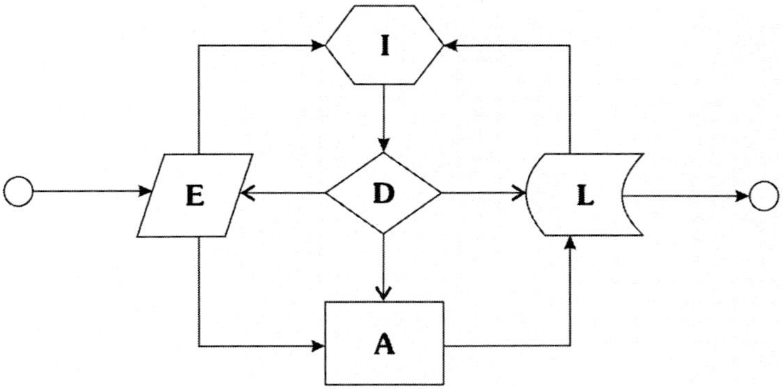

Definition. The five IDEAL learning styles are as follows:

1. The *Empiricist*. Empiricists have a preference for using the IDEAL Evidence component **E**.
2. The *Idealist*. Idealists have a preference for using the IDEAL Iteration component **I**.
3. The *Theorist*. Theorists have a preference for using the IDEAL Algorithm component **A**.
4. The *Activist*. Activists have a preference for using the IDEAL Decision component **D**.
5. The *Conformist*. Conformists have a preference for using the IDEAL Log component **L**.

Notation. It is convenient to summarise these and further mappings in tabular form, thus:

IDEAL component		IDEAL learning style
E	Evidence	Empiricist
I	Iteration	Idealist
A	Algorithm	Theorist
D	Decision	Activist
L	Log	Conformist

Notation. The names of the learning styles relate to their preferred sources of learning:

1. Empiricists have a preference for learning through *observation*, which is closely related to the data-gathering function of the IDEAL Evidence component.
2. Idealists have a preference for learning through comparing and correlating information within a pre-existing *framework*, which is closely related to the data comparison function of the IDEAL Iteration component.
3. Theorists have a preference for learning through constructing and operating representative *models*, which is closely related to the analytical function of the IDEAL Algorithm component.
4. Activists have a preference for learning through *action and reaction*, which is closely related to the control function of the IDEAL Decision component.
5. Conformists have a preference for learning through *reference* to an established authority, which is closely related to the data storage function of the IDEAL Log component.

IDEAL learning style	Source of learning
Empiricist	Observation
Idealist	Framework
Theorist	Models
Activist	Action and reaction
Conformist	Reference

Proposition. IDEAL learning styles may be associated with distinctive personality traits:

IDEAL learning style	Personality factor
Empiricist	Openness
Idealist	Neuroticism
Theorist	Agreeableness
Activist	Extroversion
Conformist	Conscientiousness

IDEAL learning style	Virtue	Vice
Empiricist	Enquiring	Interfering
Idealist	Detached	Passive
Theorist	Resourceful	Pedantic
Activist	Dynamic	Controlling
Conformist	Loyal	Reactionary

IDEAL learning style	Positive emotion	Negative emotion
Empiricist	Attraction	Disgust
Idealist	Joy	Sorrow
Theorist	Inspiration	Fear
Activist	Excitement	Anger
Conformist	Love	Hate

IDEAL learning style	Positive reaction	Negative reaction
Empiricist	Embrace	Flee
Idealist	Proclaim	Lament
Theorist	Create	Fake
Activist	Act	Threaten
Conformist	Serve	Oppose

Proposition. *Omnis extremus, sed non in extremis.*[1] There are significant learning benefits in engaging with all five IDEAL learning styles in a balanced fashion. There is a benefit, too, in switching between different learning styles at frequent intervals. Conversely, excessive dependence on any one learning style may be associated with an 'extremist' approach to seeking after truth, and has even been suggested as the basis of a taxonomy for mental illness:

IDEAL learning style	'Extremist' truth seeker	Caricature
Empiricist	Empirical scientist	Explorer
Idealist	Mystic	Guru
Theorist	Theoretical scientist	Philosopher
Activist	Activist	Conqueror
Conformist	Religious devotee	Priest(ess)

[1] "To be every extremist—but none too much."

IDEAL learning style	Mental illness	Caricature
Empiricist	Childhood psychiatric disorders	Fox
Idealist	Anxiety/adjustment disorders	La Rage
Theorist	Delusional disorders	Werewolf
Activist	Personality disorders	Red Dog
Conformist	Mood disorders	Black Dog

Proposition. As a person grows to maturity, he or she typically passes through five 'ages of man' characterised by the five IDEAL learning styles in the following sequence: (i) Empiricist; (ii) Idealist; (iii) Activist; (iv) Conformist; (v) Theorist. In this interpretation, 'mature behaviour' at any age may be defined as the extent to which a person can manifest its virtues while resisting its vices.

Definition. 'IDEAL man' is that person who has lived by the maxim *Omnis extremus, sed non in extremis* through all the ages of man. This definition applies to men and women equally.

Proposition. "The States are as the men are; they grow out of human characters." [2] That is, social structures such as the family, the community, the workplace, the market-place and the nation-state each reflect the characteristics of the five IDEAL learning styles.

Investigation. Introduced for its convenience, the tabular format is a surprisingly powerful means of summarising complex relationships between concepts. Too powerful, indeed, as it facilitates the lazy assumption that any given description or system may be expressed in terms of a set of five 'factors', regardless of the availability of supporting evidence. The absurdity of this approach can be illustrated by compiling an arbitrary list of five 'things' that may be used as factors, for example:

1. Five fingers on each hand—still the basis of our counting system.
2. Five senses (sight, hearing, taste, touch, smell).
3. Five elements (earth, air, fire, water, quintessence).
4. Five Platonic solids (cube, tetrahedron, octahedron, dodecahedron, icosahedron).
5. Five planets known to ancient astronomers (Mercury, Venus, Mars, Jupiter, Saturn).
6. Stars on national flags are invariably five-pointed. These include the single star on the flags of Algeria, Burkina Faso, Cameroon, Central

[2] Plato, *The Republic* (*circa* 350 BC), tr. Benjamin Jowett (1856-93).

African Republic, Chile, Democratic Republic of Congo, Djibouti, Ethiopia, Ghana, Guinea-Bissau, Liberia, Morocco, Northern Mariana Islands, Pakistan, Senegal, Somalia, Surinam, Togo, Tunisia, Turkey; multiple stars on the flags of Iraq, New Zealand, Saint Kitts and Nevis, Samoa, Solomon Islands, Syria, USA; the communist star on the Chinese, Soviet, Cuban and Vietnamese flags; and so on. Incidentally, the five points of the communist star represent the five sectors of society (youths, workers, peasants, intellectuals, soldiers). Also, starfish have five legs.

7. The map of the world on the UN flag has five concentric circles of latitude. There are five permanent members of the UN Security Council (China, France, Russia, UK, USA).
8. The Olympic flag has five rings, representing five continents.
9. The pentathlon (running, jumping, wrestling, discus, javelin).
10. The five D's of *Dodgeball* (dodge, duck, dip, dive and dodge).
11. In the UK there are five nationwide terrestrial television channels and five nationwide BBC radio channels.
12. *The Famous Five* series by Enid Blyton.
13. Five, V, The Jackson Five, Dave Clark Five, Five Americans, Five Man Electrical Band, Motor City Five, Five Blind Boys of Alabama, Band of Five Names, and so on.
14. The pentatonic musical scale.
15. The Jewish Pentateuch (Genesis, Exodus, Leviticus, Numbers, Deuteronomy).
16. The five duties of Islam (recognition of God, prayer, almsgiving, fasting, pilgrimage).
17. The five K's of Sikhism (uncut hair, comb, knife, wristcord, underclothes).
18. The five castes of Hinduism, that is, four brahminical castes (brahmins, kshatriyas, vaishyas, shudras) plus outcast pariahs.
19. The pentacle or pentagram.
20. A pentagon.
21. The Pentagon in Washington DC. Apparently, the Washington monument is 555 ft high.

The list is endless, and it offers limitless opportunities to the unscrupulous. For example, 'fiver' numerology features prominently in Dan Brown's *The Da Vinci Code*. FACT: 'Brown' has five letters. 'B' is for 'bee', buzzing around as it explores its territory like an *Empiricist*; 'R' is for 'round', signifying completion, unity, the single framework of the *Idealist*;

'O' is for 'ooh!', the *Theorist*'s expression on making a creative discovery; 'W' is for 'war', the *Activist*'s answer to any problem; and 'N' is for 'n', a letter to be found only in '*Conformist*':

IDEAL learning style	Brown
Empiricist	B
Idealist	R
Theorist	O
Activist	W
Conformist	N

This trivial numerology may seem no more than a bit of harmless fun, but it can quickly become very serious indeed. Firstly, the unthinking conviction that there *must* be a complete set of related factors underlying momentous events directly generates the alternative 'explanations' that we call 'conspiracy theories'. Thus we have, for example, Philby, Burgess, Maclean, Blunt and... the 'Fifth Man'. More recently, the four suicide bombers who struck three tube trains and one bus in London on '7/7' (7 July 2005) were so alike in their youth and inexperience, they *must* have been groomed in their task by a 'master-bomber': a foolish assumption, in retrospect, but at the time it did not seem so foolish, and indeed this assumption appears to have influenced the direction of police enquiries. Secondly, even where it is generally accepted that there is a well-defined set of related factors underlying particular descriptions or systems, a careless misallocation can have serious repercussions. I would hate to be on the hit list of a militant Trekkie who disagreed with my characterisation of Captain Kirk as an 'Activist', for example. To guard against these and similar dangers, five criteria have been established for the acceptance of a theory:

1. Does it correspond to the known facts?
2. Can it be understood in the context of its frame of reference?
3. Does it compare with established theories, both in the manner of its derivation and in the finesse of its application?
4. Does it make claims or predictions that can be tested?
5. Has it taken account of the current literature in the field?

It is suggested that *all* of these criteria must be satisfied for a theory to be deemed acceptable. Clearly, a 'theory' based solely on the identification of five factors in a description or system is unlikely to survive this examination. This sceptical outlook must always be borne in mind when reading the following tabulations mapping IDEAL learning styles to "the received wisdom of past masters". Indeed, as befits the suspension of critical analysis that is the stated operating framework of the present discussion, *none* of the following tabulations have been tested using all of these criteria. As indicated above, the purpose here is not to lay down uncontestable truths, rather it is to suggest tentative correlations between IDEAL learning styles and established insights.

Disclaimer. What follows is personal opinion; it is not to be treated as established fact.

The individual

How should I live my life? In times past the answer seemed clear: "Thou shalt love the Lord thy God with all thy heart, and with all thy soul, and with all thy strength, and with all thy mind; and thy neighbour as thyself."[3] And what of taxes? "Render to Caesar the things that are Caesar's, and to God the things that are God's."[4] What about work? "Get a good job with more pay and you're OK."[5] Yes, but why does that unconventional bass rhythm unsettle me? Do I *really* have to get a mortgage? What about marriage? The upbringing of children? Why conform to the conventional life at all, why not live in a monastery or wander the earth as a free spirit? I've heard great things about magic mushrooms. Perhaps the answer isn't so clear, after all.

Proposition. The human brain has five main parts, corresponding to the five components of IDEAL. If the brain is to remain healthy, all five parts must be nurtured carefully and in a balanced fashion—none to the exclusion of the others. Hence the maxim, *Omnis extremus, sed non in extremis*.

Investigation. "To be every extremist—but none too much." What does this mean in practice? Can anything be learnt from the lives of others? What do the idealised examples of Buddha or Jesus or Muhammad mean to me *as an individual*? Very little, I fear. They were extraordinary individuals and I am not. They provide no example of how to live an ordinary life. Perhaps, for a good example, I should look closer to home: my parents, their parents, and the generations before them. I am fortunate to have a well-documented ancestry. My father's grandmother's grandmother's grandfather was John Millar:

---

[3] *Luke* 10:27 (KJV).

[4] *Mark* 12:17 (KJV).

[5] Pink Floyd, *Money*.

> **Millar, John** (1735-1801) A leading figure in the Scottish Enlightenment of the late eighteenth century, who is sometimes acknowledged as an early sociologist, on the grounds that his essay on *The Origin of the Distinction of Ranks* (1771) offers a theory of the evolution of societies (which connects forms of property-holding to types of authority and government), and an early account of the division of labour in society.[6]

Lehmann[7] makes the following observations on Millar as a person:

> It has already been indicated that Millar was very much a family man. A few further glimpses into his domestic life will prove revealing. Besides being a man of sanguine temperament, though self-restrained at times to a fault, he was a man of very fine sensibilities and always entered "with the greatest warmth into the feelings of every person around him". He attended personally with great care to the education, both moral and intellectual, of all of his children, and as they grew up, took them often into his confidence in his own intellectual pursuits. To quote his biographer:
>
>> He had long been in the habit of consulting Mrs. Millar with regard to his literary works, and some of his children being [by the time his *Historical View* was in composition] competent judges of composition, he occasionally read over to his family the most amusing and interesting passages, and listened with much attention to their various criticisms. By these means, besides increasing the mutual confidence which ever subsisted between him and his family, he had the means of detecting any little errors which had escaped his own observation, and formed the taste while he improved the judgement of his children.
>
> Another echo of his family life, with four boarding students in residence, will be found in these notes from the *Melbourne Papers*. In a letter to his mother, Lady Melbourne, Frederick, the younger of the Lamb brothers, writes—this was in the last year of Millar's life—"All the ladies [here] are contaminated with an itch for philosophy and learning, and such a set of fools it was never my lot to see... They are all philosophers..." That this matter of "fools" is not to be taken too literally, and that such "philosophy" did not rob this enlarged family life of all gaiety, is shown by the next observation. Besides remarking that one of the daughters was "very pretty", and that his oldest brother William (the future Prime Minister) was reading poetry to these young ladies all the time, he gives an account of table manners and table scenes, observing among other things:
>
>> One exclusive custom I have remarked here is a devilish good one which ought to be adopted everywhere. After cheese they

---

[6] Gordon Marshall (ed.), *The Oxford Concise Dictionary of Sociology* (Oxford 1994).

[7] William Lehmann, *John Millar of Glasgow 1735-1801, His Life and Thought and his Contributions to Sociological Analysis* (Cambridge 1960).

> hand around the table a bottle of whisky and another of brandy, and the whole company, males and females, in general, indulge in a dram. It is very comfortable and exhilarating, and affords an opportunity for many jokes.

Sounds like fun! Then why, at the same time, did Millar risk everything with his unfashionably liberal views concerning the abolition of slavery and the independence of the American colonies?

Also amongst my ancestors is John Napier (1550-1617), mathematician, inventor, agriculturist, alchemist, astrologer and Presbyterian theologian[8]. Napier undertook these activities in complete isolation, at a time when any display of independence of spirit or originality of intellect placed a person in great danger of being denounced as a heretic or Devil-worshipper and burned at the stake. So why didn't Napier confine himself to mathematics? Why did he feel the need to indulge in secret inventions, prophecy, the black art, and the rest? Why is it that the hallmark of a great mind is not a clever invention (which may have been obtained by chance or deceit), but other 'discoveries', less-renowned and often less-welcome, that always accompany the headline citation like a dark shadow to a brilliant light?

Proposition. A great mind is a free mind. Such a mind wanders through every experience, delighting in the diversity and the unity of nature and ideas, generating descriptions and explanations all the while, some priceless, others worthless. It knows no limits and it is oblivious to danger. However, this freedom of mind does not extend to methodology. On the contrary, it is clear that both Millar and Napier were uncompromising in their application of the methodological rule that *every problem must be scrutinised from each and every perspective*. This is the 'secret of learning': to be every kind of truth seeker, exercising complete freedom of thought—within a rigid methodological framework. In other words: "To be every extremist—but none too much."

---

[8] For a more detailed account of Napier's exploits, see **4. Why?**

Example. Advice to a loved son.

Rudyard Kipling, *If*— (1895)	IDEAL learning style
If you can keep your head when all about you	Activist
Are losing theirs and blaming it on you,	Activist
If you can trust yourself when all men doubt you	Activist
But make allowance for their doubting too;	Activist
If you can wait and not be tired by waiting,	Idealist
Or being lied about, don't deal in lies,	Idealist
Or being hated, don't give way to hating,	Idealist
And yet don't look too good, nor talk too wise:	Theorist
If you can dream—and not make dreams your master;	Theorist
If you can think—and not make thoughts your aim;	Theorist
If you can meet with Triumph and Disaster	Idealist
And treat those two impostors just the same;	Idealist
If you can bear to hear the truth you've spoken	Idealist
Twisted by knaves to make a trap for fools,	Idealist
Or watch the things you gave your life to, broken,	Idealist
And stoop and build 'em up with worn-out tools:	Activist
If you can make one heap of all your winnings	Activist
And risk it on one turn of pitch-and-toss,	Activist
And lose, and start again at your beginnings	Activist
And never breathe a word about your loss;	Activist
If you can force your heart and nerve and sinew	Conformist
To serve your turn long after they are gone,	Conformist
And so hold on when there is nothing in you	Conformist
Except the Will which says to them: 'Hold on!'	Conformist
If you can talk with crowds and keep your virtue,	Empiricist
Or walk with kings—nor lose the common touch,	Empiricist
If neither foes nor loving friends can hurt you,	Empiricist
If all men count with you, but none too much;	Empiricist
If you can fill the unforgiving minute	IDEAL man
With sixty seconds' worth of distance run,	IDEAL man
Yours is the Earth and everything that's in it,	IDEAL man
And—which is more—you'll be a Man, my son!	IDEAL man

Example. *The five virtues of chivalry.* It is said that the medieval code of chivalry required knights to adhere to the five virtues of charity, courtesy, fellowship, generosity and purity. Apparently Sir Gawain embodied all five virtues and was considered to be the 'perfect knight'. It is not known whether his example has been matched by any non-mythical knight.

IDEAL learning style	Chivalric virtue
Empiricist	Fellowship
Idealist	Purity
Theorist	Generosity
Activist	Charity
Conformist	Courtesy

Example. *The Prince.*

> For this reason a prince ought to take care that he never lets anything slip from his lips that is not replete with the above-named five qualities, that he may appear to him who sees and hears him altogether merciful, faithful, humane, upright, and religious.[9]

IDEAL learning style	Princely quality
Empiricist	Humane
Idealist	Religious
Theorist	Upright
Activist	Merciful
Conformist	Faithful

Example. *Body parts.* "A young man who is not a radical has no heart, and an old man who is not a conservative has no head." This saying—attributed to a number of epigrammatists including Oscar Wilde and Georges Clemenceau—highlights the fact that our language is littered with phrases relating our attitudes and responses to body parts and associated functions. It suggests the following mapping:

IDEAL learning style	Faculty
Empiricist	Physical senses
Idealist	Heart
Theorist	Intellect
Activist	Stomach
Conformist	Memory

---

[9] Nicolò Machiavelli, *The Prince* (*circa* 1505), tr. W. K. Marriott (1908).

Example. *Future minds.* Howard Gardner has identified five 'minds for the future'[10]:

IDEAL learning style	Mind
Empiricist	Respectful
Idealist	Synthesising
Theorist	Creating
Activist	Disciplined
Conformist	Ethical

Example. *Hierarchy of needs.* Abraham Maslow[11] has identified a five-layer pyramid of human needs, where the fulfilment of each layer is dependent upon the prior fulfilment of those beneath it: (i) Physiological; (ii) Safety; (iii) Love/belonging; (iv) Esteem; (v) Self-actualization. These map as follows:

IDEAL learning style	Need
Empiricist	Physiological
Idealist	Love/belonging
Theorist	Self-actualization
Activist	Esteem
Conformist	Safety

With one exception this hierarchy follows the sequence of five 'ages of man' identified earlier[12]. 'Safety' appears second in Maslow's list, possibly because he is considering primal needs, whereas the initial 'ages of man' assume this secure environment to have been provided by parents or the community.

Investigation. When we place too much emphasis on one learning style, to the exclusion of the others, we can expect a cumulative diminution of understanding and an increased separation from the world and its affairs. In its mildest form this dissociation is a harmless quirk; in more serious cases, it amounts to mental illness. The following examples span this range.

---

[10] Howard Gardner, *Five Minds for the Future* (Harvard 2007).

[11] Abraham Maslow, 'A Theory of Human Motivation', *Psychological Review*, vol. 50, pp. 370-96 (1943).

[12] That is: (i) Empiricist; (ii) Idealist; (iii) Activist; (iv) Conformist; (v) Theorist.

Example. *Television and radio preferences.*

IDEAL learning style	Terrestrial TV	BBC radio
Empiricist	ITV	Radio 1
Idealist	BBC 2	Radio 3
Theorist	Channel 4	Radio 4
Activist	Five	Radio 5 Live
Conformist	BBC 1	Radio 2

Example. *Five types of anorak.* 'Anorak' is a mildly pejorative term for someone (male) who has a spare-time interest or hobby. We know them well:

1. The *Enthusiast*, who enjoys his hobby for its own sake.
2. The *Master*, who is driven to possess the totems of his hobby.
3. The *Perfectionist*, who knows every fine detail of his hobby.
4. The *Ritualist*, whose hobby involves the precise repetition of a set of complex procedures.
5. The *Set-collector*, who is compelled to collect complete sets of totems of his hobby.

IDEAL learning style	Type of anorak
Empiricist	Enthusiast
Idealist	Set-collector
Theorist	Perfectionist
Activist	Master
Conformist	Ritualist

Example. *Five stages of grief.* Elizabeth Kübler-Ross[13] describes five stages in the process by which individuals experience grief and tragedy: (i) Denial; (ii) Anger; (iii) Bargaining; (iv) Depression; (v) Acceptance.

IDEAL learning style	Type of grief
Empiricist	Bargaining
Idealist	Denial
Theorist	Acceptance
Activist	Anger
Conformist	Depression

[13] Elizabeth Kübler-Ross, *On Death and Dying* (Routledge 1973).

Example. *Five types of fool.* Apparently the Jewish Bible contains five different words for 'fool':

1. *Eviyl*, meaning a silly fool.
2. *Keciyl*, meaning a sensual fool.
3. *Luwts*, meaning a scorning fool.
4. *Nabal*, meaning a steadfast fool.
5. *Pethiy*, meaning a simple fool.

IDEAL learning style	Type of fool
Empiricist	Simple
Idealist	Scorning
Theorist	Silly
Activist	Sensual
Conformist	Steadfast

Example. *Five types of stalker.* In a recent study[14], five different types of stalker were defined:

1. *Incompetent suitors*, who are looking for a first date.
2. *Intimacy seekers*, who are in love with their victims and are looking for an intimate relationship.
3. *Predatory stalkers*, who intend a sexual assault.
4. *Rejected suitors*, who are often seeking revenge on an ex-partner.
5. *Resentful stalkers*, who believe that their victims have mistreated them.

IDEAL learning style	Type of stalker
Empiricist	Intimate
Idealist	Resentful
Theorist	Incompetent
Activist	Predatory
Conformist	Rejected

The team

Take a group of perhaps a dozen people drawn from the population at random but around the same age. Give them a task that requires them to work together as a team. Invariably the people in the group will organise

[14] Paul Mullen, Michele Pathé and Rosemary Purcell, *Stalkers and their Victims* (Cambridge 2000).

themselves to fulfil particular roles—without being told to do so. One will start to direct the work, another will gather information, a third will commence on the task itself, and so on. When opting for a particular role, an individual in the group will undoubtedly be guided by his or her preferences, which will have been conditioned by prior training and experience. However, not everyone gets the role they want, and it is remarkable how many individuals are prepared to be flexible in their role—just as long as they have one. Equally, it is remarkable how many individuals become agitated or disaffected if they are unable to agree on the distribution of roles. It is almost as if there is a set of team roles, implicit and undefined but nevertheless clear and distinct within some kind of 'collective unconscious', which people feel compelled to adopt for themselves and impose on others, in order to feel safe and secure.

Proposition. *Team roles*. One way of assessing a management structure is in terms of Belbin team roles[15]. These nine roles appear to map to the five IDEAL learning styles as follows:

IDEAL learning style	Belbin team role
Empiricist	Resource investigator
Idealist	Monitor/evaluator, Completer/finisher
Theorist	Plant, Specialist
Activist	Co-ordinator, Shaper
Conformist	Implementer, Teamworker

Alternatively, for an office environment, the following synonyms seem to be appropriate:

IDEAL learning style	Team role
Empiricist	Information acquisition
Idealist	Conceptualist
Theorist	Technical expert
Activist	Leader
Conformist	Researcher

[15] Meredith Belbin, *Team Roles at Work* (Heinemann 1993).

Similarly, Peter Senge identifies five vital 'disciplines' of a learning organisation[16]:

IDEAL learning style	Discipline
Empiricist	Team learning
Idealist	Building shared vision
Theorist	Mental models
Activist	Personal mastery
Conformist	Systems thinking

Example. *Information sharing in operational headquarters.* Team roles are particularly apparent in highly-organised administrative structures such as military or civil emergency headquarters:

IDEAL learning style	HQ
Empiricist	Information acquisition
Idealist	Advisers
Theorist	Analysts
Activist	Command and control
Conformist	Information retrieval

Example. *Psychological profiling of terrorists.* The following team structure[17] has been proposed for the '7/7' London suicide bombers:

1. The entrepreneur.
2. The drifter.
3. The misfit.
4. The protégé.

To make up the five we include the hypothetical 'master-bomber' that many people assumed was behind the outrage (erroneously, as it turned out):

IDEAL learning style	Terrorist team
Empiricist	Drifter
Idealist	Misfit
Theorist	Master-bomber
Activist	Entrepreneur
Conformist	Protégé

[16] Peter Senge, *The Fifth Discipline—The Art and Practice of the Learning Organization* (Doubleday 1990).

[17] Peter Nessen, Norwegian Defence Research Establishment (2006).

Example. *Roles in the family*. Anecdotally, the role that a person gravitates towards in life appears to be determined by his or her position in their family. This seems to be the case regardless of race, creed or culture[18].

IDEAL learning style	Family member
Empiricist	Middle child(ren)
Idealist	Father
Theorist	Youngest child
Activist	Eldest child
Conformist	Mother

Clearly, as children grow up and start families of their own then they are required to take on new roles. This is part of the maturing process described earlier. Conversely, the breakdown of the conventional family structure removes this maturing imperative on young men (at least), with potentially far-reaching consequences for society as a whole.

Example. *Football teams*. Positions on—and off—the football field often say a great deal about the individuals occupying those positions:

1. Defenders must be robust and resourceful.
2. Goal-keepers must be reliable and predictable.
3. Midfield players must be able to discover their opponents' weaknesses.
4. The team manager must *appear* to have a high degree of insight.
5. Strikers must be ruthlessly efficient.

IDEAL learning style	Position
Empiricist	Midfield
Idealist	Manager
Theorist	Defence
Activist	Striker
Conformist	Goal-keeper

[18] See, for example, *Brideshead Revisited* and *The Simpsons*, analysed below.

Example. *Rock bands.* When they start out, rock bands like to think of themselves as unique and original. It is striking, therefore, how many of them can be caricatured in a simple tabulation:

IDEAL learning style	Rocker
Empiricist	Lead guitar
Idealist	Composer
Theorist	Bass guitar
Activist	Vocalist
Conformist	Percussion

It is possible that these five band parts derive from the five traditional aspects of music:

IDEAL learning style	Music
Empiricist	Harmony
Idealist	Form
Theorist	Timbre
Activist	Melody
Conformist	Rhythm

Since most rock bands have few members, they have a high chance of a mismatch in their team structure: two Activists and no Idealists, for example. This might explain the notorious propensity for rock bands to self-destruct.

Example. *Dysfunctional team roles.* When teams go wrong[19].

IDEAL learning style	Anti-team role
Empiricist	Self-preserver
Idealist	Voice in the wilderness
Theorist	Wimp
Activist	Bully
Conformist	Sidekick

[19] See, for example, *Lord of the Flies* and *The Bridge on the River Kwai*, analysed below.

Society

The development of particular roles within society is a natural consequence of the 'division of labour' which since Adam Smith's *The Wealth of Nations* (1776) has been seen as the basis of economics and the organisation of modern society. Smith's colleague John Millar investigated the relationship between the division of labour and the development of societal roles, but his work was swiftly forgotten after his death and when the field of 'sociology' was inaugurated a century later it took a different direction.

Investigation. *The Origin of the Distinction of Ranks*[20]. Millar's chapter headings identify five 'ranks':

1. "Of the rank and condition of women in different ages."
2. "Of the jurisdiction and authority of a father over his children."
3. "The authority of a Chief over the members of a tribe or village."
4. "The authority of a Sovereign… over a society composed of different tribes or villages."
5. "The authority of a Master over his Servants."

The following observations assist the mapping of Millar's ranks to the IDEAL learning styles:

1. For 'Women', Millar clearly endorses the Conformist role: "Loaded by nature with the first and most immediate concern in rearing and maintaining the children, she is endowed with such dispositions as fit her for the discharge of this important duty, and is at the same time particularly qualified for all such employments as require skill and dexterity more than strength, which are so necessary in the interior management of the family."
2. Normally the 'Father' would take the Idealist role in the family, but Millar does not hold with this tradition. This is clear both from his own example and from his words: "In those European nations which have made the most improvement in commerce and manufactures, great liberty is usually enjoyed by the members of every family; and the children are no farther subjected to the father than seems necessary for their own advantage." Millar's 'Father' is not a sovereign Idealist but a benevolent philosopher, that is, a Theorist.
3. The "chief of a rude tribe" "is at first the commander of their forces, and has merely the direction of their measures during the time of an engagement." That is, the 'Chief' is an Activist.

---

[20] John Millar, *The Origin of the Distinction of Ranks* (third edition, 1779), reprinted in William Lehmann, *ibid.*

4. Consistent with other mappings, the 'Sovereign' occupies the Idealist role. Millar does not subscribe to the notion of the 'divine right' of kings, however: "To say that a king ought to enjoy absolute power because a father has enjoyed it, is to defend one system of oppression by the example of another."
5. Referring to the abolition of slavery, Millar wrote: "In the history of mankind, there is no revolution of greater importance to the happiness of society than this which we have now had occasion to contemplate." There is no place for the 'Master' in Millar's world, and a 'Servant' is free to experience the world in his or her own way, the same as any other citizen.

IDEAL learning style	Rank
Empiricist	Servant
Idealist	Sovereign
Theorist	Father
Activist	Chief
Conformist	Women

There are strong resonances between this mapping and those for Plato's systems of governance, Freeden's list of modern ideologies, and a separation of powers between government institutions[21]:

IDEAL learning style	System	Ideology	Institution
Empiricist	Democracy	Liberalism	Electorate
Idealist	Aristocracy	Communism	Sovereign
Theorist	Timocracy	Socialism	Legislature
Activist	Tyranny	Fascism	Executive
Conformist	Oligarchy	Conservativism	Judiciary

A similar pattern is found for the Hindu castes, as well:

IDEAL learning style	Caste	Role
Empiricist	Shudra	Servant, menial
Idealist	Pariah	Without caste
Theorist	Vaishya	Farmer, merchant
Activist	Kshatriya	Warrior, ruler
Conformist	Brahmin	Priest

[21] These mappings are proposed in **4. Why?**

On the subject of governance, veteran British politician Tony Benn has formulated five questions that he would put to anyone proposing to exercise power over others[22]: (i) What power have you got; (ii) Where did you get it from; (iii) In whose interests do you exercise it; (iv) To whom are you accountable; and—the killer!—(v) How can we get rid of you? These are the political equivalents of the five theory-acceptance criteria discussed earlier.

Investigation. *The Art of War*[23]. The administration of military operations has been cited already as a convenient, well-defined case study for the understanding of societal roles. *The Art of War* is the world's oldest military treatise. It appears that the author had something of a fixation on the number five, listing five determining factors in warfare, five essentials for victory, five types of spy, and other quintets. These are analysed in turn.

Five determining factors in warfare:

1. "The Moral Law causes the people to be in complete accord with their ruler, so that they will follow him regardless of their lives, undismayed by any danger."
2. "Heaven signifies night and day, cold and heat, times and seasons."
3. "Earth comprises distances, great and small; danger and security; open ground and narrow passes; the chances of life and death."
4. "The Commander stands for the virtues of wisdom, sincerity, benevolence, courage and strictness."
5. "By method and discipline are to be understood the marshalling of the army in its proper subdivisions, the graduations of rank among the officers, the maintenance of roads by which supplies may reach the army, and the control of military expenditure."

IDEAL learning style	Determining factor in war
Empiricist	Heaven
Idealist	Commander
Theorist	Method and discipline
Activist	Earth
Conformist	The Moral Law

22 Copied from a blackboard displayed in the Museum of the History of Science in Oxford, May 2005.

23 Sun Tzu, *The Art of War* (*circa* 500 BC), tr. Lionel Giles (1910).

Five essentials for victory:

1. "He will win who knows when to fight and when not to fight."
2. "He will win who knows how to handle both superior and inferior forces."
3. "He will win whose army is animated by the same spirit throughout all its ranks."
4. "He will win who, prepared himself, waits to take the enemy unprepared."
5. "He will win who has military capacity and is not interfered with by the sovereign."

In current military terminology, these five phrases correspond to 'situational awareness', 'flexible control', 'coherent objectives', 'operational tempo' and 'institutional support', respectively:

IDEAL learning style	Essential for victory
Empiricist	Situational awareness
Idealist	Coherent objectives
Theorist	Flexible control
Activist	Operational tempo
Conformist	Institutional support

Even today, all of these factors are considered to be of critical importance in the waging of war. For example, an influential model of 'operational tempo' is the Boyd 'OODA loop':

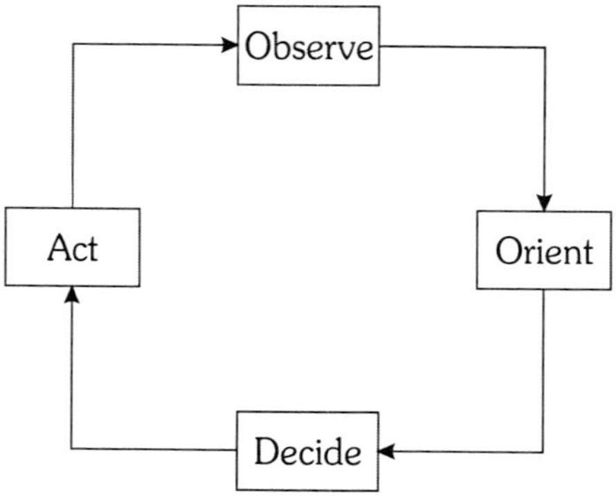

Boyd argued that a combatant can defeat a stronger opponent simply by undertaking the OODA loop at a greater operational tempo. The same idea underpins the earlier point that learning can be optimised by switching between different IDEAL learning styles at frequent intervals.

Five types of spy:

1. "Having local spies means employing the services of the inhabitants of a district."
2. "Having inward spies, making use of officials of the enemy."
3. "Having converted spies, getting hold of the enemy's spies and using them for our own purposes."
4. "Having doomed spies, doing certain things openly for purposes of deception, and allowing our spies to know of them and report them to the enemy."
5. "Surviving spies, finally, are those who bring back news from the enemy's camp."

IDEAL learning style	Type of spy
Empiricist	Local
Idealist	Doomed
Theorist	Converted
Activist	Surviving
Conformist	Inward

Investigation. *Civilisation*. Arnold Toynbee[24] comments that "This pseudo-Latin word is a modern French coinage, and Dr. Johnson refused to include the English counterpart of it in his dictionary of the English language." In fact it appears that Johnson eventually followed the fashion and included the word in his fourth (1773) edition, by which time it had already appeared in Ferguson's *An Essay on the History of Civil Society* (1767) and Millar's *The Origin of the Distinction of Ranks* (1771)[25]. Toynbee identifies five civilisations that he considers are "unaffiliated to others": (i) Sumero-Akkadian; (ii) Egyptiac; (iii) Aegean; (iv) Indus; (v) Sinic. In addition he lists 29 civilisations that are secondary in nature, being "affiliated to others", "satellite civilizations", "abortive civilizations" or "unrelated to others" by reason of their isolation. Quite arbitrarily:

---

[24] Arnold Toynbee, *A Study of History* (Oxford 1972).

[25] Jane Rendall erroneously ascribes priority to Millar. She also dates the first usage in French to "around 1766". If this is the case then it seems that Johnson missed a trick, as his dictionary was first published in 1755. See Jane Rendall, '"The grand causes which combine to carry mankind forward": Wollstonecraft, History and Revolution', *Women's Writing*, vol. 4, pp. 155-72 (1997).

IDEAL learning style	Civilisation
Empiricist	Aegean
Idealist	Sinic
Theorist	Indus
Activist	Sumero-Akkadian
Conformist	Egyptiac

It is clear, however, that Toynbee's five 'unaffiliated' civilisations are distinguished largely by *antiquity* and *geography*, which of course has nothing to do with competing *learning styles*. Reselecting on the basis of proximity in time and space, and taking into account the different *religious* inclinations in the ancient world, we obtain the following:

IDEAL learning style	Civilisation
Empiricist	Aegean
Idealist	Semitic
Theorist	Great Goddess
Activist	Roman
Conformist	Egyptiac

Here, 'Semitic' civilisation is taken to include the monotheistic religions of Judaism, Christianity and Islam; the 'Great Goddess' civilisation is taken to include the worship of the ancient triple goddess that once prevailed throughout the Middle East, India and beyond[26]; and the 'Roman' civilisation is taken to include the Persian, Macedonian and Spanish empires.

Investigation. *Religion.* Is it tempting to extend the last exercise in order to analyse current world religions in relation to one another. There are two reasons to desist, however. The first is the very real threat of a *fatwa*; no-one believing in the exclusive primacy of their religion will be happy to see it juxtaposed with others. The second is the practical difficulty of comparing 'living' faiths that are at different stages of development. Recalling earlier comments concerning the similarities between social structures and human characteristics, and the existence of five 'ages of man', one can hypothesise that religions also have a five-stage lifecycle, for example: (i) Revelation; (ii) Charismatic evangelism; (iii) Schism; (iv) Retrenchment; (v) Individualised observance. Given this lifecycle, it makes no sense to compare religions of different 'ages' in the same table.

---

[26] Robert Graves, *The White Goddess* (Faber 1948).

Investigation. *Five ages of man.* Hesiod described the historical development of man as having five ages[27]:

1. "The so-called golden race, subjects of Cronus, who lived without cares or labour, eating only acorns, wild fruit, and honey that dripped from the trees, drinking the milk of sheep and goats, never growing old, dancing, and laughing much; death, to them, was no more terrible than sleep."
2. "Next came a silver race, eaters of bread, likewise divinely created. These men were utterly subject to their mothers and dared not disobey them, although they might live to be a hundred years old."
3. "Next came a brazen race, who fell like fruits from the ash-trees, and were armed with brazen weapons. They ate flesh as well as bread, and delighted in war, being insolent and pitiless men."
4. "The fourth race of man was brazen too, but nobler and more generous, being begotten by the gods on mortal mothers."
5. "The fifth race is the present race of iron, unworthy descendants of the fourth. They are degenerate, cruel, unjust, malicious, libidinous, unfilial, treacherous."

Mapping these in the established sequence of (i) Empiricist, (ii) Idealist, (iii) Activist, (iv) Conformist and (v) Theorist, we obtain:

IDEAL learning style	Age of man
Empiricist	Golden
Idealist	Silver
Theorist	Iron
Activist	Brazen, warlike
Conformist	Brazen, generous

By the time of the Scottish Enlightenment these stages of society had been reformulated as: (i) Hunting and fishing; (ii) Gathering and herding; (iii) Agriculture; (iv) Manufacture and trade; (v) Modern civilisation. Karl Marx took this a stage further with: (i) Primitive communism; (ii) Slave society; (iii) Feudalism; (iv) Capitalism; (v) Socialism (which he saw as a temporary interregnum); (vi) Communism. More recently Walt Rostow[28] identified five stages of economic growth: (i) The traditional society; (ii) The preconditions for take-off; (iii) The take-off; (iv) The drive to

---

27 Quotations from Robert Graves, *The Greek Myths* (Penguin 1955).

28 Walt Rostow, *The Stages of Economic Growth: A Non-Communist Manifesto* (Cambridge 1960).

maturity; (v) The age of high mass-consumption. Interpolating these variants, we obtain the sequence: (i) Nomadic *hunting*; (ii) Feudal/caste/slave *farming*; (iii) Military empire-*building*; (iv) Capitalist *trading* (that is, trading under agreed tax and interest laws); (v) Global *networking*.

IDEAL learning style	Economic stage
Empiricist	Hunting
Idealist	Farming
Theorist	Networking
Activist	Building
Conformist	Trading

Investigation. *The 80:20 rule.* In 1906, Italian Vilfredo Pareto estimated that 80% of the land in his country was owned by 20% of the people. This 'Pareto principle' or '80:20 rule' has since been invoked in a wide range of circumstances, for example, 80% of workplace successes are associated with 20% of the staff, 80% of management problems are associated with 20% of the staff, and so on. The rule is empirical and bears no obvious relationship to known statistical distributions. But let us suppose that, for a wide range of circumstances, 20% of the population respond differently from the rest. Of course, it is not always the *same* 20% that respond: different circumstances will favour different groups, each making up 20% of society. In which case, the 80:20 rule could arise from the existence of five equally-sized groups in society:

IDEAL learning style	Proportion (%)
Empiricist	20
Idealist	20
Theorist	20
Activist	20
Conformist	20
Total	**100**

In order for this explanation to hold, a sixth group—'IDEAL man'—must be sufficiently marginalised and disadvantaged that it does not register, as might be expected in times of extreme social polarisation[29].

[29] See, for example, *The Seven Samurai*, analysed below.

Values and symbols

The following mappings concern value systems, motifs, symbols, and gods. Since there is little or no connection between the tables, they are all identified as 'examples'. Examples of *what*, I cannot say.

Example. *Five types of love.* It is conventional to use the Greek words: (i) *Agape*, meaning divine, unconditional love; (ii) *Eros*, meaning sexual, romantic love; (iii) *Philia*, meaning friendship, brotherly love; (iv) *Storge*, meaning familial, motherly love; (v) *Xenia*, meaning hospitality, love of foreigners. This list appears to encompass most interpretations. For example: Erich Fromm, *The Art of Loving* (1956), lists Brotherly love, Erotic love, Love of God, Motherly love, Self-love; C. S. Lewis, *The Four Loves* (1960), lists Agape, Eros, Philia, Storge; Everett Shostrom, *The Caring Relationship Inventory* (1966), lists Agape, Eros, Empathy, Friendship, Self-love. 'Self-love' appears to be the 'odd one out', but arguably this is the counterpart of Xenia, given the imperative to love "thy neighbour as thyself"[30]. I might add that there is a sixth type of love, 'Universal love', which is all of the others—but none too much. I look forward to the day when this inclusive definition replaces the repressive 'Agape good, Eros bad' dualism.

IDEAL learning style	Love
Empiricist	Xenia
Idealist	Agape
Theorist	Philia
Activist	Eros
Conformist	Storge
IDEAL man	Universal love

Example. *Six Christian values.*

> If I speak in the tongues of men and of angels, but have not love, I am a noisy gong or a clanging cymbal. And if I have prophetic powers, and understand all mysteries and all knowledge, and if I have all faith, so as to remove mountains, but have not love, I am nothing. If I give away all I have, and if I deliver my body to be burned, but have not love, I gain nothing.[31]

[30] This interpretation also decodes the five modes of loving listed in *Luke* 10:27, cited earlier.

[31] 1 *Corinthians* 13:1-3 (RSV).

IDEAL learning style	Value
Empiricist	Speech
Idealist	Prophesy
Theorist	Understanding
Activist	Self-sacrifice
Conformist	Faith
IDEAL man	Love

Example. *Universal Declaration of Human Rights.*

> *Whereas* recognition of the inherent dignity and of the equal and inalienable rights of all members of the human family is the foundation of freedom, justice and peace in the world...

Does this constitute a universal set of values? If so, what about love? Perhaps love is equivalent to 'all of the others—but none too much', in which case, as the song goes, "All you need is love":

IDEAL learning style	Value
Empiricist	Freedom
Idealist	Peace
Theorist	Equality
Activist	Justice
Conformist	Dignity
IDEAL man	Love

Example. *Five trust criteria.* Renn and Levine[32] identify five criteria for a 'risk communicator' to be trusted:

IDEAL learning style	Trust criterion
Empiricist	Objectivity
Idealist	Consistency
Theorist	Fairness
Activist	Competence
Conformist	Good faith

[32] Ortwin Renn and Debra Levine, 'Credibility and Trust in Risk Communication', in Roger Kasperson and Pieter Jan Stallen (eds.), *Communicating Risks to the Public* (Kluwer 1991). See also the analysis of five truth criteria in **2. Where and When?**

Example. *Five compatibility criteria for a life partner.* If your partnership score is 80% or more then you'll be just fine, son. Probably.

IDEAL learning style	Compatibility
Empiricist	Similar interests
Idealist	Mutual attraction
Theorist	Similar ways of doing things
Activist	Similar goals
Conformist	Similar moral code

Example. *Five motives.* Why do you do what you do?

IDEAL learning style	Motive
Empiricist	Interest
Idealist	Unity
Theorist	Truth
Activist	Power
Conformist	Duty

Example. *Five motifs.* As part of his study of Sundaland—the drowned continent of Southeast Asia—Oppenheimer[33] identifies five myth motifs. These may be mapped as follows:

IDEAL learning style	Motif
Empiricist	Serpent, bird and tree
Idealist	Tree of life
Theorist	Moon
Activist	Warring brothers
Conformist	Ark

In this mapping, the 'serpent, bird and tree' corresponds to the caduceus of Hermes; the 'tree of life' corresponds to the 'King of the Wood' in *The Golden Bough*; the 'moon' is the symbol of Artemis; the 'warring brothers' motif corresponds to the Activist's preference for learning through action and reaction; and the 'ark' represents a place of security and refuge.

Example. *Roman numerals.* Undoubtedly based on finger-counting, the Roman numerical system throws up the interesting quirk that DCLXVI is the same as 666, the number of the beast.[34]

33 Stephen Oppenheimer, *Eden in the East* (Weidenfeld and Nicolson 1998).

34 Robert Graves, *The White Goddess* (Faber 1948).

> A lunatic is easily recognized. He is a moron who doesn't know the ropes. The moron proves his thesis; he has a logic, however twisted it may be. The lunatic, on the other hand, doesn't concern himself at all with logic; he works by short circuits. For him, everything proves everything else. The lunatic is all *idée fixe*, and whatever he comes across confirms his lunacy. You can tell him by the liberties he takes with common sense, by his flashes of inspiration, and by the fact that sooner or later he brings up the Templars.[35]

The same might be said whenever the number 666 crops up. This should be borne in mind when perusing the following tabulations. Beware!

Example. *Tarot cards.* Modern 52-card decks do not have the knight.

IDEAL learning style	Tarot card
Empiricist	Page/Jack
Idealist	King
Theorist	Ace
Activist	Knight
Conformist	Queen

Example. *Tarot suits.* Modern 52-card decks do not have the separate trump suit.

IDEAL learning style	Tarot suit	Modern equivalent
Empiricist	Trumps	Joker
Idealist	Swords	Spades
Theorist	Wands	Clubs
Activist	Pentacles	Diamonds
Conformist	Cups	Hearts

Example. *Five elements.*

IDEAL learning style	Element
Empiricist	Quintessence
Idealist	Air
Theorist	Fire
Activist	Earth
Conformist	Water

[35] Umberto Eco, *Foucault's Pendulum* (1988).

Example. *Colours of the rainbow.*

IDEAL learning style	Colour
Empiricist	Green
Idealist	Purple
Theorist	Yellow
Activist	Red
Conformist	Blue
IDEAL man	White

Example. *Heavenly bodies.*

IDEAL learning style	Sphere
Empiricist	Mercury, Venus
Idealist	Jupiter
Theorist	Moon, Saturn
Activist	Mars
Conformist	Earth
IDEAL man	Sun

Example. *Greek gods and goddesses.* For this mapping two different methods were tried.

Method 1: (i) From the twelve Olympian gods (Zeus, Hades, Poseidon, Apollo, Hermes, Ares, Hera, Demeter, Athene, Artemis, Aphrodite, Hestia), collect recognised 'sets', for example, {Zeus, Hera}, {Zeus, Hades, Poseidon}; (ii) Collect further sets by interpreting some gods as 'aspects' of others, for example, Ares may be taken to represent the warlike aspect of Athene; (iii) Thereby select the five gods or goddesses that best represent the twelve.

IDEAL learning style	Greek god/goddess	Aspects
Empiricist	Hermes	Aphrodite
Idealist	Zeus	Hades, Poseidon, Hera, Demeter
Theorist	Apollo	Artemis
Activist	Athene	Ares
Conformist	Hestia	–

Method 2 does not downselect the Olympians, rather it allocates the gods and goddesses separately to the *six* IDEAL learning styles, including 'IDEAL man', which now represents the (fivefold!) triple god or goddess.

IDEAL learning style	Greek god	Greek goddess
Empiricist	Hermes	Aphrodite
Idealist	Poseidon	Demeter
Theorist	Apollo	Artemis
Activist	Ares	Athene
Conformist	Hades	Hestia
IDEAL man	Zeus	Hera

It is not known which of these mappings best represents the 'true' nature of the gods.

Example. *Greek heroes and heroines*. This is a small sample only:

IDEAL learning style	Greek hero or heroine
Empiricist	Adonis, Orestes
Idealist	Odysseus, Agamemnon
Theorist	Teiresias, Asclepius
Activist	Heracles, Achilles
Conformist	Penelope, Clytaemnestra

Example. *Egyptian gods*. The Egyptian calendar had a 360 + 5 day year, the additional five being the birthdays of Horus, Isis, Nephthys, Osiris and Set. Thoth is the Egyptian god of learning.

IDEAL learning style	Egyptian god or goddess
Empiricist	Horus
Idealist	Osiris
Theorist	Thoth
Activist	Set
Conformist	Isis, Nephthys

Example. *Norse gods*. In this interpretation, Loki is a 'dark trickster' and the sacrificed Baldur is equivalent to Adonis and Horus.

IDEAL learning style	Norse god or goddess
Empiricist	Loki, Baldur
Idealist	Odin
Theorist	Heimdall
Activist	Thor
Conformist	Freya

Ancient myth and modern fiction

Some ancient myths are based on actual events, others are not. However, all myths attempt to describe or explain something about the human world, and all have been reinterpreted many times. On both counts we might expect that these myths say more about human psychology and the learning styles of their narrators than about the original events that they claim to report. To lend weight to this expectation we start with something heavy.

Investigation. *The Golden Bough*. James George Frazer's *opus magnum* is a magnificent, unreadable tome. Magnificent because of its scope, unreadable because of its pedantry. Having merely skimmed through an abridged version[36], I am not qualified to pass judgement. Therefore the following comments constitute 'first impressions' only.

Frazer's all-encompassing study of myth, ritual and belief is framed by his description of the rites of Nemi. These rites involve: (i) The 'King of the Wood', who dies or is sacrificed, only to be reborn; (ii) A challenger, who aims to take the place of the king; (iii) The goddess Diana Nemorensis, bearer of the golden bough, the totem of the rite. Frazer focusses almost exclusively on the first of these roles, in its many manifestations across all cultures. However, it suits my purpose to retain all three of the Nemi roles, and to add a further two, the 'shaman' and the 'trickster', that appear intermittently throughout *The Golden Bough* and other myth studies. These five roles may be mapped to IDEAL learning styles as follows:

IDEAL learning style	Role
Empiricist	Trickster
Idealist	Dying and rising king
Theorist	Shaman
Activist	Challenger
Conformist	Totem bearer

In emphasising the role of the 'dying and rising king', Frazer gives great credence to the concept of the 'scapegoat'. However, he appears not to have known that this is a relatively recent concept, for the word makes its first appearance in William Tyndale's 1526 translation of the Bible. Tyndale's usage survives in the King James Bible:

> And he shall take the two goats, and present them before the Lord at the door of the tabernacle of the congregation. And Aaron shall cast

[36] James Frazer, *The Golden Bough* (1890-1915; Oxford 1994).

> lots upon the two goats; one lot for the Lord, and the other lot for the scapegoat. And Aaron shall bring the goat upon which the Lord's lot fell, and offer him for a sin offering. But the goat, on which the lot fell to be the scapegoat, shall be presented alive before the Lord, to make an atonement with him, and to let him go for a scapegoat into the wilderness.[37]

This is based on a misreading of 'Azazel' ('Goat-god') as 'ezazel' ('the goat that departs', hence Tyndale's '(e)scape-goat') present in the fifth-century Vulgate Bible. It is corrected in the Revised Standard Version:

> Then he shall take the two goats, and set them before the Lord at the door of the tent of meeting; and Aaron shall cast lots upon the two goats, one lot for the Lord, and the other lot for Azazel. And Aaron shall present the goat upon which the lot fell for the Lord, and offer it as a sin offering; but the goat on which the lot fell for Azazel shall be presented alive before the Lord to make atonement over it, that it may be sent away into the wilderness to Azazel.[38]

Christian theology conflates these two goats as two aspects of Christ: (i) The innocent sacrifice; (ii) The bearer of our sins. Thus "Christ died so that our sins may be forgiven". Frazer, following common usage, similarly conflates the two concepts in the single word 'scapegoat'. However, the original meaning was quite different, and much simpler: one goat was sacrificed to God, the other was sent to the Devil together with our accumulated sins. If theologians had maintained this interpretation then the two 'goats' would have been Christ and Barabbas respectively, and we would be saying "Christ died and Barabbas lived so that our sins may be forgiven". This change of emphasis suggests that Frazer should have drawn a greater distinction between the 'dying and rising king' and the 'scapegoat', as indeed there is a distinction between "the sacred king who dies at midsummer" and "the son who avenges him"[39]—Agamemnon and Orestes, for instance.

Five reasons why Frazer should have been influenced by John Millar:

1. Millar has many interesting things to say about the relationship between cultural practices and societal roles, much of it of considerable relevance to Frazer.
2. Millar's liberal Scottish Enlightenment outlook would have appealed to Frazer.
3. Like Frazer, Millar was a scion of Glasgow.

---

[37] *Leviticus* 16:7-10 (KJV).

[38] *Leviticus* 16:7-10 (RSV).

[39] Robert Graves, *The Greek Myths* (Penguin 1955).

4. Frazer's mother was a keen family historian. Did she not know that Millar's living descendants were Frazer's distant cousins?
5. In composing *The Golden Bough* Frazer demonstrated an incredible appetite for research. Although Millar's works had been neglected by scholars for a century, it is surprising that Frazer did not find them.

Frazer should have been influenced by Millar—but he wasn't. Why not?

Investigation. *From Ritual to Romance.* In *Apocalypse Now*, based on Conrad's *Heart of Darkness*, Kurtz is portrayed reading the poetry of T.S. Eliot. His other reading matter, at his bedside, is *The Golden Bough* and Jessie Weston's *From Ritual to Romance.* Eliot was strongly influenced by Conrad and Weston, and Weston in turn was strongly influenced by Frazer. Between them, these authors established descriptions of mythological archetypes that have been woven in to much of modern fiction[40]. Weston's contribution was to identify the archetypes associated with the grail legend[41]:

1. The dying and rising king, personified as the 'Fisher King'.
2. The 'Hero'.
3. The 'Medicine Man'.
4. The 'female grail messenger'.

One role that Weston did not explore is that of the wizard, in Arthurian legend personified by Merlin. Perhaps she did not wish to add to an already huge literature on the subject. Nevertheless, it is curious that she did not include wizardry in her discussion of medicine. In any case, it is clear that we have five main roles, similar to those in *The Golden Bough* and reminiscent of the five fields of study of Doctor Faustus[42]:

IDEAL learning style	Role	Field of study
Empiricist	Wizard	Magic
Idealist	Dying and rising king	Divinity
Theorist	Healer	Medicine
Activist	Hero	Logic
Conformist	Grail messenger	Law

Weston analyses the symbols associated with the grail legend—the lance and the grail, in particular—and relates them to the four tarot suits of

[40] See, in particular, *Lord of the Flies*, analysed below.

[41] Jessie Weston, *From Ritual to Romance* (1920; Princeton 1993).

[42] See **4. Why?**

swords, cups, pentacles and wands. The sword is the symbol of the king (Excalibur, for example), the cup is the grail, and the pentacle is the symbol of the perfect knight[43]:

'Wand' is ambiguous, as it has been illustrated both as a short stick and as a stout staff, neither of which corresponds to Weston's 'lance':

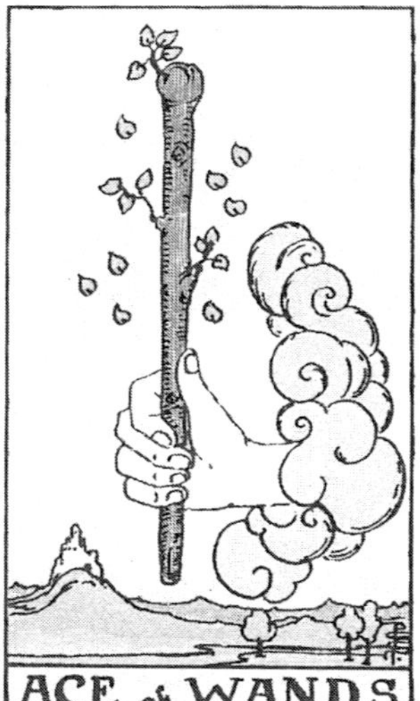

[43] Rider Tarot Cards, conceived by A. E. Waite and drawn by Pamela Colman Smith (Rider and Company 1910).

Indeed, the tarot wand appears to be a conflation of the wizard's magic wand based on the caduceus of Hermes (left), and the healer's staff of Asclepius (right):

Unpicking this conflation, we obtain the following mapping:

IDEAL learning style	Role	Symbol
Empiricist	Wizard	Wand (caduceus)
Idealist	Dying and rising king	Sword
Theorist	Healer	Wand (staff)
Activist	Hero	Pentacle
Conformist	Grail messenger	Cup

Investigation. *The durability of myth.*

> Nineteenth-century theories tended to see the subject matter of myth as the natural world and to see the function of myth as either a literal explanation or a symbolic description of that world. Myth was typically taken to be the 'primitive' counterpart to science, which was assumed to be wholly modern. Science rendered myth not merely redundant but outright incompatible, so that moderns, who by definition are scientific, had to reject myth... The biggest difficulty for Tylor's and Frazer's view of myth as the primitive counterpart to science is that it conspicuously fails to account for the retention of myth in the wake of science. If myth functions to do no more than science, why is it still around?[44]

There is an obvious need for a framework in which to juxtapose not just science and myth, but also religion, mysticism, and that other agent of mass appeal, direct action. Can all these diverse activities be interpreted as attempts to 'seek the truth'? If so, then IDEAL provides the framework:

[44] Robert Segal, *Myth—A Very Short Introduction* (Oxford 2004).

IDEAL learning style	'Extremist' truth seeker	Caricature
Empiricist	Empirical scientist	Explorer
Idealist	Mystic	Guru
Theorist	Theoretical scientist	Philosopher
Activist	Activist	Conqueror
Conformist	Religious devotee	Priest(ess)

Investigation. *Mythological archetypes and fictional stereotypes.* The preceding analyses of *The Golden Bough* and *From Ritual to Romance* have established five 'mythological archetypes':

IDEAL learning style	Archetype
Empiricist	Trickster/Wizard
Idealist	Dying and rising king
Theorist	Shaman/Healer
Activist	Challenger/Hero
Conformist	Totem bearer/Messenger

The idea of the 'archetype' was first conceived by Carl Gustav Jung at around the same time that Frazer and Weston were developing their own ideas. From a scientific point of view, Jung's analysis is critically handicapped by his disinclination to define a small 'basis set' of archetypes from which one might construct the remainder. However, Jung's descriptions are rich with insight and can be made the basis of a reasonably-convincing argument, if one is prepared to follow the usual custom of picking out the favourable features and ignoring the rest. Thus, for example, Christopher Booker identifies 'dark' and 'light' versions of five main archetypes[45]:

Negative/centred on the ego	Positive/centred on the Self
Dark Father/Tyrant/Dark Magician	Light Father/Good King/Wise Old Man
Dark Mother/Dark Queen/Witch	Light Mother/Good Queen/ Wise Old Woman
Dark Rival/Dark Alter-Ego	Light Alter-Ego/Friend and Companion
Dark Other Half/Temptress	Light Other Half (light *anima*/*animus*)
Child	

45 Christopher Booker, *The Seven Basic Plots* (Continuum 2004). This table is copied from page 306.

These map to the 'Frazer/Weston' archetypes as follows:

IDEAL learning style	Frazer/Weston	Jung/Booker
Empiricist	Trickster/Wizard	Child
Idealist	Dying and rising king	King
Theorist	Shaman/Healer	Alter-Ego
Activist	Challenger/Hero	Other Half
Conformist	Totem bearer/Messenger	Queen

Mythological archetypes may appear to be dry-as-dust abstractions, but they are the underlying basis of the key stereotypes that populate modern fiction:

1. The innocent *seeker* who discovers his or her true path in life.
2. The other-worldly *guru* (or *fiend*), unconstrained by physical limitations.
3. The clever *detective* who unravels a mystery.
4. The unfazed action *hero* (or *villain*), not troubled by fear or doubt.
5. The loyal *devotee* who proves his or her love.

IDEAL learning style	Fictional stereotype
Empiricist	Seeker
Idealist	Guru or fiend
Theorist	Detective
Activist	Hero or villain
Conformist	Devotee

From our understanding of IDEAL learning styles and our ample exposure to fictional stereotypes it is possible to infer likely relationships between these types of people. For example:

1. An Idealist may be killed but never 'dies'.
2. An Idealist is a Theorist with only one explanation for events.
3. Empiricists and Theorists are complementary.
4. Idealists cannot be controlled by Activists, and Activists do not listen to Idealists, so generally they are in conflict.
5. Conformists (usually female) are wont to attach themselves to Activists (usually male).

Investigation. *Cautionary tales.* Fictional stereotypes appear in their clearest form in 'cautionary tales', simplified moral stories that are designed to highlight the virtues and vices associated with characteristic behaviours. To what extent do the five fictional stereotypes based on IDEAL learning styles feature in the best-known compendium of cautionary tales, *Aesop's Fables*? A simple statistical analysis[46] reveals the following:

1. There are 207 fables. Of these, 138 (67%) feature the interaction of animals. (The remainder are based on humans, gods, the seasons and so on.)
2. A count was made of the individual occurrences of each of the creatures in each of the fables. The Fox made 29 separate appearances; Lion, 26; Dog, 23; Ass, 21; Wolf, 15; Sheep, 7; Snake, 7; and so on down. Of the 252 separate appearances made by all of the animals, 114 (45%) were made by one of the 'Big Five': Fox, Lion, Dog, Ass, Wolf.
3. Of the 'animal' fables, 78 (57%) feature one or more of the 'Big Five'.

Even without further analysis and interpretation (treating the Eagle as a surrogate Lion, for instance), the main result is plain to see: five animals stand out as having far more occurrences than the rest. Typically, these five each perform the following well-defined roles:

1. The Fox is an impostor.
2. The Lion is a monarch.
3. The Dog is a protector.
4. The Ass is a clever fool.
5. The Wolf is a predator.

IDEAL learning style	Archetype	Stereotype	Animal
Empiricist	Trickster/Wizard	Seeker	Fox
Idealist	Dying and rising king	Guru or fiend	Lion
Theorist	Shaman/Healer	Detective	Ass
Activist	Challenger/Hero	Hero or villain	Wolf
Conformist	Totem bearer/Messenger	Devotee	Dog

Proposition. *Modern fiction.* The genre of any piece of modern fiction may be inferred from the stereotypical behaviour of its leading character:

IDEAL learning style	Leading character	Genre
Empiricist	Seeker	Rites of passage
Idealist	Guru or fiend	Rebirth
Theorist	Detective	Mystery
Activist	Hero or villain	Overcoming the monster
Conformist	Devotee	Romance
IDEAL man	All—but none too much	Comedy

[46] This analysis was undertaken using *Aesop's Fables* tr. S.A. Handford (Penguin 1954).

These genre can be related to Christopher Booker's *Seven Basic Plots*[47], which are 'Overcoming the Monster', 'Rags to Riches', 'Quest', 'Voyage and Return', 'Comedy', 'Tragedy' and 'Rebirth'. Two further plots, 'Rebellion Against 'The One'' and 'Mystery', Booker discards because of their perceived rarity and banality respectively. His analysis is an application of Jung's archetypes, and it inherits the same features, good and bad. The good news is that Booker's succinct single-paragraph summaries of hundreds of plot lines are often brilliantly evocative. The bad news is that his selection of seven basic plots is quite arbitrary, being founded on a simple classification of the stories with which he happens to be acquainted. As with Jung, Booker's analysis lacks a convincing theoretical framework having clear limits. As a result, his disparaging comments about stories that do not fit into his classification have to be treated as simply a matter of opinion. To get from Booker's seven-plus-two plots to the six IDEAL genre, we observe the following:

1. 'Rags to Riches', 'Quest' and 'Voyage and Return' all appear to be variants of the IDEAL 'Rites of passage' genre.
2. Booker's 'Comedy' is what most of us call romance, but he doesn't like this word because what most of us call romance he would dismiss as meaningless and sentimental. The IDEAL genre of 'Comedy' is a subset of Booker's, based on his comment that "Only in Comedy is it the general tendency for all the characters to be brought to light and reconciled, to produce the story's closing image of a little world wholly united". This principle is a useful 'rule of thumb' but, as its author discovers, it is too general to be the only means of discrimination. Accordingly Booker admits as 'Comedy' other stories that do not fulfil this criterion in any obvious way, and it is these numerous misfits that constitute the IDEAL 'Romance' genre.
3. Booker's 'Tragedy' plot simply comprises 'dark' versions of the other 'light' plots. This simplistic black-and-white classification prejudges the outcome of a story and leads Booker to reject many stories as 'unresolved', when in fact their endings give a very clear idea of what happens when people fail to break out of narrow stereotypical behaviour. Indeed, these 'unresolved' stories are a valuable indication of the limitations of certain types of behaviour, analogous to the role played by failed tests in the development of a scientific theory. Accordingly, I have left aside the 'dark' and 'light' classification, and with it the separate definition of 'Tragedy'.
4. Similarly, 'Rebellion Against 'The One'' appears to be a dark version of 'Rebirth', into which it may be subsumed.

---

[47] Christopher Booker, *ibid.*

IDEAL genre	Booker's basic plots
Rites of passage	Rags to Riches, Quest, Voyage and Return, Tragedy (part)
Rebirth	Rebirth, Rebellion Against 'The One', Tragedy (part)
Mystery	Mystery, Tragedy (part)
Overcoming the monster	Overcoming the Monster, Tragedy (part)
Romance	Comedy (part), Tragedy (part)
Comedy	Comedy (part), Tragedy (part)

In the following, these six IDEAL genre are investigated through a number of examples taken from modern fiction (that is, anything that is not ancient myth). Most of the tables are given without any commentary, in order to minimise additional interpretation.

Rites of passage

The Rites of passage genre is taken to have an Empiricist as a leading character (indicated in *italics*).

Example. *Brideshead Revisited* by Evelyn Waugh (1945).

IDEAL learning style	Character
Empiricist	*Charles, Sebastian, Julia*
Idealist	Lord Marchmain
Theorist	Cordelia
Activist	Brideshead, Rex
Conformist	Lady Marchmain

Example. *Great Expectations* by Charles Dickens (1861).

IDEAL learning style	Character
Empiricist	*Pip*
Idealist	Estella
Theorist	Herbert Pocket
Activist	Magwitch
Conformist	Miss Havisham

Example. *Hamlet* by William Shakespeare (*circa* 1601).

IDEAL learning style	Character
Empiricist	*Hamlet*
Idealist	Ghost of Hamlet's father
Theorist	Polonius
Activist	Claudius
Conformist	Gertrude, Ophelia

Example. *Harry Potter* (any story) by J. K. Rowling (1997-2007).

IDEAL learning style	Character
Empiricist	*Harry Potter*
Idealist	Dumbledore
Theorist	Hermione
Activist	Voldemort
Conformist	Ron

Example. *The Jungle Book* by Rudyard Kipling (1894).

IDEAL learning style	Character
Empiricist	*Mowgli*
Idealist	Akela, Hathi
Theorist	Tabaqui, Kaa
Activist	Shere Khan, Bagheera
Conformist	Raksha, Baloo

Example. *Kim* by Rudyard Kipling (1901). Kim appears twice in this table because he has a persistent identity crisis: "'I am Kim. I am Kim. And what is Kim?' His soul repeated it again and again."

IDEAL learning style	Character
Empiricist	*Kim*
Idealist	Lama
Theorist	Hurree Baba
Activist	Mahbub Ali
Conformist	Kim

Example. *Lord of the Flies* by William Golding (1954). Golding was strongly influenced by the works of Frazer, Weston, Eliot and others of similar persuasion.

IDEAL learning style	Character
Empiricist	*Ralph*
Idealist	Simon
Theorist	Piggy
Activist	Jack
Conformist	Roger

Example. *The Lord of the Rings* by J. R. R. Tolkein (1954-5). This is one of several storylines operating in parallel.

IDEAL learning style	Character
Empiricist	*Frodo*
Idealist	Gandalf
Theorist	Gollum*
Activist	Gollum*
Conformist	Sam

* Gollum has a persistent identity crisis.

Example. *The Matrix.*

IDEAL learning style	Character
Empiricist	*Neo*
Idealist	Morpheus, The Oracle
Theorist	Cypher
Activist	Agent Smith
Conformist	Trinity

Example. *Star Wars.*

IDEAL learning style	Character
Empiricist	*Luke Skywalker*
Idealist	Obi-Wan Kenobi
Theorist	R2D2, C3P0
Activist	Darth Vader, Han Solo
Conformist	Princess Leia

Example. *The Third Man.*

IDEAL learning style	Character
Empiricist	*Holly Martins*
Idealist	Harry Lime
Theorist	Sgt. Paine
Activist	Maj. Calloway
Conformist	Anna Schmidt

Example. *The Three Musketeers* by Alexandre Dumas (1845).

IDEAL learning style	Character
Empiricist	*D'Artagnan*
Idealist	Athos
Theorist	Aramis
Activist	Porthos
Conformist	Constance

Example. *Titus Groan* and *Gormenghast* by Mervyn Peake (1946).

IDEAL learning style	Character
Empiricist	*Lord Titus Groan*
Idealist	Lord Sepulchrave Groan
Theorist	Lady Fuschia
Activist	Steerpike
Conformist	Lady Gertrude Groan

Example. *Treasure Island* by Robert Louis Stevenson (1882).

IDEAL learning style	Character
Empiricist	*Jim*
Idealist	Ben Gunn
Theorist	Dr. Livesey
Activist	Long John Silver
Conformist	Pirates

Example. *The Wonderful Wizard of Oz* by L. Frank Baum (1900).

IDEAL learning style	Character
Empiricist	*Dorothy*
Idealist	Tin Man
Theorist	Scarecrow
Activist	Cowardly Lion
Conformist	Toto

Rebirth

The Rebirth genre is taken to have an Idealist as a leading character (indicated in *italics*).

Example. *Crime and Punishment* by Fyodor Dostoyevsky (1866).

IDEAL learning style	Character
Empiricist	Dunya
Idealist	*Raskolnikov**
Theorist	Pofiry
Activist	Raskolnikov*
Conformist	Sonya

* Raskolnikov has a persistent identity crisis.

Example. *Dr. Strangelove, or How I Learned to Stop Worrying and Love the Bomb.*

IDEAL learning style	Character
Empiricist	Gen. 'Buck' Turgidson
Idealist	*Dr. Strangelove*
Theorist	President Merkin Muffley
Activist	Brig. Gen. Jack D. Ripper
Conformist	Maj. T. J. 'King' Kong

Example. *The Godfather.*

IDEAL learning style	Character
Empiricist	Michael
Idealist	*Don Vito Corleone*
Theorist	Tom Hagen
Activist	Santino (Sonny)
Conformist	Mama Corleone, Luca Brasi

Example. *The Government Inspector.*

IDEAL learning style	Character
Empiricist	Tony Blair
Idealist	*David Kelly*
Theorist	Andrew Gilligan
Activist	Alistair Campbell
Conformist	Susan Watts

Example. *The Greatest Story Ever Told.*

IDEAL learning style	Character
Empiricist	Pilate
Idealist	*Jesus*
Theorist	Judas Iscariot
Activist	Caiaphas
Conformist	Mary Magdalene

Example. *Heart of Darkness* by Joseph Conrad (1902).

IDEAL learning style	Character
Empiricist	Marlow*
Idealist	*Kurtz*
Theorist	Harlequin
Activist	Marlow*
Conformist	Helmsman

* Marlow has a persistent identity crisis.

Example. *King Lear* by William Shakespeare (*circa* 1606).

IDEAL learning style	Character
Empiricist	Lear*
Idealist	*Lear**
Theorist	Kent, Fool
Activist	Regan, Goneril
Conformist	Cordelia, Gloucester

* Lear has a persistent identity crisis.

Example. *The Trigan Empire.* This requires some explanation. *The Trigan Empire*, a comic strip in the *Look and Learn* children's magazine, was essential reading during my formative years. The central characters are:

1. Trigo, Emperor of the Trigans, "a great leader, who having defeated his country's enemies, built the spendid city of Trigan," which curiously takes on the appearance of great antiquity even though Trigo himself scarcely ages. Indeed, Trigo's person and his rule appear to be indestructible and everlasting, in spite of continual challenges and disruptions.
2. Brag, Trigo's brother. Brag is a simple, uncomplicated and utterly loyal supporter of the Empire. However, he is also slow-witted and as a result he is occasionally duped into schemes that threaten his brother's rule. Sooner or later these nefarious plots backfire, much to Brag's embarrassment and disadvantage.
3. Janno, Brag's son. The presumed heir of his uncle Trigo, whom he closely resembles in appearance and personality, Janno is nevertheless spared the burden of running the Empire, and instead he is free to express his adventurous and impetuous spirit. This lands him in all sorts of situations that are variously foolish, perilous or accidentally heroic, but which always end up enhancing the power and prestige of the Empire.
4. Peric, Trigo's wise and venerable adviser, who is capable of inventing all manner of devices from space rockets to invisibility rays, but is not a great leader. Thus on one occasion Trigo concludes: "As a General you make a very good scientist, Peric! The orders you have given would have ensured one thing… *the utter destruction of the Trigan Empire!*"

Trigan Empire storylines tend to follow a set formula that after several repeats is quite recognisable:

1. At the beginning of each tale a new threat to the Empire is introduced in the form of an 'episodic adversary'.
2. Trigo is removed from the scene by imprisonment, incapacitation or exile. Occasionally this 'removal' is effected through following the adventures of Janno in some far-flung corner of the planet where Trigo's rule has broken down or has yet to be established.
3. There is a struggle for power featuring one or more of the central characters in a pivotal role.
4. The episodic adversary is defeated and Trigo's power is restored or enhanced.

IDEAL learning style	Character
Empiricist	Janno
Idealist	*Trigo*
Theorist	Peric
Activist	Episodic adversary
Conformist	Brag

Mystery

The Mystery genre is taken to have a Theorist as a leading character (indicated in *italics*).

Example. *The Name of the Rose* by Umberto Eco (1980).

IDEAL learning style	Character
Empiricist	Adso
Idealist	Jorge
Theorist	*William of Baskerville*
Activist	Bernardo Gui
Conformist	The Abbot

Example. *Nineteen Eighty-Four* by George Orwell (1949).

IDEAL learning style	Character
Empiricist	Julia
Idealist	Emmanuel Goldstein
Theorist	*Winston Smith*
Activist	O'Brien
Conformist	Big Brother

Example. *Poirot, Miss Marple* (any story) by Agatha Christie (1920-1976).

IDEAL learning style	Character
Empiricist	Naïve initiate
Idealist	Femme fatale
Theorist	*Sleuth*
Activist	Dashing gent
Conformist	Butler

Example. *Sherlock Holmes* (any story) by Arthur Conan Doyle (1887-1928).

IDEAL learning style	Character
Empiricist	Stupid policeman
Idealist	Mysterious stranger
Theorist	*Sherlock Holmes*
Activist	Nasty piece of work
Conformist	Dr. Watson

Example. *Tinker, Tailor, Soldier, Spy* by John Le Carré (1974). "There are three of them and Alleline..."

IDEAL learning style	Character	Codename
Empiricist	Toby Esterhase	Poorman
Idealist	Bill Haydon	Tailor
Theorist	*George Smiley*	*Beggarman*
Activist	Roy Bland	Soldier
Conformist	Percy Alleline	Tinker

Overcoming the monster

The Overcoming the monster genre is taken to have an Activist as a leading character (indicated in *italics*). In addition to the examples given here, there are many fictional storylines that exploit the Activist's preference for 'action and reaction', in particular, 'buddy movies' that explore the 'intimate enemy' relationship between an Activist and his or her foil[48].

Example. *The Bridge on the River Kwai.*

> In the end, Clipton's cry of "madness" is not just the madness of war but of men with distorted values, the madness of a distracted dreamer. It is the insanity not just of combat but of codes which make enemies of men with much in common, which compels tired and bleeding soldiers to march proudly into a prison camp, which can twist an ordinary, constructive act such as bridge-building into an abnormal one.[49]

IDEAL learning style	Character
Empiricist	Shears
Idealist	Clipton
Theorist	Warden
Activist	*Nicholson**
Conformist	Nicholson*, Saito

* Nicholson has a persistent identity crisis.

---

48 'Intimate enemies' are described by Daniel Goleman, *Emotional Intelligence* (Bloomsbury 1995). **4. Why?** is an extended example of the use of this device.

49 Alain Silver and James Ursini, *David Lean and his Films* (Silman-James 1992).

Example. *Citizen Kane.*

IDEAL learning style	Character
Empiricist	Susan Alexander Kane
Idealist	Jedediah Leland
Theorist	Mr. Bernstein
Activist	*Charles Foster Kane*
Conformist	Walter Parks Thatcher

Example. *I, Robot.*

IDEAL learning style	Character
Empiricist	Sonny
Idealist	VIKI
Theorist	Dr. Alfred Lanning
Activist	*Detective Del Spooner*
Conformist	Dr. Susan Calvin

Example. *James Bond* (any of the *films*).

IDEAL learning style	Character
Empiricist	Bond girl
Idealist	Episodic adversary
Theorist	Q
Activist	*James Bond*
Conformist	M

Example. *Macbeth* by William Shakespeare (*circa* 1606).

IDEAL learning style	Character
Empiricist	Macbeth*
Idealist	Duncan
Theorist	Banquo
Activist	*Macbeth**
Conformist	Lady Macbeth

* Macbeth has a persistent identity crisis.

Example. *The Man who would be King* by Rudyard Kipling (1888).

IDEAL learning style	Character
Empiricist	Kipling
Idealist	Daniel Dravot
Theorist	Billy Fish
Activist	*Peachey Carnehan*
Conformist	Priests

Example. *Star Trek* (any story). In this interpretation, Captain Kirk and his crew are not explorers but serial invaders, boldly meddling where no man has meddled before.

IDEAL learning style	Character
Empiricist	Grateful aliens
Idealist	Ungrateful aliens
Theorist	Spock
Activist	*Captain Kirk*
Conformist	Crew of Enterprise

Romance

The Romance genre is taken to have a Conformist as a leading character, or as the object of the affections of the leading character (indicated in *italics*).

Example. *Casablanca.*

IDEAL learning style	Character
Empiricist	Capt. Louis Renault
Idealist	Victor Laszlo
Theorist	Sam
Activist	*Rick Blaine*
Conformist	Ilsa Lund

Example. *Far from the Madding Crowd* by Thomas Hardy (1874).

IDEAL learning style	Character
Empiricist	*Bathsheba Everdene*
Idealist	Fanny Robin
Theorist	William Boldwood
Activist	Sgt. Troy
Conformist	Gabriel Oak

Example. *Gone with the Wind* by Margaret Mitchell (1936). A tragic twist of the genre: Scarlett's tragedy is that she is *anything other* than a Conformist, except when it's too late.

IDEAL learning style	Character
Empiricist	*Scarlett O'Hara*
Idealist	Tara
Theorist	Ashley Wilkes
Activist	Rhett Butler
Conformist	Melanie Hamilton

Example. *A Passage to India* by E. M. Forster (1924).

IDEAL learning style	Character
Empiricist	Adela Quested*, Aziz
Idealist	Godbole
Theorist	Mrs. Moore
Activist	Ronny
Conformist	*Adela Quested**

* Adela Quested has a persistent identity crisis.

Example. *Pride and Prejudice* by Jane Austen (1813). Something strange is going on here: unlike *Gone with the Wind*, *Pride and Prejudice* is not a tragedy; unlike Adela Quested, Elizabeth Bennet is not experiencing a crisis of identity; and yet neither she nor Darcy fit the description of 'Conformist', so this story cannot legitimately be called a 'Romance'. The answer, I suggest, is that *Pride and Prejudice* is a Comedy, in which all roles play a part—but none too much:

IDEAL learning style	Bennet sister	Male character
Empiricist	Kitty	Mr. Bingley
Idealist	Elizabeth	Mr. Darcy
Theorist	Mary	Mr. Bennet
Activist	Lydia	Mr. Wickham
Conformist	Jane	Mr. Collins

Example. *Romeo and Juliet* by William Shakespeare (*circa* 1595).

IDEAL learning style	Character
Empiricist	Romeo
Idealist	Montague, Capulet
Theorist	Friars, Apothecary
Activist	Mercutio, Tybalt
Conformist	*Juliet*

Example. *Wuthering Heights* by Emily Brontë (1847). Heathcliffe is the classic rejected suitor out for revenge.

IDEAL learning style	Character
Empiricist	Catherine Earnshaw
Idealist	Isabella Linton
Theorist	Edgar Linton
Activist	Hindley Earnshaw
Conformist	*Heathcliffe*

Comedy

The Comedy genre is taken to have no single leading character, rather several different characters interact in a close-knit ensemble. An ensemble of this nature is a fundamental prerequisite for the portrayal of witty repartee, confusion, misunderstandings, and other elements of what we consider to be funny. Accordingly, many of the Comedy plots aim to amuse. However, as some of the examples indicate, the Comedy genre can also accommodate plots that are not at all funny.

Example. *Animal Farm* by George Orwell (1945).

IDEAL learning style	Character
Empiricist	Squealer, Mollie, Cat
Idealist	Old Major, Raven
Theorist	Snowball, Benjamin
Activist	Napoleon, Boxer
Conformist	Dogs, Sheep, Clover

Example. *The Brothers Karamazov* by Fyodor Dostoyevsky (1880).

IDEAL learning style	Character
Empiricist	Alyosha
Idealist	Smerdyakov
Theorist	Ivan
Activist	Mitya
Conformist	Fyodor

Example. *Dad's Army.*

IDEAL learning style	Character
Empiricist	Pte. Pike
Idealist	Capt. Mainwaring
Theorist	Sgt. Wilson
Activist	Cpl. Jones
Conformist	Privates

Example. *Father Ted.* Priests are *supposed* to be Conformists.

IDEAL learning style	Character
Empiricist	Father Dougal
Idealist	Father Ted
Theorist	Father Jack
Activist	Mrs. Doyle
Conformist	–

Example. *The Guns of Navarone* by Alistair MacLean (1957).

IDEAL learning style	Character
Empiricist	Lieut. Andy Stevens
Idealist	Capt. Keith Mallory
Theorist	Cpl. Dusty Miller
Activist	Col. Andrea Stavros
Conformist	Petty Officer Casey Brown

Example. *The Ladykillers.* According to John Cleese, the criminal gang in *The Ladykillers* comprises the perfect comedy ensemble.

IDEAL learning style	Character
Empiricist	Harry/'Mr. Robinson'
Idealist	Professor Marcus
Theorist	Claude/'Major Courtney'
Activist	Louis/'Mr. Harvey'
Conformist	One-Round/'Mr. Lawson'

Example. *Nostromo* by Joseph Conrad (1904).

IDEAL learning style	Character
Empiricist	Nostromo
Idealist	Dr. Monygham
Theorist	Decoud
Activist	Charles Gould
Conformist	Mrs. Gould

Example. *The Secret Life of Walter Mitty* by James Thurber (1941).

IDEAL learning style	Character
Empiricist	The Fighter Pilot
Idealist	The Undefeated Condemned
Theorist	The Expert Surgeon
Activist	The Defiant Accused
Conformist	The Reliable Commander
IDEAL man	Walter Mitty

Example. *Shichinin no samurai* (*The Seven Samurai*).

IDEAL learning style	Character	Role
Empiricist	Katsushiro	Apprentice samurai
Idealist	Kambei	Leader of samurai
Theorist	Kyuzo [3]	Expert swordsman
Activist	Kikuchiyo [4]	Would-be samurai
Conformist	Shichiroji	Kambei's friend
IDEAL man 1	Heihachi [1]	Good-natured samurai
IDEAL man 2	Gorobei [2]	Wise warrior

Numbers in square brackets indicate the sequence in which the samurai die. It is interesting to note that Heihachi and Gorobei are the first to go; clearly, these are trying times for people of a balanced disposition. The mapping for the derivative *The Magnificent Seven* is similar, except that the Activist role is now shared between Lee (the coward) and Calvera (the villain). This classic Hollywood device for the portrayal of 'action and reaction' changes the sequence of fatalities, but little else:

IDEAL learning style	Character
Empiricist	Chico
Idealist	Chris
Theorist	Britt [3]
Activist	Lee [2], Calvera
Conformist	Vin
IDEAL man 1	Harry Luck [1]
IDEAL man 2	Bernardo [4]

Example. *The Simpsons.*

IDEAL learning style	Character
Empiricist	Lisa
Idealist	Homer
Theorist	Maggie
Activist	Bart
Conformist	Marge

Example. *Twelve Angry Men.* Numbers in square brackets indicate the sequence in which the jurors vote 'Not Guilty'. 'Compassionate' versus 'Egocentric' is a relative distinction introduced only to give additional structure to the tabulation. The juxtaposition is fascinating, however.

IDEAL learning style	Compassionate	Egocentric
Empiricist	Juror 8 (Architect) [1]	Juror 12 (Salesman) [9/10/11]
Idealist	Juror 9 (Old man) [2]	Juror 3 (Father) [12]
Theorist	Juror 2 (Accountant) [5/6]	Juror 4 (Stockbroker) [9/10/11]
Activist	Juror 1 (Foreman) [7/8]	Juror 7 (Baseball fan) [7/8]
Conformist	Juror 11 (Immigrant) [4]	Juror 10 (Bigot) [9/10/11]
IDEAL man	Juror 6 (Simple man) [5/6]	Juror 5 (Poor man) [3]

Example. *War and Peace* by Leo Tolstoy (1865-8).

IDEAL learning style	Character
Empiricist	Natasha
Idealist	Nikolai
Theorist	Pierre
Activist	Napoleon
Conformist	Maria

Example. *Winnie-the-Pooh* by A. A. Milne (1926).

It went on raining, and every day the water got a little higher, until now it was nearly up to Piglet's window ... and still he hadn't done anything.

"There's Pooh," he thought to himself. "Pooh hasn't much Brain, but he never comes to any harm. He does silly things and they turn out right. There's Owl. Owl hasn't exactly got Brain, but he Knows Things. He would know the Right Thing to Do when Surrounded by Water. There's Rabbit. He hasn't Learnt in Books, but he can always Think of a Clever Plan. There's Kanga. She isn't Clever, Kanga isn't, but she would be so anxious about Roo that she would do a Good Thing to Do without thinking about it. And then there's Eeyore. And Eeyore is so miserable anyhow that he wouldn't mind about this. But I wonder what Christopher Robin would do?"

IDEAL learning style	Character
Empiricist	Piglet
Idealist	Eeyore
Theorist	Owl
Activist	Rabbit
Conformist	Kanga
IDEAL bear	Winnie-the-Pooh
IDEAL boy	Christopher Robin

Epilogue

If five people meet together to seek for truth, they must begin by cutting themselves free from all their own special conditions and renouncing all preconceived ideas. In order to find truth we must give up our prejudices, our own small trivial notions; an open receptive mind is essential. If our chalice is full of self, there is no room in it for the water of life. The fact that we imagine ourselves to be right and everybody else wrong is the greatest of all obstacles in the path towards unity, and unity is necessary if we would reach truth, for truth is *one*.[1]

1 Abdul Baha, *Paris Talks* (eleventh British edition, UK Bahai Publishing Trust 1979).